How to Vote Progressive in Australia

How to Vote Progressive in Australia

Labor or Green?

Edited by Dennis Altman and Sean Scalmer

© Copyright 2016
Copyright of this collection in its entirety is held by Dennis Altman and
Sean Scalmer.
Copyright of the individual chapters is held by the respective chapter authors.

All rights reserved. Apart from any uses permitted by Australia's Copyright
Act 1968, no part of this book may be reproduced by any process without
prior written permission from the copyright owners. Inquiries should be
directed to the publisher.

Monash University Publishing
Matheson Library and Information Services Building
40 Exhibition Walk
Monash University
Clayton, Victoria 3800, Australia
www.publishing.monash.edu

Monash University Publishing brings to the world publications which
advance the best traditions of humane and enlightened thought.

Monash University Publishing titles pass through a rigorous process of
independent peer review.

www.publishing.monash.edu/books/hvp-9781925377149.html

Series: Politics

Design: Les Thomas

National Library of Australia Cataloguing-in-Publication entry:
    Title: How to vote progressive in Australia : Labor or Green?
                / edited by Dennis Altman and Sean Scalmer.
    ISBN: 9781925377149 (paperback)
    Subjects: Australian Labor Party.
                Green Party (Australia).
                Labor movement--Australia.
                Green movement--Australia.
                Political leadership--Australia.
                Australia--Politics and government--21st century.
    Dewey number: 324.294

Printed in Australia by Griffin Press an Accredited ISO AS/NZS
14001:2004 Environmental Management System printer.

The paper this book is printed on is certified against
the Forest Stewardship Council ® Standards. Griffin
Press holds FSC chain of custody certification SGS-
COC-005088. FSC promotes environmentally
responsible, socially beneficial and economically
viable management of the world's forests.

Contents

Introduction. Caught Between Red and Green:
The Electoral Dilemma............................. 1
  Dennis Altman

1. The Effect of the Institutional Settings on the
   ALP–Greens Relationship....................... 17
   Nicholas Barry, Stewart Jackson and Narelle Miragliotta

2. Progressive Voting, Party Organisation, and Political
   Reform: A Historical View 37
   Sean Scalmer

3. Leaving Labor for the Greens 54
   Ellen Sandell

4. How I Fell out of Love with the Greens:
   A Personal Story about the Labor Party 65
   Van Badham

5. What's Left – Progressive?...................... 78
   Carmen Lawrence

6. We're Not There Yet: Labor's Past, Present and
   Future as a Party of Government................. 91
   Andrew Giles

7. Which Way for a Progressive Voter in 2016?....... 106
   Scott Ludlam

8. 'Australia the Beautiful': A Dangerous Myth 115
   David Mejia-Canales

9. Burying Margaret Mead: Environment and the
   Labor Party 140
   Felicity Wade

10. Why Progressives Should be Pro-Growth......... 163
    Andrew Leigh

11. Making Progressive Government Happen 179
    Adam Bandt

12. Labor, the Greens and the Union Movement 203
    Shaun Wilson

13. Progressivism at an Industry Level: Reflections
    on a Successful Unaffiliated Trade Union 230
    James Tierney

14. Does Turnbull Offer a Progressive Alternative? 245
    Peter Van Onselen

15. Labor or Green: The Left and the Crisis of Politics... 259
    Simon Copland

Contributors 279

Introduction

Caught Between Red and Green: The Electoral Dilemma

Dennis Altman

Politics can change fast. When we started discussing this project there was a real fear that Tony Abbott's government might succeed in imposing a set of policies on welfare, taxation, climate change, asylum seekers and human rights that would be more reactionary than anything yet envisioned in Australia. As the year unfolded he ran into increasing difficulties – both in implementing all his policies and in the public response – with a series of opinion polls that suggested Labor was on track to win the 2016 election. Months later Abbott was replaced by Turnbull, and the polls reversed.

Too much of our political debate revolves around individuals – Gillard versus Rudd versus Abbott versus Turnbull – which ignores the realities that leaders are constrained by their parties, but even more so by the larger social, economic and cultural environment. Across the western world, traditional political parties are struggling to retain members and cohesion, as new issues arise and new political parties emerge on both left and right. The problems for Labor of finding a coherent response to rapidly changing social and economic conditions is shared by social democratic parties across the western world, symbolised by the repeated electoral success of moderate conservative parties in Britain, Germany and New Zealand. While the Australian Labor Party (ALP/Labor) remains the only realistic alternative governing party it faces the possibility of losing some of its inner-city base to the Australian Greens (Greens).

In April 2015, I took part in an Open Labor discussion entitled: *Should Labor talk to the Greens*. The title was somewhat misleading; as one of the speakers pointed out Labor is constantly talking to the Greens, and under Julia Gillard developed a working, if sometimes tense, relationship with them in federal Parliament. In the short term this alliance seemed to work against both; Labor was consistently attacked as being held hostage by the Greens, and the Greens lost support because they were seen simultaneously seen as part of the system and as too radical – tree-hugging crazies who would destroy the economy, according to the Murdoch press and the Labor Right.

Open Labor is a group of people, mainly party members, who are trying to democratise the Labor Party and reduce the power of factions and party apparatchiks in what David Marr has referred to as the brutal world of the Victorian ALP.[1] Not surprisingly, the focus of the evening was less on how to work with the Greens than whether or not the Greens posed an ongoing and substantial threat to Labor's ability to build electoral majorities.

What was most interesting was that in a room of Labor supporters there was far more anger and frustration directed at Labor than at the Greens, who for many of the audience offered a model for Labor to emulate. While some people

---

1   David Marr, *Faction Man: Bill Shorten's Path to Power*, Quarterly Essay 59 (2015): 52.

mistrusted the Greens as unrealistic and unprincipled, more in the audience admired their stand on asylum seekers and the willingness to question the limits to growth. The attitude of some party officials, that the Greens are a major enemy who should be opposed even if it means doing preference deals with the Liberals, appeared a minority view in the room. Most of the people present were passionate about the need to challenge injustice and inequality, and angry at what seemed Labor's inability to offer clear alternatives to the [then] Abbott government.

Summing up the debate James Button and Tom Bentley wrote: 'Can Labor and the Greens cooperate on any level, or are they locked in a fight that can produce only one winner?'.[2] Framing the question in this way is important, because we are used to thinking of politics as a zero sum game, in which only one team can win. With bitter memories of the problems of managing a Parliament in which there was no clear majority there is a strong mood within Labor that they can only govern with an absolute majority, despite the considerable legislative achievements of the Gillard government.

The question is whether Labor and the Greens can find ways of working together while struggling for the same supporters. For those of us who belong to neither party it seems that far too much energy is spent in squabbles between two groups who share a common desire for a more progressive politics, even while disagreeing on several fundamental points. Just what these are, and whether they can be sufficiently reconciled, is the theme of this book. To answer this question means asking fundamental questions about larger social and economic

---

2 http://www.openlabor.net.au/open-labor-blog/should-labor-talk-to-the-greens-a-report-of-our-first-debate.

changes, even as electoral politics revolve around leadership styles and management competence rather than competing visions.

One of the clichés of contemporary Australian political analysis is to claim that Labor is increasingly unable to hold together the alliance of traditional working-class voters and a socially progressive 'new class', often referred to sneeringly as latté-sipping inner-city sophisticates, needed to win electoral majorities. There are those within Labor who would cede some of these votes to the Greens in favour of a greater populist appeal to suburban and provincial voters, assumed to be mainly concerned with economic issues; others argue for attacking the Greens head-on in their inner-city strongholds, a problem when they need ensure their preferences elsewhere. In a discussion with Michele Grattan frontbencher Sam Dastyari, a power broker within the NSW Labor Right, argued that Labor needed to respond more aggressively to the Greens, while nominating issues, such as climate change and same-sex marriage, where the more Labor seeks to differentiate itself from the Liberals the more it appears to be merely following the Greens.[3] For Victorian right-winger, Michael Danby, the real gulf between the two parties is on matters of national security.[4]

Some of the political commentariat seem agreed that the Greens will dwindle away under the pressure of some apparently immutable need for a binary party divide. Even as sensible a reporter as Jennifer Hewett has suggested that

---

3 *The Conversation*, 16 October 2015.
4 Michael Danby, 'Liberal deal with Greens could compromise our national security,' *Australian*, 14 January 2016.

'we just politely ignore the Greens as irrelevant'.[5] George Megalogenis's overview of Australian political history and future, published in 2016,[6] has literally no mention of the Greens, even though they were consistently polling between 12 and 16 per cent in opinion polls since the 2013 elections. Amanda Lohrey seemed more accurate in her cover story for the *The Monthly* declaring the Greens were now hitting the mainstream.[7]

Minor parties are hardly new in Australian politics, and they benefit from an electoral system that allows greater possibilities for representation than the first-past-the-post voting used in Britain and the United States. Australian politics are deeply shaped by a complex electoral system, which means preferences of minor parties are essential in the House of Representatives and can become byzantine in the Senate, leading to the changes to Senate voting pushed through by the Turnbull government with the support of the Greens in March 2016. What is new is a party that can seriously contest Labor's claim to occupy the more progressive side of Australian politics, and sees itself as becoming a serious contender for government.

When the Greens emerged out of battles to preserve the Tasmanian wilderness they seemed likely to be no more than a boutique party, capable perhaps of winning a few Senate seats and using their electoral position to highlight certain environmental issues. But with the demise of the Democrats

---

5   J. Hewett, 'Labor script not in Abbott plot,' *Australian Financial Review*, 17 October 2013.
6   George Megalogenis, *Australia's Second Chance*, Penguin, Australia, 2015.
7   Amanda Lohrey, 'The new Greens,' *The Monthly*, June, 2015.

in the first few years of this century, the Greens were able to appeal to both those voters who distrusted the two major groupings and those Labor voters who were increasingly disillusioned with what seemed an abandonment of progressive principles. In both New South Wales and Victoria, the Greens have won state seats from the conservatives [Ballina; Prahran] and former Nationals Leader, Larry Anthony, has warned of Greens inroads in traditional National territory.

While the Menzies government depended heavily on Democratic Labor Party (DLP) preferences after the Labor split of 1955, this was in a period when the major party groupings enjoyed a much larger share of the popular vote than they do today. Since 1949, when Menzies ushered in his remarkable twenty-three years of Liberal reign, Labor has only once won over 50 per cent of the popular vote [in 1954: an election it lost]. Hawke came close in 1983, but since that election Labor's primary vote has steadily declined. Hawke won the 1990 election with just under 40 per cent of first preferences, and Kevin '07 achieved 43 per cent in 2007.

Since then Labor has consistently struggled to win 40 per cent of the electorate, and in practice can only win government with a consistent flow of Greens preferences and the support of Greens members, where they exist, in Parliament. Both parties need each other to win seats, while simultaneously competing for the same group of voters, people who see themselves as 'progressive', and are likely to give high priority to issues such as climate change, civil liberties and immigration policies.

As Labor cautiously tries to position itself as 'progressive' on these issues – with the notable exception of asylum seekers – it runs up against a Greens party that is moving towards a more social democratic position. When Richard di Natale took over leadership of the Greens in 2015 he laid out a program that could well have been nominated by a Labor leader, and in practice the Greens have often seemed more interested in economic redistribution than has Labor. Di Natale has even floated the possibility of a formal Labor/Greens coalition government, with himself as Health Minister.[8] Given that such a coalition could only be established by the Greens winning some Labor held seats it is unlikely to be an attractive proposition to the ALP.

State politics have already seen various forms of Labor/ Greens coalitions. In 1989 the Tasmanian Labor/Greens Accord allowed the formation of a Labor government which lasted until the following year, when disputes over forestry policy saw the accord collapse and Premier Michael Field compare the relationship between Labor and the Greens to a 'forced marriage' which ended in a 'very acrimonious divorce'. So bitter were the relations between the parties that in 1998 Labor joined the Liberals in cutting back the size of the lower house to squeeze out the Greens, but between 2010 and 2014 Labor formed a government in formal coalition with the Greens who held several ministerial positions. That coalition was ended by Premier Lara Giddings in 2014 in the lead-up to a state election that saw major swings against both parties.

Between 2008 and 2012 the Greens supported a Labor government in the Australian Capital Territory (ACT), though without formal participation in the ministry; the Greens

---

8 James Massola, 'Richard Di Natale eyes cabinet post in future Labor-Greens Government as Malcolm Turnbull brings him in from the cold,' *Sydney Morning Herald*, 22 October 2015, http://www.smh.com.au/federal-politics/political-news/richard-di-natale-eyes-cabinet-post-in-future-laborgreens-government-as-malcolm-turnbull-brings-him-in-from-the-cold-20151022-gkfq7i.html.

were reduced to one seat in 2012 but the one member, Shane Rattenbury, became a minister in the Labor government. Like Tasmania the ACT uses proportional representation to elect its lower house; but in both Victoria and NSW in recent state elections the Greens have won lower house seats, and have members [though not the balance of power] in the upper houses.

It is common to complain that Labor has lost any sense of purpose beyond winning elections, and that it is increasingly a cabal of union-dominated professional politicians that at best will govern with a slightly more egalitarian tone. Yet for the foreseeable future Labor remains the alternative government. There is a real danger that the more successful are the Greens in attracting smart young recruits the harder it will be for Labor to attract sufficient members and candidates with a diversity of backgrounds. (It is difficult to get accurate figures for party membership; Labor still seems to have around 50,000 members, while the Greens have 10,000, numbers having surged for Labor when members were given a role in the choice of party leader.)

For the Greens the corresponding danger is that in order to attract more votes they will sound increasingly like Labor. The Greens webpage at the time of writing (October 2015) highlighted four issues: 'national biosecurity'; 'denticare for everyone'; 'standing up for small business' and 'build high speed rail'. It is hard to detect in these any policies with which Labor might disagree.

Labor no longer even identifies itself as a democratic socialist party, as Gillard made clear in an address during her Prime ministership:

> I come here to this union's gathering as a Labor leader. I'm not the leader of a party called the progressive party. I'm not the leader of a party called the moderate party. I'm not the leader of a party even called the socialist democratic party. I'm a leader of the party called the Labor Party deliberately because that is what we come from. That is what we believe in and that is who we are.[9]

In a world where fewer people identify as workers is this sufficient?

* * *

This book grew out of discussions with Nathan Hollier and Sean Scalmer in early 2015, and a shared concern that mainstream opposition to the Abbott government too often was bogged down in bitter disputes between the Labor Party and the Greens. Out of our discussions came invitations to a range of possible contributors to what we hoped would be a real conversation about the possibilities for progressive politics in Australia, meaning an emphasis on equity, social justice, human rights and a more generous and internationalist vision of our place in the world. More specifically, we were interested in how our contributors saw the choice between Labor and Green, and where they saw it most productive to put their energy.

Amongst our contributors there are different visions of what a progressive politics might encompass. Ours was an open-ended invitation, and each author has chosen to answer the

---

9 Julia Gillard, speech, Australian Workers' Union National Conference, 18 February 2013.

question in ways that reveal the very different priorities and preoccupations of people engaged in political debate. Many of those we would have liked to have contributed were not able to, for a variety of reasons, and inevitably some issues have been neglected, most particularly the ongoing shame of Australia's relationship to its Indigenous citizens. Anyone who has compiled a collection of essays, especially one with tight deadlines, will recognise the frustration when careful attempts at gender and geographic balance are undone by authors who, often for the best of reasons, are unable to complete the task.

We deliberately sought a balance between sitting politicians from both parties and activists and commentators from outside, who are clearly freer to express their doubts in and demands of the political system. Some contributors write from within the academy, others have chosen a far more personal style. We deliberately chose not to impose a template on our contributors, and we have organised the book as an on-going conversation, not seeking to prioritise any one position or way of approaching the question.

My Own Ambivalences

For me, as for many others, the topic of this book explores a personal conundrum. I grew up a gut Labor voter, probably due to the influence of my mother, but during the post-Tampa election of 2001 I was tempted for the first time to give an effective first preference to the Greens in the lower house (as I then lived in the electorate of Melbourne this was more than a merely symbolic vote). It was only on entering the polling booth that I finally resolved to vote Labor, partly because my then member, Lindsay Tanner, had indicated his own discomfort with the hard line on asylum seekers to which Beazley had committed the Australian Labor Party (ALP).

That indecision has remained with me ever since; I have consistently voted Greens in the Senate, and in 2010 I voted for Adam Bandt in the House of Representatives; however in the following year's state election I voted Labor in a seat (Richmond) where, again, the choice was meaningful. In that instance, I felt as the ALP seemed likely to win state government it was better to have the local member, Richard Wynne, in government, and such has proved to be the case.

I know and respect some of the major figures in both parties; I understand both those Greens who are disgusted by Labor's factional deals and those Labor supporters who see the Greens, in Peter Garrett's terms, as sanctimonious, 'promising a nirvana that couldn't be delivered and castigating everyone else as moral inferiors'.[10] Politics, it is often said, is the art of the possible. But what is possible is in turn politically constructed, and it is here that a Labor–Greens alliance offers new prospects for opening up a debate that goes beyond Labor's current attempts to appear progressive while being unwilling to challenge the basic assumptions of neoliberal economics. The ubiquitous attacks on high taxation (in reality, Australians are relatively lowly taxed), on 'the nanny state' and on the incompetence of the public sector are as much product of the much touted reforms of the Hawke–Keating period as are lower tariffs and a more open economy.

Rudd's victory in 2007 should remind us that Labor wins when it appears clearly more progressive than its opponents: think Gough Whitlam in 1972, Bob Hawke in 1983 and Paul

---

10 Peter Garrett, *Blue Sky*, Allen & Unwin, 2015, 276.

Keating in 1993. Attempts by Labor to position itself as a better manager of the status quo – Kim Beazley's tactic in 2001 – are less successful because the party can't outbid the Liberals on that ground unless the Liberals overreach (as Howard did with Work Choices) or run out of steam. What's different now is that Labor no longer has a monopoly of progressive views.

Some in the Labor Party understand this new political environment, and recognise that there needs to be real change in the way the party governs itself and proposes to govern Australia. But I doubt that Labor has the internal reserves to do this alone. The left–right division within the party is no longer much more than a way of distributing party spoils, and the goodwill briefly generated by the 2014 leadership contest between Shorten and Albanese was quickly dissipated by the cynical manipulation of caucus's vote for shadow cabinet by the factional groups. More significant even than party reform, Labor needs to radically rethink the legacy of the Hawke–Keating policies in light of the growing significance of global warming and the ongoing decline of manufacturing industry, which is probably irreversible given our population and the bipartisan zeal for free trade. Labor might save some shipyards; I doubt whether they will be able to resuscitate a domestic car industry.

Just as Liberals and Nationals have found ways of working together to build a coalition, despite moments of deep tension, the left needs to find ways of working together if we are to be relevant in face of a resurgent populist right. Every time Labor attacks Greens voters it reduces the possibilities of winning back the growing number of voters who are not willing merely to support Labor out of some residual sense that it is the party of those who are worse off. Labor may lose several inner-city seats to the Greens; it should worry more that it currently holds virtually no provincial electorates outside Victoria, except in Newcastle and Wollongong.

Coalition does not mean agreement; indeed the experience of the Labor-Greens coalitions in Tasmania have has disappointed many on both sides. But it does mean some mutual respect and discussion, and a willingness to swap preferences even where there are major disagreements about policy or candidates. While any alliance will be seized on by conservatives to attack Labor, a sensible dialogue would allow both parties to maintain a distinct identity while avoiding dissipating energies better directed at the right.

Politics is both about the allocation of economic resources and the recognition of diversity and inequality based less on money than on factors such as race, ethnicity, gender and sexuality. The Labor Party grew out of a passion to improve the lot of the working class, and class inequality remains a reality in Australia today, as so much of our popular culture – think of Christos Tsiolkas's novel *Barracuda* or television shows such as *Kath and Kim* or Upper *Middle Bogans* – reminds us. But we can no longer depend on the union movement to represent the worst off in society, nor can Labor claim a monopoly of concern for the dispossessed.

The Greens have grown beyond their original focus on the environment to embrace a range of issues that are concerned with social equity and justice. Precisely because they cannot become a party of government they are able to take a longer-term view on some of the key issues that face us, and on issues such as asylum seekers, climate change and international development they are a necessary corrective to those in Labor who are unwilling to think beyond the next election.

The 2013 election saw worrying signs of American-style politics, as Clive Palmer demonstrated that well-funded right-wing populism can be successful, but the swing to the right was also a consequence of Labor's failure to develop a genuine counter-narrative to that which defines conventional economic management and facilitating individual acquisitiveness as the central aims of government. A genuinely progressive politics would be one that questions some of the basic assumptions that have enabled the constant attacks on taxation and regulation, and demonstrates that in a country of growing urbanisation, an ageing population and environmental fragility we depend more, not less, on government.

Most Australians recognise the need for a disability insurance scheme, better-funded public schools, vastly improved public transport and a national broadband network, and acknowledge that this means increased taxation. Beware the constant mantra of the financial press about the need for more economic reforms: these are often code for new ways of increasing economic inequality, which, as Labor MP Andrew Leigh has demonstrated, is already rising in Australia.[11] The market can't do much about growing transport gridlock or the increasing fragilities of an ageing population, though it seems very effective in increasing the wealth gap between a small part of the population and the rest.

Political parties remain essential mechanisms for allowing a liberal democracy to function, but they cannot alone create major changes to the status quo. At best they can articulate new demands and build on progressive forces, as Whitlam did in recognising the case for women's equality and Aboriginal

---

11 Andrew Leigh, *Battlers and Billionaires: The Story of Inequality in Australia*, Black Inc. Redback, Carlton, 2013.

land claims, as Keating did in his reframing of our links with Asia, as Gillard did in her espousal of the national disability scheme.

Both Labor and the Greens grew out of significant social movements, and it is the role of social movements and of intellectuals to constantly challenge the status quo, and to place new issues on the political agenda. Political parties by themselves can't change the political culture, even though the best politicians find ways of articulating new ways of seeing the world. Those of us who believe deeply in a progressive agenda will inevitably be disappointed by the compromises and failures of elected governments, but rather than attacking politicians we to need find ways of creating sufficient popular support for them to take bolder steps.

It is the nature of electoral politics that it concentrates on the immediate rather than the long term, on incremental rather than radical change. Even so, there is a timidity in current Australian political thought, expressed in declining satisfaction with the political system and disillusionment with current political leadership. The belief that we might create a better society, that political debate might be creative rather than managerial, seems to have largely vanished. It is our hope that the conversations in this book might rekindle a larger sense of political possibility.

Chapter 1

The Effect of the Institutional Settings on the ALP–Greens Relationship

Nicholas Barry, Stewart Jackson and Narelle Miragliotta

The long-term decline in the Australian Labor Party's (ALP) primary vote and the growing electoral success of the Australian Greens (Greens) has led to speculation about the future relationship between the two parties. Comments by the federal leader of the Greens, Richard Di Natale, have raised the prospect of Greens serving as ministers in a future ALP-Greens coalition government,[1] with one commentator, Brad Orgill,[2] going so far as to suggest that the amalgamation of the two parties is a viable option. Others have emphasised that the parties are rivals and some within the ALP have argued that the party should adopt a more aggressive electoral strategy towards the Greens.[3]

These discussions, however, often fail to consider the ways in which the institutional context shapes the relationship

---

1 Massola, 'Richard Di Natale eyes cabinet post.'
2 Brad Orgill, *Why Labor Should Savour its Greens: Rebuilding a Fractured Alliance*, Scribe, Brunswick, 2013.
3 John Ferguson and Verity Edwards, 'Party in revolt on PM's deal with Greens,' *Australian*, 19 August 2013, 1.

between the two parties. This chapter focuses on this issue, exploring how Australia's political institutions are likely to affect the ALP-Greens relationship over the medium to longer term. We argue that these institutions militate against close and sustained cooperation between the two parties, particularly a coalition arrangement. The current institutional framework favours, at best, weak and opportunistic forms of cooperation between the parties.

The Parties Compared

It is easy to assume that the similarities between the ALP and the Greens (for example, their roots in a radical democratic heritage) are greater than their differences. However, this ignores the fact that the ALP and the Greens formed in very different historical contexts in response to very different political circumstances. The ALP is a creature of the trade union movement, emerging out of the materialist struggles to secure jobs, decent wages, education, and health care for the working class and the poor. The Greens, however, have their roots in the late twentieth century new social movements championing post-materialist concerns concentrated around social justice, the environment, peace and disarmament and participatory democracy. Although the ALP has broadened its platform to incorporate these issues since the 1970s, this continues to sit alongside more traditional materialist concerns.[4] Within the ALP, there remains strong resistance towards some aspects of the post-materialist agenda among influential party figures. In fact, part of the motivation for

---

4 John Warhurst, 'Transitional hero: Gough Whitlam and the Australian Labor Party,' *Australian Journal of Political Science* 31(2) (1996): 243–252.

the formation of the Greens was the belief that a number of post-materialist issues were not being adequately addressed by the ALP.[5]

There are also differences in the parties' respective bases of support. The Greens have their organisational roots in the radical participatory democratic culture of the late twentieth century and its constituents are generally younger than major party identifiers, with the highest proportion aged 18–24 and the lowest in the 65+ bracket. They are more likely to hold a tertiary qualification, to be employed in one of the professions, and they are predominately urban dwelling.[6] The ALP has also attracted significant support from tertiary-educated urban professionals and those involved in the new social movements. Nonetheless, its traditional support base is among working-class voters, and although this has weakened in recent decades, one of the major differences between the parties is that the ALP continues to be heavily dependent on support from manual workers.[7]

The different political, social and economic forces which propelled their formation, as well as their different bases of voter support, suggest that a merger would be an unlikely scenario and also extremely difficult to achieve. It has never

---

[5] Narelle Miragliotta, 'From local to national: Explaining the formation of the Australian Green Party,' *Party Politics* 18(3) (2012): 409–425, at 417.

[6] Narelle Miragliotta, 'The Australian Greens: Carving out space in a two-party system,' *Environmental Politics* 22(5) (2013): 706–727, at 712.

[7] The figures were 38 per cent for the ALP and 7 per cent for the Greens in the 2013. See Clive Bean and Ian McAllister, 'Documenting the inevitable: Voting behaviour at the 2013 Australian Election,' in *Abbott's Gambit: The 2013 Australian Federal Election*, ed. Carol Johnson, John Wanna and Hsu-Ann Lee, ANU Press, Canberra, 2015.

been seriously entertained by elites or the membership of either party. This is because amalgamation would require the two parties to collapse their respective structures to create a new party organisation. While there are some areas of overlap in the ideology and voter base of the two parties, there are also major areas of differences across values, policy and organisational formats that would prove difficult to reconcile.

Nor does either party have a compelling reason to contemplate amalgamation. While it has been suggested that amalgamation might be a way of potentially re-energising the ALP's moribund branch structure,[8] the ALP has a continuous organisational history that spans over 125 years. The ALP is also the only party capable of consistently forming government in its own right. The Greens too have emerged as a stable and resilient parliamentary party capable of influencing legislation and government formation. It consistently wins seats in jurisdictions that use proportional electoral systems to elect members, and it has begun to achieve significant victories in inner metropolitan state and federal lower house electorates.[9] The party's electoral growth has been modest, but steady, and there are indications that it has acquired a small but committed partisan base of support.[10] While the Greens is a younger party than the ALP, it has now existed as a genuinely national party organisation for more than twenty years.

Some believe amalgamation would strengthen the position of the left in Australia, but it might in fact produce the opposite

---

8 Kate Crowley, 'Against Green minority government? Themes and traditions in Tasmanian politics,' *Tasmanian Historical Studies* 14 (2009): 137–153.
9 Since the early 2000s, approximately ten Greens have been elected to single member lower houses electorates.
10 Miragliotta, 'The Australian Greens.'

effect. The ALP is able to reach a much broader spectrum of voters than the Greens, which has a narrower electoral base primarily consisting of inner metropolitan tertiary-educated professionals. Moreover, the parties' core constituencies will prove difficult to unite. The Greens' base is affluent, progressive and holds values and supports policies that many in the ALP's traditional working class and trade union base at best do not prioritise, and at worst, reject. The risk in amalgamation is that the new party would struggle to accommodate both constituencies, resulting in the new organisation attracting fewer votes than the combined support base of the ALP and Greens presently.

Partial amalgamation between the ALP and the Greens – as might occur if a schism in one party results in a significant proportion of its members leaving to join a second party – is also an unlikely scenario.[11] Both parties are certainly riven by internal divisions. In the case of the ALP, these divisions are open and formalised in factions, while in the case of the Greens, the divisions are generally less organised and often subterranean.[12] However, in either case, the cleavages that

---

11 The closest example of partial amalgamation occurred when the ALP split over the issue of conscription in 1916. The then ALP Prime Minister, William Hughes, along with four ministers and 26 other members of caucus, resigned from the party and eventually joined with Liberals to form the Nationalist party.

12 Although, see Cate Faerhmann, 'Greens won't get much further If we repeat poll blunders,' *Sydney Morning Herald*, 7 April 2011, http://www.smh.com.au/federal-politics/political-opinion/greens-wont-get-much-further-if-we-repeat-poll-blunders-20110406-1d4e7.html#ixzz3n0R1hd7f; and Andrew Crook, '"The new normal": Rhiannon forces triumph in NSW Greens,' *Crikey*, 21 October 2013, http://www.crikey.com.au/2013/10/21/the-new-normal-rhiannon-forces-triumph-in-nsw-greens/?wpmp_switcher=mobile.

presently exist, while occasionally disruptive, are not of the kind likely to produce the kind of ruptures last seen in the ALP in the Split of 1955. While some members have left the Greens over internal differences over the years, these have been in very small number.

There is also little likelihood of party elites defecting to the other party. Recent history suggests politicians have good reason to be wary of crossing from minor parties to major parties and vice versa. The story of Cheryl Kernot and her defection from the Australian Democrats to the ALP is particularly instructive. Kernot left the Democrats while still a high profile party leader. Although she was enticed across to the ALP, she was not welcomed by local ALP branches, and she held the federal seat of Dickson for just one term before losing. Equally, state politicians who have left the ALP and joined the Greens (Ronan Lee in Queensland and Kris Hanna in South Australia) have faced suspicion and distrust within the party. While Lee lost his subsequent re-election bid, Hanna quit the Greens prior to the 2006 South Australian state election to successfully contest his seat as an Independent, sensing perhaps correctly that ALP voters were more likely to accept him as an Independent than as a Greens candidate.

For these reasons, it is highly likely that the two parties will continue to operate as separate organisations for the foreseeable future. Whether this relationship is cooperative or antagonistic is, however, likely to be strongly shaped by the institutional framework within which they operate. We explore this in the next section.

Navigating the National Institutional Context

The conventional wisdom was that the Australian system is primarily majoritarian in character with a two-party, or on some accounts, a two-and-a-half party system. The government–opposition dynamic is dominant and relations between the major parties are antagonistic. One of the major factors contributing to this is the use of the single-member preferential system for House of Representatives elections.[13] This makes it difficult for minor parties – other than the Nationals – to gain representation as they generally lack a sufficient concentration of support in any one geographical area to win a seat. This produces highly disproportionate vote-to-seat share outcomes, with major parties securing more seats in parliament than their vote share warrants, while minor parties gain much fewer seats. By way of example, the Liberal–National Coalition (Coalition) received 45.5 per cent of the first preference vote and 60 per cent of the seats in the House at the 2013 federal election.[14] In contrast, the Greens secured 8.7 per cent of the vote but only won the seat of Melbourne. The ALP and the Coalition between them won a total of 145 out of 150 seats.

A further consequence of vote-to-seat disproportionality is that the ALP or the Coalition is almost always able to form government in its own right. The second Gillard–Rudd Government (2010–13) was a notable exception, becoming the first minority government in the postwar period. The

---

13 For more, see Arend Lijphart, *Patterns of Democracy*, Yale University Press, New Haven, 1999, 143–170.

14 'House of Representatives votes and seats won, national summary,' Australian Politics and Elections Database, University of Western Australia, http://elections.uwa.edu.au/elecdetail.lasso?keyvalue=1872, accessed 19 January 2016.

combination of stable parliamentary majorities for the governing party/parties alongside Australia's relatively high levels of party discipline, effectively gives the party leadership control of the House of Representatives. It is rare for the opposition or the small number of minor parties managing to win seats to have much legislative impact in the House because the government does not normally need their support to pass legislation. This fosters a bipolar dynamic to party politics in Australia, which is primarily oriented around an antagonistic contest between the ALP and the Liberal–National Coalition for office.

However, these majoritarian features of the Australian system sit alongside other more consensual elements that can encourage limited forms of cooperation between the parties.[15] Senate elections are conducted under proportional representation using the single transferable vote. When teamed with multi-member statewide electoral districts, more proportionate outcomes are produced, giving minor parties a greater opportunity to gain parliamentary representation. At the 2013 Senate election, the Liberal–National Coalition received a total of 37.7 per cent of the first preference vote and won 42.5 per cent of the seats, while the Greens received 8.7 per cent of the first preference vote and won 10 per cent of the seats.[16] Overall, 11 of the available 40 seats were won by parties other than the Coalition or the ALP.

---

15 Arend Lijphart, 'Australian democracy: Modifying majoritarianism,' *Australian Journal of Political Science* 34(3) (1999): 313–326.

16 'Senate votes and seats won, and seats held, national summary,' Australian Politics and Elections Database, University of Western Australia, http://elections.uwa.edu.au/elecdetail.lasso?keyvalue=1863, accessed 19 January 2016.

Another important consequence of the Senate electoral system is that it is rare for the governing party to have a majority of seats. The John Howard Coalition Government had a majority in the Senate from July 2005 until it lost office in October 2007, but that was the first time since 1981 this had occurred. When this is combined with the strongly bicameral nature of the Parliament – legislation cannot pass without going through the Senate – this adds an important element of consensus democracy into the Australian system.[17] For the government to get its legislation through the Parliament, it must negotiate with the Opposition or the minor parties who hold the balance of power in the Senate. Parties have an incentive to cooperate and negotiate with each with other, at least some of the time. This is not to deny that there are many occasions when major bills are blocked by minor parties and/or the Opposition in the Senate, but the vast bulk of government-initiated legislation is passed.[18]

The use of forms of preferential voting in both houses of parliament is another feature of the Australian political system conducive to cooperation between the parties. For House of Representatives elections, there is an incentive for major parties to do deals with minor parties to attract preferences in key seats. The same thing occurs in the Senate, although there is also an incentive for minor parties to do deals with each other in the hope of obtaining enough of the surplus vote to meet the quota and get elected.

---

17 See, for example, Lijphart 'Australian democracy.'
18 Harry Evans, 'The case for bicameralism,' in *Restraining Elective Dictatorship: The Upper House Solution?*, eds Nicholas Aroney, Scott Prasser and John Nethercote, UWA Press, Crawley, 2008; Stanley Bach, 'Senate amendments and legislative outcomes in Australia, 1996–2007,' *Australian Journal of Political Science*, 43(3) (2008): 395–423.

A similar blend of majoritarian and consensual features exists at state and territory level in Australia. Four jurisdictions – Western Australia, South Australia and Victoria and the Northern Territory – have single-member electoral districts in the lower house of parliament and use compulsory full preferential voting, which requires voters to number all squares on the ballot paper in descending order of preference. In two other states – New South Wales and Queensland – the system is optional preferential voting, where voters may elect to number past one candidate, or stop before numbering all candidates. These electoral systems make it difficult for minor parties to get elected, and politics tends to have a highly majoritarian character in these jurisdictions. In New South Wales, Victoria, Western Australia and South Australia, this is partly off-set by the use of proportional representation in the upper house, which facilitates greater minor party representation, and encourages a more consensual dynamic between the parties. The two exceptional jurisdictions in Australia are Tasmania and the Australian Capital Territory (ACT), which use the Hare-Clark system for lower house elections. This is a form of proportional representation that is much more likely to produce parliaments where the minor parties have the balance-of-power, making various forms of cooperative arrangements, including coalitions, more likely, as discussed below.

In sum, outside of Tasmania and the ACT, the institutional framework of the Australian system is highly majoritarian in certain respects, producing a two-party/two-and-a-half party dynamic that is conducive to highly antagonistic relations between the two major blocs. However, there are also elements of the system associated with consensus democracy

– particularly strong bicameralism, the Senate electoral system and preferential voting for elections of the lower house – which encourage more cooperative forms of interaction between the parties. This is why Lijphart has described the Australian system as a form of 'modified majoritarianism'.[19] The next section will look specifically at what this means for the prospects of an ALP-Greens coalition.

The Options Considered

Coalition

As mentioned above, the idea of an ALP–Greens coalition has been floated on occasions. Coalitions are formal written agreements that set down executive power sharing between two or more parties. Such an arrangement enables two or more parties to form government, particularly in circumstances where neither has sufficient support to govern alone. While a coalition arrangement preserves the organisational independence of the parties, it diminishes the autonomy of their parliamentary wings.

Greens internationally have been involved in a number of governing coalitions with parties from both the left and right. The situation of the Greens in the German states of Hamburg and Hesse – where they are in coalition with the Social Democrats (SPD) and Christian Democrats (CDU) respectively – is an example of a successful coalition arrangement between the Greens and establishment parties. Within Australia, there have also been examples of ALP–

---

19 Lijphart, 'Australian democracy.'

Greens coalitions in Tasmania (2010–14) and the ACT (2012–16).

However, ALP–Green coalitions have tended to occur in jurisdictions that use proportional representational systems to elect the lower house. The majoritarian electoral system used for House of Representative elections makes it difficult for minor parties to win enough seats to make coalitions necessary. In addition, minor parties are competing in an environment in which almost three-quarters of voters continue to identify as Liberal, ALP or National, even if the strength of partisanship has declined over time.[20] The effect of this is to limit minor party gains to areas where they have some natural advantage, such as the Nationals in rural and regional areas. The only apparent Greens party advantage appears to be in inner urban areas in major cities, although there are still very few electorates that are likely to produce a result where a high Greens primary vote can be translated into a win.

This being the case, the likelihood of the Greens securing a sufficient number of seats in the lower house to be a viable coalition partner for the ALP is low. This has not occurred in those states most likely to have the population in inner urban areas to elect Greens (New South Wales and Victoria), although a number of Greens MPs have been elected successfully to lower house seats. Greens tend to be corralled into upper houses of parliaments, with favourable multi-member electoral systems, and remain unviable as a coalition partners for the ALP.[21]

---

20 Ian McAllister, *The Australian Voter: 50 Years of Change*, UNSW Press, Sydney, 2011, 38–43.

21 Charnock examined the Greens as a replacement for the Australian Democrats and noted the difficulty the Greens would have in respect

The Tasmanian and ACT experience also suggests there are electoral risks for the Greens in entering a formal coalition arrangement with the ALP. In 2014, the Greens in Tasmania found themselves on the wrong side of an electoral backlash against the Giddings ALP Government. At this election, the Greens haemorrhaged a third of their vote and lost two of their five MPs. In the ACT, the Greens reached a formal agreement to support the ALP government after the 2008 election. They held the parliamentary Speakership, but did not formally enter into a coalition arrangement. However, at the 2012 election, they lost a third of their vote, and three of their four MPs. This rather disastrous election was salvaged by their remaining MP, Shane Rattenbury, being in the balance of power and able to negotiate a Cabinet position in the ALP government. Nonetheless, it is clear that being seen as too close to the government can have distinctly a negative electoral impact for the Greens.[22]

Accords and Agreements

Another option would be for the Greens and ALP to enter into an accord or agreement relating to the formation of government and securing Supply. An accord is similar to a

---

of losing their base if they moved to a centrist position occupied by the Democrats. See David Charnock, 'Can the Australian Greens replace the Australian Democrats as a 'third party' in the Senate?,' *Australian Journal of Political Science* 44(2) (2009): 245–258.

22 Wolfgang Rüdig, 'Is government good for Greens? Comparing the electoral effects of government participation in Western and East-Central Europe,' *European Journal of Political Research*, 45 (2006): 127–154; Stewart Jackson, *The Australian Greens: From Activism to Australia's Third Party*, Melbourne University Press, Carlton, 2016.

coalition agreement in that it is manifest in a formalised pact between parties. However, it differs from a coalition in an important respect. Accords do not deal with sharing executive office but rather set out the terms for mutual support in exchange for very particular policies or other demands (such as regular consultation with the Prime Minister). This generally affords the signatories freedom to operate as independent legislative actors, while avoiding the spectre of legislative and governmental instability.

The Greens have negotiated parliamentary and electoral agreements with governments, especially in the ACT and Tasmania. The Greens' support for Tasmania's Tony Rundle Liberal Government from 1996 to 1998 is a notable example. At the 1996 state election, the incumbent Ray Groom Liberal Government lost its majority in the Legislative Assembly, while the Greens emerged with four seats. Although the ALP and the Greens could have entered into a coalition, the then ALP leader, Michael Field, refused to do so. Instead, the Greens reached an informal arrangement with the Liberals to allow them to govern as a minority government.

Although the Rundle Government lost the 1998 election, bedevilled by high and persistent unemployment, this Government was successful in some regards.[23] But the clear downside for the Greens was that, even though they demonstrated responsibility in working with the minority

---

23 For a full discussion of how the Greens operated in relation to the Rundle Liberal government see Kate Crowley, 'Strained parliamentary relations: Green-supported minority government in Tasmania,' *Australasian Parliamentary Review*, 17(2) (2003): 55–71; and Richard A. Herr, 'Reducing parliament and minority government in Tasmania: Strange bedfellows make politics – badly,' *Australasian Parliamentary Review*, 20(2) (2005): 130–143.

Rundle government, at the end of the term a tacit agreement emerged between the Liberal and ALP parties on electoral reform to reduce the size of the House and attempt to exclude the Greens.

In spite of the risks for minor parties in negotiating formal alliances with major parties, there are benefits in doing so. Minor parties may be able to bargain for particular policies, or at least moderate government policies they oppose. But the general effect is that any policy 'wins' will be claimed by the major party, and any 'losses' (particularly where there is a negative impact for electors) will be blamed on the actions of the minor party. While it is also possible that a minority government might be necessary to maintain 'stable government,' a media compliant or supportive of the government, such as existed at the time of the Rundle government, can be utilised to prosecute the view that the minor party is hindering reform or economic growth. In a state such as Tasmania, with persistent high unemployment, this is a strategy that can easily be invoked by the major party to shift the blame.

From the ALP's perspective, this suggests that there may be some subtle benefits from the presence of the Greens in parliament. However, the first experiment with an ALP–Greens Agreement in Australia left many in the ALP wondering if it was possible to work with the Greens. This agreement was struck in 1989 between the Fields ALP Government and the Greens. It floundered when the ALP, under pressure from the forestry industry, sought to secure the continuation of the industry. Legislation to this effect was supported by both major parties, and the Greens withdrew support for the Government, forcing an early election, which the Liberal Party won. Many in the ALP at the time thought the Greens could not be trusted again. However, since then the experience has been generally more positive. The ALP Lara Giddings Government that was formed after the 2010 state election was able to govern with the Greens in Cabinet, with the then Greens Leader, Nick McKim, even prepared to deliver unwelcome news on budget cuts to the electorate.

The Greens' success at the 2010 federal election, and in the subsequent negotiations over the terms of their support for the Gillard–Rudd ALP Government, might point to the potential for future such arrangements with the ALP. However, poor opinion poll results, a concerted campaign against the ALP and Prime Minister Julia Gillard from a conservative press and the Opposition Leader Tony Abbott led to a collapse in confidence in the Gillard Government, with the Green-negotiated carbon price as its most hated element. Just as Tasmanian Premier, Michael Fields discovered with the ALP–Green Agreement in 1982, at some point the divergent ideologies of the major parties and the Greens will eventually dent any lasting agreement. While it may be possible to win and hold government with Green support, this strategy appears to work most successfully when serving as a prop to weak governments nearing the end of their tenure, and not in the form of stability offered by the Nationals to the Liberals.

Competition

Given that the prospects of a long-term ALP–Greens coalition or formal accord are fairly remote at this point in time, and agreements are only likely on a case-by-case basis, this seems to leave both parties in ongoing competition for the constituency of progressive, tertiary-educated professionals.

While the Greens are heavily dependent on this constituency, it is also vital to the ALP's electoral success in a number of inner metropolitan seats. The likelihood of continued electoral warfare between both parties vexes those progressive thinkers who believe that the viability of the left requires some sort of formal coalition or accord between the ALP and the Greens.

However, there are possibilities for informal forms of cooperation between the parties that fall short of full coalition or a formal accord. Given that the Greens are permanent fixtures of the Australian political system, the ALP will need to accommodate and adapt to this situation. The nature of the Greens' core constituency means that its core base is likely to remain concentrated in inner-city electorates and so will not threaten the ALP heartland areas in the working-class dormitory suburbs such as in western Sydney and Melbourne.[24] If an informal electoral agreement could be reached to not compete except in certain agreed circumstances, then the prospects of both parties prospering would be increased. This would mean, for example, that the ALP would not run candidates against a sitting Greens MP such as Adam Bandt, who wins a seat in an inner-city electorate, while the Greens would not run candidates against the ALP in an agreed set of key ALP seats. This would allow the ALP to concentrate their campaign resources on seats at threat from the Coalition, while the Greens could concentrate their resources on shoring up their Senate vote. It would also pave the way for a general

---

24 Notwithstanding the occasional exception, such as the regional electorate of Ballina, where the electoral dynamics have altered due to the arrival of 'tree changers' who previously voted in inner-city electorates, and the issue of coal-seam gas mining. See Jackson, *The Australian Greens*, for a broader discussion of the activist and voter makeup of the Australian Greens.

preference swapping agreement between party elites where the ALP would agree to preference the Greens over other parties in the House and the Senate, while the Greens would agree to preference the ALP.

These moves could be combined with ad hoc arrangements for securing stable minority government. These ad hoc arrangements could be negotiated after an election that produces a hung parliament, as occurred in 2010. However, they could be the result of a verbal agreement between the two party leaders rather than signed in a formal document, potentially helping avoid the perception of a de facto coalition. This arrangement would guarantee Supply for a minority ALP government, while still allowing both parties to pursue their own policy and legislative goals. While this would appear to keep the ALP beholden to the Greens, the reality of electoral politics is in fact the reverse. It is the major party that has the upper hand in terms of agenda setting and media access. However, there would still be potential benefits for the Greens in allowing them an open line to policy makers through regular consultation with key ministers, and a greater prospect of implementing Green policies.

Although the informal arrangements relating to electoral competition outlined above are not completely infeasible, in the current environment, it is doubtful that either party would agree to them. It is not clear that the ALP would benefit much from the absence of Green competition in seats under threat from the Coalition as these are rarely seats attracting a high Green vote. In fact, it is in seats where the Green vote is higher – such as Sydney, Batman, or Fremantle – that the ALP would benefit most from not having to divert resources to campaign against the Greens, but these are the seats the Greens want to win, so they are unlikely to agree to include them in any agreement that limits competition. The ALP is also unlikely to be prepared to concede long-held inner-city electorates such as Melbourne to the Greens when they are lost. An on-going across-the-board preferencing arrangement between the parties also seems unlikely as both the ALP and the Greens would be likely to depart from any such arrangement and deal with other parties when they think it would be electorally expedient. The most likely scenario, then, is a continuation of the status quo.

Conclusion

The institutional setting creates some incentives for the ALP and the Greens to work together but these incentives are not sufficient to generate sustained forms of cooperation at the national level, such as amalgamation, coalition, or even informal agreements to limit electoral competition. The structure of incentives within the institutional setting, and its tendency to produce a zero-sum game in relation to electoral and legislative rewards, generates a very specific understanding among parties about the benefits and the costs of forging close ties. In the case of the Greens, closer ties with the ALP is largely understood in terms of its potential to provide access to, and experience of, power on the long road to supplanting the ALP as the main progressive party. The benefits for the ALP exist only to the extent that it may help them to form government, to win seats in close competition with conservative parties, and securing some of its legislative outcomes in parliament.

The fact that the institutional setting mostly inspires competition between parties ultimately makes it difficult for them to overcome the fundamental differences that exist between them. The ALP is a centre-left party, adept at winning and holding government by appealing to the median voter. The Greens sit further to the left, with no clear cleavage constituency other than inner-city dwellers: the 'culture-creatives'. Close and formalised cooperation between the parties would require them to shed policy, position and principles. This is likely to be opposed by the voter base and activist core of both parties, and it is strongly discouraged by the institutional rules of the game.

Chapter 2

Progressive Voting, Party Organisation, and Political Reform: A Historical View

Sean Scalmer

The pioneers of the Australian Labor Party understood their actions as a contribution to progress: an expression of the 'increasing intelligence of the age', read one 1890 statement;[1] a means of uniting electors in pursuit of 'democratic and progressive legislation', read another.[2] Over more than a century, the Party's leaders have persistently described themselves as modernisers: 'generators of change', 'breaking new ground',[3] bearers of the 'demands and opportunities of the future'.[4] Labor is the party of 'initiative', many political

---

1 Report of the First Annual Session of the General Council, A.L.F., Brisbane, 1 August 1890, in *The Australian Labor Movement 1850–1907*, ed. R.N. Ebbels, Australasian Book Society, Sydney, 1960, 205.
2 Labor Electoral League's objects, cited in George Black, *History of the N.S.W. Labor Party*, Sydney, 1910, reprinted in Ebbels, *Australian Labor Movement*, 210.
3 Terms used by Bob Hawke (1991) and Andrew Fisher (1911), reproduced in *Labor National Platform: A Smart, Modern, Fair Australia*, 2015, http://www.alp.org.au/national_platform, 10.
4 Gough Whitlam, *Australian Labor Party Policy Speech, 1972*, http://whitlamdismissal.com/1972/11/13/whitlam-1972-election-policy-speech.html, 1.

scientists have agreed.[5] The current Labor platform declares a continuity of purpose: 'For us, the true reward of politics is progress'.[6]

But what might it mean to be a party of 'progress'? The term implies forward movement or advancement. In consequence, the label has been embraced by a diversity of political actors; it lacks a stable referent. For those Labor candidates elected to the first Commonwealth Parliament, 'progressive' legislation included racial exclusion, a citizen army and compulsory arbitration; all three would now more commonly be seen as regressive.[7] Likewise, the advocates of state ownership in the early twentieth century claimed to be bearers of progress, while the privatisers and free-marketeers of the 1980s and '90s deployed a similar rhetoric. And if Laborites have aspired to represent 'progressive' politics, then this is equally true of Liberals of various kinds. Robert Menzies famously embraced the middle class as the basis of a 'dynamic democracy': 'the strivers, the planners, the ambitious ones'.[8] National progress, he argued, came through policies that rewarded 'the efforts of the individual'.[9]

---

5   There are also notable dissenters. See Henry Mayer, 'Some conceptions of the Australian party system 1910–1950', *Historical Studies: Australia and New Zealand* 7(27) (1956): 253–270.

6   *Labor National Platform*, 10.

7   Stuart Macintyre, 'The first Caucus', in *True Believers: The Story of the Federal Parliamentary Labor Party*, eds John Faulkner and Stuart Macintyre, Allen & Unwin, St. Leonards, 2001, 18.

8   Robert Menzies, 'The forgotten people', http://www.liberals.net/theforgottenpeople.htm.

9   Robert Menzies, 'Election speech, 1946', http://electionspeeches.moadoph.gov.au/speeches/1946-robert-menzies.

In this context, it is difficult to establish a definition of 'progressive policy', much more to identify it with a single party. Historically, however, Labor's claim to embody 'progress' has rested not just on the Party's sponsorship of particular policies. Rather, it has emphasised perhaps more strongly the Party's claim to represent a political organisation of a new and superior kind.

Formed in the aftermath of devastating strike defeats at the beginning of the 1890s, the new institution was established by trade unionists: conscious of the power of state repression, anxious to use government to defend their interests. Its then novel structure reflected such a collective mission. The Labor representative in parliament was to be a delegate of the movement, pledged to implement Party policy; that policy was to be formed at a Labor conference, made up of representatives from affiliated trade unions and from local Labor leagues.

Traditionally, Westminster parliaments emphasised the duty of the representative to serve constituency rather than party and to follow the dictates of individual conscience over collective discipline. The rise of Labor therefore reshaped the practice of democracy. This was a political organisation of a new kind. Through the procedures of Labor conference, the policies to be submitted to the election might be determined by Labor members and affiliates. By the imposition of new controls on politicians, the activity of representatives could be directed and constrained. With the rapid growth of the new institution, working people might now successfully contest elections against the wealthy and well connected.

Labor's distinctive version of democracy won precocious success. The party stormed into colonial parliaments, generating an enormous sense of belonging and commitment. It seemed to some a kind of political religion. The Party's opponents recognised that Labor in government formed but one part of a broader movement; it campaigned without end. Labor leaders even spoke of a 'light on the hill' – a 'great objective' that transcended the quest for improved conditions, extending, almost mystically, to the 'betterment of mankind... anywhere we might give a helping hand'.[10]

And yet, when Vere Gordon Childe – a socialist, prehistorian and a former secretary to a Labor Premier – analysed *How Labour Governs* in 1923, he wrote with a sense of controlled disappointment. Labor's vaunted theory of democratic collectivism had been thwarted in practice. A great progressive promise had not been fulfilled.

Propelled into Parliament and thence into the Ministry, members of Labor Governments, Childe observed, were apt to lose touch with the movement's animating spirit. The need to win the votes of those outside the union movement weighed heavily. The decisions of Labor Conference were often ignored; its delegates powerless to enforce their will upon the politicians they had helped to elect. At the gatherings to determine party policy, genuine collective discussion was frequently trumped by factional manoeuvring. The numbers spoke loudest; the battle for control rested mostly on covert intrigue and wire pulling. Solidarity could not be preserved when serious political conflicts emerged; the party split over conscription, economic emergency, and communism.[11]

---

10 J. B. Chifley, 'For the betterment of mankind – anywhere', in *Things Worth Fighting For: Speeches by Joseph Benedict Chifley*, ed. A. W. Stargardt, Melbourne University Press, Carlton, 1952, 65.

11 Vere Gordon Childe, *How Labour Governs: A Study of Workers' Representation in Australia*, 2nd edn, Melbourne University Press, Carlton, 1964 [1st edn, 1923] lays out the arguments later used by many other critics.

If these weaknesses have long been evident, then the events of the last few decades have raised further and more fundamental problems for Labor's democratic mission. The Party that brought miners and engine drivers into national leadership is now dominated by professional politicians: former staffers, union functionaries, party officials, with little direct experience of work or business. Trade union membership has declined precipitously, particularly in the private sector. The most dynamic and successful unions of recent years – the nurses and teachers – are not affiliated to the ALP. In fact, more than 90 percent of Australian workers do not belong to unions affiliated to the putative 'party of labour'.[12] Local labour leagues have reduced in number and importance; more than 100 ALP branches folded in New South Wales in the decade leading up to 2009, alone.[13] In consequence, Labor's internal processes can no longer be considered anything but the most indirect expression of the views of working people. The Labor machine works commendably as a ladder of opportunity for the ambitious. It is not an effective means of bending the parliament to the people's will.

Political mobilisations evident especially since the 1970s have drawn attention to the limits of Labor's progressive vision, in any case. In waves of connected protests, liberationists have claimed greater freedom and equality for women, gay men, and lesbians; concerned citizens have demanded enhanced protection of animals and the environment; Indigenous people have asserted the right to land, self-government, and recognition; migrant communities have sought to maintain

---

12 Rodney Cavalier, *Power Crisis: The Self-destruction of a State Labor Party*, Cambridge University Press, Melbourne, 2010, 32.
13 Cavalier, *Power Crisis*, 47.

their own ways of living, and their equal status in a new land. Bearers of hopes that transcended class identities, these groups have aimed to create their own political spaces, where they might share distinctive experiences, clarify particular concerns, and articulate independent demands. The Labor party has not always been able to recognise the importance of these new aspirations. Its organisational rituals, and its culture, have often failed to accommodate the ways and priorities of quite different political campaigns.

Perhaps the most vigorous challenge has been launched by the environmental movement. Though celebration of the natural world has a venerable history, political campaigns in defence of the environment emerged most powerfully only a few decades ago. In opposition to the damming of wild rivers in Tasmania, a new electoral organisation, the United Tasmania Group, was formed in the early 1970s. It has since been claimed as the world's first green party.[14] Its failure to halt government's plans provoked more militant tactics. When a further dam menaced the Franklin river system on the island's south-west coast, a major movement emerged in its defence. The campaign to save the Franklin encompassed mass civil disobedience on land and water; rallies in major centres of population; legal challenge; and political lobbying. Its success helped to establish an abiding movement and an enduring repertoire of contention.[15] It was succeeded by many similar campaigns to protect Australia's native forests.

---

14 Amanda Lohrey, *Groundswell: The Rise of the Greens*, Black Inc., Melbourne, 2002.

15 *The Franklin Blockade*, by the Blockaders, Wilderness Society, Hobart, 1983; James McQueen, *The Franklin: Not Just a River*, Penguin, Ringwood, 1983; Peter Thompson, *Bob Brown of the Franklin River*, George Allen & Unwin, Sydney, 1984.

Labor acted to incorporate or tame the new movement, with at least some success while it held office.[16] But the more devoted and impatient protectors of the environment also began to enter parliaments as independent and Green candidates of various kinds. In 1992 they formed their own national party, 'The Greens'.[17] Without question, it now constitutes a third force in Australian politics. In Tasmania, the ACT, and nationally, Greens parliamentarians have supported minority Labor governments, extracting major concessions and wielding genuine influence; they have also been prepared to negotiate deals with non-Labor parties. The Greens holds seats in lower and in upper houses in Commonwealth and state parliaments.

If the Labor Party's roots in industrial battles bequeathed a culture of collective solidarity and disciplined number-crunching, then the character of campaigning to defend the environment has also shaped the political culture of the Greens. The party claims to have been 'founded on the principle of grassroots democracy'.[18] Like Labor, the Greens privilege a National Conference: the 'supreme governing body' of the party.[19] Unlike Labor, the Constitution of the

---

16 Nicholas Economou, 'Greening the Commonwealth the Australian Labor Party government's management of national environmental politics, 1983–1996', PhD, University of Melbourne, 1998; Timothy Doyle, *Green Power: The Environment Movement in Australia*, UNSW Press, Sydney, 2000.

17 Bob Brown and Peter Singer, *The Greens*, Text Publishing, Melbourne, 1996.

18 Greens, *Standing Up For What Matters: The Greens' Plan for a Better Australia*, http://greens.org.au/platform, 51.

19 Greens, 'The Charter and Constitution of the Australian Greens', http://greens.org.au/sites/greens.org.au/files/AG-Constitution-Nov-2014-1-2.pdf, 13.

Greens affirms that: 'Serious attempt will be made to make decisions by consensus at all meetings'.[20] The decision to move to a vote (technically a 'procedural motion') is made only after persistent disagreement; it requires a two-thirds majority. Any vote subsequently taken to change the status quo also needs two-thirds support.[21] Likewise, individual attendance and participation of party members in 'All meetings of the Greens' is explicitly welcomed.[22] Collective deliberation is therefore much more strongly emphasised than internal vote-winning.

These principles of design are matched by a looser and less tightly policed political culture. The Charter of the Greens formally accepts that electoral politics 'is by no means the only step' towards a better society. It pledges support for 'grassroots movements and community initiatives' that share the party's overriding goals.[23] Green representatives elected to Parliament tend to define themselves as activists rather than politicians,[24] and to work to promote heightened community involvement in law making.[25] Questioned by political scientists, the majority of Green parliamentarians continue to emphasise the import of participatory democracy.[26] The concept of 'grassroots

---

20 Ibid., 16.

21 Ibid., 17.

22 Though in practice this may be tempered at the 'discretion' of the major 'delegated meetings: Ibid., 17.

23 Ibid., 3.

24 Nick Turnbull and Ariadne Vromen, 'The Australian Greens: Party organisation and political processes,' *Australian Journal of Politics and History*, 52(3), 2006: 459.

25 Ariadne Vromen and Anika Guaja, 'Protesters, parliamentarians, policymakers: The experiences of Australian Green MPs,' *Journal of Legislative Studies*, 15(1), 2009: 101.

26 Vromen and Guaja, 'Protesters,' 107.

participatory democracy' constitutes one of the party's 'four pillars', or most prized objectives.[27] And there is no distinct career path to becoming a Greens MP.[28]

This is a political institution that much more closely resembles the ways and assumptions of contemporary campaigning than the bureaucratised procedures of the venerable Labor machine. Animated by the looming horizon of environmental emergency, broadened by an increasing engagement with economic and social equality, elevated by the principled advocacy of its MPs, the Greens have enjoyed rapid growth. Like the Labor Party of the late nineteenth century, its propaganda claims a special capacity to meet contemporary challenges ('you cannot solve problems with the same mindset that created them').[29] In the eyes of increasing numbers, it is the home of progressive politics.

Still, the long history of Labor's achievements and disappointments here provides some pause. When Labor members first entered parliament, they also seemed more idealistic and committed than their established forbears. When plunged into the maelstrom of parliament, however, they found it difficult to retain a dual commitment to electoral success and radical purpose. Until recently, the Greens have mostly been protected from these tensions by their relative marginality. As they emerge as a genuine 'third force', so they also face increased scrutiny and pressure. If the Labor Party's elaborate organisation has not preserved democratic vitality, then the danger also threatens that Green decision-

---

27 Greens, 'Charter and Constitution,' 7.
28 Vromen and Guaja, 'Protesters,' 91.
29 Greens, *Standing Up for What Matters*, 5.

making will not be able to cope with significant involvement in legislature and executive, either.

The structure and culture of the party presents some possible dangers. Consensus decision-making has long been criticised for its openness to manipulation: a so-called 'tyranny of structurelessness', in which elites mask their direction of group decisions, and informal networks wield a covert power.[30] Reflecting a reluctance to assert organisational control, a substantial minority (around three in ten) of surveyed Green activists do not believe that their elected representatives should be bound by party policy.[31] Green parliamentarians themselves appear to have widely divergent views on the matter.[32] Under these conditions, adherence to progressive reform cannot simply be assumed.

Tendencies toward increased centralisation and professionalisation of the institution have also recently been observed.[33] And the positional authority of the Party leader has recently been described as a 'highly contentious' issue among Green MPs.[34] The 2015 resignation of one Federal party leader, Christine Milne, and the rapid appointment of a successor, Richard Di Natale, seemed to resemble the internal machinations of Labor and Liberal apparatchiks much more than

---

30 Jo Freeman, 'The tyranny of structurelessness,' 1970, http://www.jofreeman.com/joreen/tyranny.htm.

31 Stewart Jackson, 'Thinking activists: Australian Greens Party activists and their responses to leadership,' *Australian Journal of Political Science*, 47(4), 2012: 602.

32 Vromen and Guaja, 'Protesters,' 103–104.

33 Narelle Miragliotta, 'Minor organizational change in Green parties: An Australian case study,' *Party Politics*, 21(5), 2015: 706–707, 709.

34 Christine Cunningham and Stewart Jackson, 'Leadership and the Australian Greens,' *Leadership*, 10(4), 2014: 507.

the transparent quest for collective agreement. Comparison with Green parties elsewhere also suggests that grassroots democracy may not survive heightened participation in national government.

Controversies over party organisation and culture extend also to legislative bargaining; the deals Greens politicians have variously struck and refused over the past few years have also been the subject of some contention. Under the Rudd Government, the Greens voted down a Carbon Pollution Reduction Scheme, arguing that it lacked sufficient ambition, flexibility, or encouragement of renewable energy.[35] Some environmental organisations disagreed (among them the Australian Conservation Foundation and the World Wildlife Fund).[36] Some progressive critics have suggested that this was an opportunity lost.[37] Australia currently lacks a sure procedure for the pricing of carbon.

In 2015, the Greens agreed to support a Liberal Party proposal to reduce pension entitlements for those retired Australians with substantial assets (more than $500,000, for an individual), held in addition to the family home. In exchange, the Liberal Government agreed to a small increase in the full pension ($15 per week) and a fuller review of retirement incomes policy, as part of a white paper tax review.

---

35 'The Greens and emissions trading – your questions answered,' 14 January 2010, http://greensmps.org.au/content/news-stories/greens-and-emissions-trading-%E2%80%93-your-questions-answered.

36 Guy Pearse, 'The climate movement: Australia's patrons of climate change activism,' *The Monthly*, September 2011, https://www.themonthly.com.au/issue/2011/september/1316399650/guy-pearse/climate-movement.

37 For example, John Menadue, 'Holier than thou… but with disastrous results,' http://johnmenadue.com/blog/?p=704

These changes are strictly progressive – favouring poorer pensioners by taking from the richer. But they also further entrench the notion that the pension is a safety net payment for the improvident or needy, not an entitlement for the citizen. The ACTU opposes; the Australian Council of Social Services supports the deal.[38]

At the end of 2015, the Greens also came to an agreement with the Liberal–National Coalition Government on laws governing multinational tax avoidance. Labor and the Greens had originally opposed Government proposals, insisting that multinational companies with turnover greater than $100 million be forced to disclose their tax arrangements. While Labor held firm, the Greens ultimately relented, agreeing to lift the threshold to $200 million per annum. 'The choice is a simple one', argued Richard di Natale, 'we either get nothing or we get significant strides forward'.[39]

Many progressive voters will doubtless applaud these parliamentary decisions. But some will question their principle and their wisdom. If most progressives will have a great deal of sympathy with Greens values and aims, then the precise actions of Greens parliamentarians are likely to be much more contested and uncertain. And it is not clear that the party's structures necessarily provide the mechanisms to deal with conflicts of these kinds.

Does the Greens political organisation then offer no greater opportunities for promoting progressive reform than the

---

38 Van Badham, 'Did the Greens turn into the "bastards" on pensions?,' *Labor Herald*, 18 July 2015, https://www.laborherald.com.au/economy/greens-indistinguishable-from-other-bastards-on-pensions/.

39 http://www.abc.net.au/news/2015-12-03/coalition-and-greens-strike-deal-on-multi-national-tax-avoidance/6997328.

party of labour? Are both institutions cursed by structural and cultural weaknesses? How is progressive change best promoted? These questions are most reliably answered historically, by a consideration of the long span of Australian political reform. Such an historical survey reminds us that progressive change has been possible at several moments in Australia's past. It also suggests that it is the vitality and breadth of political campaigning, not the precise make-up of the parliament, that most influences the prospects of positive change.

* * *

Whatever the foibles and disappointments of particular parties and individuals, Australian democracy has been punctuated by several periods of major progressive reform. In the middle of the nineteenth century, propertyless men won the vote and a secret ballot (what came to be known as 'the Australian ballot' elsewhere). Striking workers, supported by a broader movement, won the eight-hour day.

Using their new parliaments to enact substantial reform, colonial citizens designed land laws to aid the settlement of farmers on small properties, and, especially, in Victoria, a system of industrial protection to nurture new businesses and thereby support mass employment. At the turn of the nineteenth century, women won the right to vote. New institutions were also established to limit the clash of labour and capital; in practice, they came to provide a floor of wages and conditions under which white men would not work. This industrial system has been called the 'wage-earners' welfare state', and it helped to define Australia (and its sister-state of NZ), as a kind of social laboratory for state experiments.

In following decades governments responded to pressures to augment social protection. Old age and invalid pensions were legislated; child endowment and widows' pensions followed; then a more substantial welfare state, in the process of wartime government and postwar planning in the 1940s. Next, under the Whitlam Government (1972–75), then later, new efforts were also made to address gender inequality; to recognise Aboriginal land rights; to register the contribution of migrants to Australian culture; and to protect animals and the environment.

While there remains much to be done, there is a clear and persistent tradition of political reform to address social need. Moreover, this has not been the work of a single institution. No party has traversed the long history of Australian political change.

Democratic reform, land legislation and industrial protection were all enacted by parliaments mostly grouped according to personal factions or only transitory forms of political organisation.[40] Driven by fear of class conflict, middle-class liberals mostly designed and enacted Australia's pioneering labour legislation.[41] Women's organisations campaigned for the extension of a wage-earners' welfare state to cover their own, neglected needs.[42] Reformist intellectuals provided much

---

40 Peter Loveday and A. W. Martin, *Parliament, Factions and Parties: The First Thirty Years of Responsible Government in New South Wales, 1856–1889*, Melbourne University Press, Carlton, 1966.
41 Stuart Macintyre and Richard Mitchell, eds, *Foundations of Arbitration: The Origins and Effects of State Compulsory Arbitration, 1890–1914*, Oxford University Press, Melbourne, 1989.
42 Marilyn Lake, *Getting Equal: The History of Australian Feminism*, Allen & Unwin, St Leonards, 1999.

of the agenda for postwar reform,[43] as they did for a great deal of the new program that the Whitlam government so assiduously implemented.[44] More recently, action to protect animals and the environment owes at least as much to independent campaigning, and to the Australian Democrats and the Greens, as it does to any party of government.

This does not imply that the work of party politics is irrelevant, and that popular campaigning automatically translates into progressive reform. On the contrary, the transfer of collective mobilisation into law and procedure is a work of great complexity. It requires a capacity for coalition-building and bargaining, a commitment to principle and an eye for the necessary compromise.

A historical understanding clearly demonstrates that no political institution has monopolised these capacities. It further demonstrates that an elaborate party machine is an insufficient condition for positive change. In the context of strong and progressive movements, politicians of many kinds have sought to remake law and institutions. In the absence of popular pressure, the election of nominally progressive politicians has rarely proved enough.

Of course, the lessons of history are not crafted on great stone tablets; they are open to competing interpretations. Still, if external pressures do play a key role in shaping progressive government, then this suggests that the presence of a more radical and uncompromising flank, to the left of the Labor

---

43 Stuart Macintyre, *Australia's Boldest Experiment: War and Reconstruction in the 1940s*, NewSouth Books, Sydney, 2015.
44 Terry Irving and Sean Scalmer, 'The public sphere and party change: Explaining the modernization of the Australian Labor Party in the 1960s,' *Labour History Review*, 65(2), 2000: 227–247.

Party, is likely to help more than hinder the broader prospects of reform. Moreover, if that party explicitly recognises the value of grassroots movements, and if its parliamentarians work to aid independent campaigns, then its ability to exert pressure for good should be further enhanced.

To the extent that the Greens play this role, they can advance progressive change. It is in their greater attachment to principle and to activism that they can help drag the polity further leftwards. Tension with the Labor Party, and an apparent unwillingness to register the 'realities' of the major parties, are a constitutive part of this political position. It is precisely by being apparently 'impractical' and 'unreasonable' that the Greens might perform their most valuable political function. Progressives who remain committed to Labor might be wise to recognise this fact, even if it is through gritted teeth.

Green parliamentarians, for their part, might recall the fate of the Australian Democrats or, more recently, the Liberal Democrats of the United Kingdom. Deals struck with conservative governments have neither advanced party nor people. Attempts to demonstrate Greens flexibility by reaching accommodation with conservatives will likely alienate Australian progressives looking for an alternative to the Labor machine. Adoption of a more 'professionalised' political form will undermine the party's distinctiveness, even as it reassures the more established or wary.

The Greens party's devotion to the principles of grassroots democracy and individual participation separates it from the older party of labour. This is the wellspring of its political energy. The more creatively and persistently the party can find continuing ways of including members and supporters in meaningful decision-making, the more strongly will it preserve its singularity and its radical power. To the extent that it does so, the party and polity will be in its debt.

Chapter 3

Leaving Labor for the Greens

Ellen Sandell

I remember the day I lost faith in the Labor Party.

It was the start of the school year in 2008 and a blistering 37 degrees.

I was a young, optimistic climate change policy advisor, working in my dream job in Labor Premier John Brumby's Department. For months, I had been working on a policy to put solar panels on every Victorian school, passionately putting in the hours to create something I believed would have a huge impact on our climate.

As I got ready for work one morning, I turned on talkback radio for background noise. My ears pricked up as parents started calling the radio, complaining their kids had to go to school on such a hot day when most classrooms didn't have air conditioners, but I didn't think much of it as I got on my bike and rode into work.

As I walked down the corridor towards my desk, still in my riding clothes and brushing sweat off my brow, I saw a piece of paper on my desk: a note from the Premier. I can't remember the exact wording of that fateful note, but, in so many words, it said: 'You know the solar panels idea? How much would it cost to put air conditioners in every Victorian school instead?'

I was crestfallen. This 180-degree-turn on policy from the Premier – from reducing pollution with solar panels to increasing energy use with air conditioners – was devastating for a young, idealistic climate advisor. All it took was a handful of parents calling talkback radio and the Premier changed his mind in an instant.

I didn't know it at the time, but that moment set me on a path to becoming the first lower-house Greens MP in the Victorian Parliament.

I never wanted to be a politician. I always wanted to be a scientist. Growing up in country Victoria, separated from Melbourne by nearly 600km of dusty highway and wheat paddocks, 'politician' was not an option the school careers advisor ever offered. I didn't know any politicians, and nobody in my family had ever been elected to public office (unless you count my dad becoming the Secretary of the local Red Cross branch, and their youngest member by about 30 years).

I, like many Greens members, grew up in a Labor household. We had a Paul Keating magnet on our fridge and my dad was a long-time member of his union. Living in a rural area, there weren't too many Labor-voting families like ours, but my parents' strong sense of social justice put their values at odds with the Liberal and National parties, who they believed stood up for the wealthy at the expense of the community and the environment. It was considered normal for mum to throw things at the television when John Howard appeared on screen.

Growing up a stone's throw from the mighty Murray River, it was impossible not to notice the impact of drought on the environment and the local growers, or the impact of overgrazing on the nearby national parks. It was also impossible not to form a strong bond with, and love for, the natural environment: the red and brown dirt, the rolling sandhills, the Mallee scrub and the big, big sky. But it wasn't until I moved to Melbourne to attend university that I learnt the long drought I had experienced during my adolescence was not just a one-off, but was potentially the new 'normal'.

Climate change was the issue that galvanised me to take action – and the issue that put science on a collision course with politics.

While I was at university learning about the dangers that climate change posed to everything I cared about: food, farmland, health, security, the environment and our way of life, I also learned pretty quickly that the barriers to action weren't scientific or technical: they were political. I still wanted to be a scientist, but we already had scientists telling us about the problem and how to fix it: what we lacked was political will.

When I graduated from university, after a short research stint at the CSIRO, I landed a job in the Office of Climate Change. Working on climate policy was the hottest thing around, as Al Gore's *An Inconvenient Truth* lent celebrity status to the issue, and Kevin Rudd signing the Kyoto Protocol gave Australians hope we might finally stop being international laggards. I started the job believing the Victorian Labor Government also wanted to act, but one too many policy backflips dampened my spirits.

Not only were my hopes crushed by the air conditioners incident, but I was constantly confused by the fact that everyone seemed to walk around with blinkers on. My colleagues would work for hours on programs to encourage people to drive their cars a little bit more conservatively to save tiny amounts of CO2, while conveniently ignoring the fact that four brown-coal power plants produce nearly half of our total pollution – far outstripping transport and agriculture. Looking at solutions for phasing out coal was not encouraged.

I have no doubt many people in the Department wanted to do the right thing, but their good intentions were stymied by the stranglehold that vested interests had on the Labor Party, and the fact that dealing with climate change was never going to be as big a priority as keeping Labor in power.

When the Federal carbon price was being debated, a consultant was engaged by the Victorian Government to tell us how badly energy companies would be affected. When the answer came back that energy companies would not be nearly as badly affected as many people imagined, I heard the consultant was asked to change the report and its assumptions, so coal companies could get more compensation than was really necessary. The writer of the report apparently quit in disgust, but nobody blew the whistle and a new report was published.

The management of Victoria's native forests was another contentious topic where industry spin, rather than scientific rigour, dominated the debate inside the bureaucracy and political circles. I couldn't have been more excited when I was tasked with writing the chapter on forestry for the climate change strategy. I put in long hours, poring over the latest peer-reviewed research from the Australian National University that indicated we should protect our native forests as carbon stores because they are some of the most carbon-dense in the whole world. Once drafted, my chapter was sent off to another Department for checking, and returned completely covered in red text, with the scientific references replaced by forest industry spin. Bureaucrats and politicians were so close to the forestry industry that they believed the spin more than they believed the peer-reviewed science from one of our top universities.

These demoralising experiences led me to three important realisations.

My first realisation was that vested interests have an incredibly strong influence over the old political parties, including Labor. I saw this play out many times during and after my stint in the Department – from the blatant direct influence of reports being changed, to the political donations from the fossil fuel industry and property developers, and the soft-power plays of industry leaders drinking with politicians in Parliament House after hours.

My second realisation was that the Labor Party is set up to deliver small, incremental change, but to essentially protect the status quo. Climate change is never going to be a higher priority to the Labor Government than jobs, or the economy, or votes in marginal seats, despite it being clear that the economy is a wholly owned subsidiary of our environment, not the other way around. Climate change, however, needs a fundamentally different approach from the status quo, because we're about to hit the tipping points that might make it impossible to avoid devastating consequences.

My third realisation was that traditional Labor and Liberal politicians rarely lead the community, but are led by pressure from the community or from vested interests, whomever is the loudest. Ultimately the game has become about staying in power no matter the cost.

I learnt that while we did need good bureaucrats, what we really needed was people pushing our politicians in the right direction, and to drown out vested interests. We needed to make it harder for politicians to stay with the status quo, and easier for them to act on important issues.

I finally understood that I could be powerful if I joined with other people to pressure politicians on climate change, so I left the Department and started working for the Australian Youth Climate Coalition (AYCC), where I would go on to become the CEO. Our mission was to create a movement strong enough to change policy on climate change and protect our future.

During my time at the AYCC, we grew to over 100,000 members across Australia. We educated tens of thousands of school students about the impacts of climate change, ran programs in the Pacific to raise the voices of those on the front-line of climate change, sent delegations to the UN climate talks, gained commitments to repower Port Augusta with solar energy, helped put climate change on the agenda during federal elections, and more. We advocated strongly for a price on carbon to curb emissions and make big polluters pay to clean up their act. Throughout my time at AYCC, I saw significant policy shifts on climate change, such as a price on carbon and $10 billion invested in clean energy through the Clean Energy Finance Corporation and the Australian Renewable Energy Agency.

These changes didn't happen because Labor or the Liberals woke up one morning and decided to do the right thing. They happened because strong, sustained community pressure showed them the cost of inaction, and the biggest gains happened when the Greens held balance of power in both houses of Parliament.

My theory that politicians act when the community pressures them to do so, and when they're scared of losing seats, has been born out many times since I left the Department.

For example, in 2010 John Brumby committed to a phase-out of Australia's dirtiest coal power station, Hazelwood. He could have done it years before, but instead he announced it during an election year, after a strong campaign by environment groups, and when the Greens looked like winning four inner-city seats from Labor.

In 2014, I was part of a similar campaign to stop the East West toll road. A strong community campaign combined with the threat of losing inner-city seats to the Greens saw Labor change their position on the toll road and promise to rip up the contracts, just months before the election.

While some people in Labor will say that they always wanted to implement these policies, and no doubt there were good people inside Labor who worked hard on them, the reality is that it wasn't until they risked losing seats that they actually acted.

I've also seen this dynamic play out in the current Victorian Government. The threat of the Greens introducing legislation to ban smoking in outdoor dining areas and for an inquiry on voluntary euthanasia led to the Labor Government putting these issues on the agenda when they otherwise had no plans to do so, or would have done so at a much, much later date.

These experiences have proven to me that the Greens are an incredibly powerful force in Australian society, and we won't achieve enough progressive change with just Labor alone.

In the short-term, pressure from the Greens can make Labor better, which is a good reason in itself to put more Greens into Parliament. The Greens can use our clout to make important issues – like climate change, refugees and public transport (or voluntary euthanasia and smoking) – a public priority, and force Labor to implement policies or talk about issues they otherwise wouldn't.

As Greens Leader Richard Di Natale has said, the challenges of the twenty-first century are challenges the Greens were set up to tackle. Addressing the challenges of climate change – equality and how to build prosperity for the public good not just private interests – are in our DNA. These are the reasons the Greens were set up in the first place.

While we've seen the two major parties' ideologies gradually converge over the past few decades, the Greens are emerging with real alternatives.

But the Greens aren't just in Parliament to be activists, asking Labor to act for us, or to raise issues for other parties to deal with. In the longer-term, we have ambitions to form government and implement our policies in full, and I wouldn't be in Parliament if I didn't see a prospect of us doing so.

The first, and very achievable, step down this path is gaining balance of power in both houses of Parliament, at a Federal and State level.

The prospect of the Greens gaining this type of power is understandably scary for the Labor Party. While the Liberals are their opponents, the Greens are an existential threat to Labor. One day soon we might replace them.

The way Labor has responded to this threat is instructive. In some cases, it has led to Labor adopting a more progressive stance on policy, and even adopting some of the Greens' policies, like cancelling the East West toll road contracts and finally starting to talk about getting rid of unfair tax concessions on superannuation. In other cases, this fear of being replaced has led Labor to some strange behaviours that are counter-productive to the progressive cause.

My friends and supporters are shocked when they watch me give a speech in Parliament, where two grey-haired male Labor MPs are often placed strategically in the chamber to howl me down so I cannot be heard. These men laugh as they trade 'shouting duties' with the most right-wing Liberals and compete for who can put me off my game, tag-teaming when one of them runs out of insults to yell. I've been subject to the dirty tactics and online trolling of Labor staffers as they put all their energy into bullying and trying to trip me up, rather than fighting the real opposition of vested interests and conservative politicians who seek to widen the gap between the rich and poor and block action on climate change. I've introduced Bills into Parliament (such as banning donations from property developers to politicians, and making Alcoa's coal operations subject to the same FOI laws as other companies) only to see Labor take the unprecedented move of voting them down at the first reading. Even though it was sensible policy, Labor did not even allow a debate, just so the Greens wouldn't get 'a win'.

I used to believe Parliament was a place for genuine debate and ideas. Then, when a Labor member yelled out across the chamber 'it's not your ideas we hate, it's just you', I realised just how entrenched the tribalism of the Labor party has become, and just how personally they take it when the Greens take a seat from them. They've lost sight of why they're in politics in the first place (surely to make change, rather than just to win the contest?).

Before the election last year, Victorian Premier-to-be Daniel Andrews held a press conference at his father's farm in Wangaratta and declared he would never do a deal with the Greens in Victoria.

It was a short-sighted move. After the election he found himself with the Greens in shared balance-of-power in the upper house and he now has to get used to negotiating with us.

It's only a matter of time before Labor finds themselves with the Greens in balance of power in the lower house as well. In that scenario, if they want to form Government they have two choices: work with the Greens or work with the Liberals. I know which one their progressive voters would prefer.

Faced with the rise of the Greens, the Labor Party can choose one of two approaches. They can take the approach of the Australian Capital Territory (ACT) Labor Party, who have realised that they have more in common with the Greens than with the Liberals, and if we form an alliance, we can keep the right-wing conservatives out of power for decades and create real progressive change. Or, the broader Victorian and Federal Labor Party can entrench their stubborn refusal to work with the Greens, even when we agree on many policies.

The public will be better served if the Labor Party realises that the Greens aren't going anywhere, and in order to achieve progressive policy in this country, we must work together. It might not be a formal coalition like exists between the Liberals and Nationals, but perhaps an election-by-election agreement to form Government together or achieve specific policy aims, as was done with Adam Bandt during the Gillard minority Government.

The Greens have shown our willingness to work with Labor, as evidenced by Greens MPs taking ministries in the Tasmanian and ACT Labor Governments, and working closely with Julia Gillard's Government to deliver a productive government that helped her pass more legislation than any other Prime Minister in Australia's history. In that government, the Greens negotiated important reforms that Labor would not have implemented on their own such as the introduction of an effective carbon price, the Clean Energy Finance Corporation, the Australian Renewable Energy Agency, the Parliamentary Budget Office for accurately costing election promises, and free denticare for kids. With those outcomes, we know the achievements of Greens in balance of power can be substantial, practical, responsible, and transformative for our country.

Now the ball's in Labor's court. Will they let go of the view that the Greens are the enemy, and put progressive policy above a desire for unbridled power, as they have in the ACT? Or will they dig their heels in, and continue to fight the Greens, to the detriment of their vote and the detriment of good policy?

Ultimately, it's a question that can only be answered by Labor.

I sincerely hope they choose to work with the Greens, rather than against us, because our country and our community will be stronger for it.

Chapter 4

How I Fell out of Love with the Greens: A Personal Story about the Labor Party

Van Badham

Indulge me. This is not going to be an academic analysis of contemporary Australian politics. It's not an essay I'd submit to the *Guardian*. It's a first-person tale – a memoirette, perhaps – of a failed political romance.

I'll admit from the outset this story heaves with cliché. The young heroine, disappointed early in her expectations, creates an object of affection from projections of her own ideological fantasy. She defends her wilful imaginings with fervour, but when confronted with an undeniable truth – spoiler alert – she leaves the relationship, a little sadder, an ocean wiser.

I write this for posterity, to share a subjective history that charts one imperfect person's most imperfect journey from political innocence to experience across roughly thirty years of Australian history, and with an intergenerational inflection. It's the story of how, after my heart was broken by Labor, I then fell out of love with the Greens. I've chosen a personal form for the telling of it because my recent experiences with the subject matter have been all too personal. Three nights ago, at midnight, I found myself on the receiving end of a Twitter trolling attack coordinated by a group of Young Greens, containing a variety of denouncements, including an 'anonymous' one (too soon exposed) that suggested I belonged in 'the KKK'.

My present rejection of the Greens is not due to this behaviour. My own history reveals that rare is the overeager, over-politicised undergraduate who can restrain themselves from punishing a perceived enemy. Rather, the experience was symptomatic of a malaise I can only describe as an 'awareness sickness' which stirred again in me six months ago, when Richard Di Natale became leader and the Greens' subsequently voted with the Coalition government to cut the aged pension. What had attracted me to the Greens was their promise to 'do politics differently'. The realisation has been nauseating for months that they are – of course – just like everybody else.

* * *

I was never an instinctive Greens voter. My family were Labor – I grew up around my mother's people who were Irish, Catholic, working class and rusted-on. These were people penniless and, unable to speak English when they emigrated, they worked as itinerant shearers. Then, the family stumbled out of retail jobs and the Erskineville Catholic ghetto and into active service in the Second World War. Our family's fortune began its transformation with this event; thanks to the *War Service Homes Act*, my returned grandfather was able to build a fibro clapboard house on the grey soil of a new and dusty Sydney suburb. The rambunctious clan moved in, and this single capital asset facilitated three generations of growing aspiration.

My father assimilated neatly into the shared values of the family sprawl. He was descended from Scots immigrants, who'd escaped the slums around the Glasgow docks where they'd built ships for new lives as retail clerks and shop hands in New Zealand. My father's father had a talent for sport and it won him a scholarship to teacher's college – but his aspirations to teach were dashed when he contracted tuberculosis. There was no welfare net to catch my father's mother; she added jobs in shops to jobs in kitchens and she stayed there. My father's only memory of his father was through the plastic wall at a tuberculosis hospital where he died when dad was three.

Both sides of my family were well-read and articulate people, who loved newspapers and adored books. It was only economic necessity that forced them out of school to work; Mum went to work in offices, Dad drifted into the world of the track and betting shop. In Australia, my family members were all members of unions, because unions fought for them, and the Labor Party fought for people represented by unions. What my grandparents saw in Curtin and Chifley, my own parents saw in Whitlam, Hawke and Keating; it was the policy determination to equalise social and economic opportunities so families like mine could have any.

Strong amongst all was the generational memory of the past where jobs were rough, poorly-paid and dangerous, education denied or threadbare, healthcare an unattainable privilege. Strong, too, was the desire amongst specifically these people, all their fine intellects thwarted merely by birth into the wrong class, that there would be educational opportunities for their children. Whitlam was more than human to my parents; the introduction of free education illuminated a world of the suddenly possible for their soon-born child. It was a light that did not dim for my parents even with Hawke's introduction of the deferred-payment HECS scheme.

They trusted a Labor that over the course of their lifetimes had created Medicare, pensions, public housing, the CES, the ABC, no-fault divorce, equal pay, superannuation, the anti-discrimination act, sewered every Australian metropolitan home, withdrawn troops from Vietnam – and so much else. When Mum and Dad were told the HECS scheme would improve the breadth and quality of education, they believed it.

So did I. And I did finish Year 12 at my suburban state school, I did do well in my exams, I did win a place at – oh my god – university. I joined the Labor Party in O-Week, an act of acknowledgment, perhaps, of my Dad's instruction: 'Never forget, Vanessa; you owe your education to the Labor Party'.

It may have been true, but my gratitude was growing uneasy. At the University of Wollongong, I never made it to a meeting of the Labor club, but I fell into student politics, anyway – and began to develop an ideological vocabulary. The Cold War had ended a couple of years before my enrolment, but state-schooled and 'first in family' to study, I developed a class consciousness as fiery as that of any vintage red. While rich kids bought themselves a discount on their HECS fees with upfront payments, and poor kids heaped debt upon themselves that ethical careers would be unlikely to repay, the realisation dawned that the system was unfair.

I had no taste for the campus's tiny socialist cults, always waving about dogmatic publications with a wan hand. It was with independent vigour I threw myself into environmental causes, the women's group, the media collective, Indigenous rights campaigns, and whatever other social justice activism was on offer. I ran with a non-aligned ticket in the student elections because they were my friends. We won, and I headed off to debut my participation in the National Union of Students (NUS). It was a conference at Southern Cross University, Lismore, 1994.

I still had my ALP membership card in my wallet when I met the student manifestation of the Labor Party for the first time.

***

Growing up, I'd absorbed talk of the 'NSW Right' for years. In truth, from Sydney there was a certain local pride in the Sussex-Street-based Labor faction that had built an unassailable machinist grip on the Party and, at that point, the nation, too. I remember as a teenager reading a Fairfax article about the takeover of Young Labor by the Right with glowing profiles of leaders Reba Meagher – now long fled politics – and Joe Tripodi, now exposed for corruption and forever disgraced. Back then, though, they presented as bright and organised, the rising generation of the bold, practical politics espoused by Paul Keating – as well as kids from suburbs just like mine. And if Paul Keating supported it, whatever 'economic rationalism' was, it sounded fair.

This was all I understood about factional politics in Labor, on the Left, or at all when I climbed into a car to get to Lismore. A Wollongong friend had organised a ride up there, driven by another non-aligned student from Macquarie and a girl from Melbourne University who, like me, seemed to have half-a-connection to the ALP. The car trip was a political initiation; our driver detailed every political sin of the state and National NUS officers, their campaign inaction on issues of import – like the environment – and their misguided spending priorities. Back in Wollongong, struggling to reorganise our student council in the wake of overturning a corrupt regime, our contact with NUS had been resentful, countering their incessant demands for money we couldn't find. I was surprised to learn that the NUS leadership who had afflicted us were all from the ALP Left.

That was, until I encountered them. We arrived in Lismore after dark, to find the conference organisers drunk and playing truth-or-dare. This was my first attack of adult 'awareness sickness' in a political context. Mostly middle-class, from Sydney University and University of New South Wales, they spilled vodka, pizza and beer on the floor of the Lismore student accommodation that NUS money had rented. Their attempts to recruit me into their ranks were not entreaties to political like-mindedness, but offerings of drinks.

Yes, we were all young – but beware the provincial purist confronted with metropolitan excess; my eyes narrowed like Martin Luther's towards Rome. The girl from Melbourne University whispered in my ear that amongst the drunken crowd, one had both an aunt who was a Labor MP, and a gold Amex card; I clung to her arm. The boy from Macquarie was running against these people for the NUS Presidency, she told me. By the end of that weekend, I had pledged my votes to him. Rare is the undergraduate, and etc.

The boy's name was Jamie Parker. He ran against Verity Firth from the Labor Left and, with votes from non-aligned leftish people like me and a deal with the ALP Right, he won. Seventeen years later, he became the first Greens lower house MP in New South Wales, beating the Labor incumbent in the seat of Balmain – the very same Verity Firth.

***

I held out for a few weeks after voting for Jamie that the Right would appear to me as some kind of beacon of 'my people' in the student movement. Then I watched them march into NUS national conference like a clone army of matching t-shirts and bound voting and I quailed. They defined themselves by defending HECS, they traded votes with – horror of horrors – Liberal students, and their bloc vote in a factional deal denied the National Presidency to the person it as clear to all was best equipped to lead it. He was a Curtin student from WA. His name was Adam Bandt.

Adam was in the 'other' non-Labor left faction to the one Jamie Parker was assembling around people like me. There are clichés of private school Marxists in the student left and that faction heaved with them; the merchant bankers' daughter who advocated 'marijuana for liberation', the shaved-head princess from the expensive Perth school brandishing her 'first up against the wall' placard, the transphobic 'radical feminist' who went to work for Rupert Murdoch within ten minutes of graduation, a parade of white boys whose sense of entitlement was curiously unimpeded by conspicuous declarations of anti-authoritarianism.

Adam, however, was distinguished by his sincerity. He was passionate, articulate and unifying. Although he was reportedly once a member of the ALP 'in his youth', he was not second-guessing a Labor career, and said what a generation of student leaders should have been screaming aloud about HECS' corrosive effect on education and compromising influence upon the universal access to other social institutions. When he spoke, even the Right listened – and they resented him for it.

The leader of the Right, Tim Lyons – twenty years later, brought undone by an unwise attempt to factionally deal himself into the leadership of the ACTU – organised Bandt's humiliating defeat in a demonstration of the efficiency of Labor's machine. All Labor's delegates – and the Liberal students – handed their votes over to be filled in for the Labor Left candidate; I can't even remember who it was.

I voted for Adam, in defiance of party allegiance, and by doing so, threw my lot in with the unbound rabble of the non-aligned left.

When I got home, I smoked cigarettes in front of my parents for the first time as I detailed the events of the conference and my disillusionment with the Party. Mum was sympathetic. Dad said: 'if you want to be a fucking communist, go and live in fucking China,' with a chuckle.

* * *

Disillusion is a hard illness to bear and an even heavier one to shift. Of course, I wasn't the only one exposed to the contaminating agents, nor was the student movement the only place disease fomented. My story is real but it's allegorical, too; by the nineties, the Labor party was lazy with power, and its Right machine vindictively gatekeeping it, too. After Keating's victory in the 'unwinnable' 1993 election, Labor decisions – like HECS and privatisation – were considered outcomes of incontrovertible logic, when they shouldn't have been. When Labor did lose in 1996, their own history of privatisations was what allowed the neoliberal fire sales of public assets engaged in by John Howard. Labor's Accord with the unions, deregistration of the Builders Labourers Federation (BLF) and suppression of the Pilots' Strike weakened the militancy of Australia's union movement and that energised Howard's relentless attempts to destroy it. Talented and ambitious young left-wing people like Jamie Parker and Adam Bandt were despised by an apparatus engaged in branch-stacking to promote the likes of Eddie Obeid. Of course they went elsewhere.

I held onto my party card as I rose myself through NUS, but when my membership lapsed I didn't renew it. Living in Wollongong, I'd watched the loveable, progressive local lefty state member Col Markham improbably lose preselection in his own seat to the deeply unpopular Noreen Hay – who, having won in the Left, jumped straight to the Right.

The promotion of candidates preselected in these worst of ways was reducing both the enthusiasm of the party's base, as well as its capacity for effective policymaking. New South Wales was a corrupt mess and everyone knew it. Historically, Labor have always struggled with Opposition, and John Howard's relentless appeals to racism and xenophobia in the electorate were seeded so well because the Labor leadership was confounded in how to confront it at inception. When during the Tampa crisis, Labor leader Kim Beazley – so beloved of the Labor family in the previous government – gave ground to Howard to allow some Australian islands to be excised from the migration zone, it enabled the onset of offshore processing system with electoral support so well-seeded by Howard's amoral genius and Labor's clumsiness that it's been an irremovable noose around the ALP's electoral neck ever since.

Labor's failure on refugees even knocked some of the rust off my parents. They were at a barbecue of old friends who were arguing that 'something had to be done about the boat people' in the wake of Beazley's cave to Howard. They stood, horrified, announced they couldn't brook this talk in Labor voters, and left, collecting another couple or two as they did.

The Greens were the party that spoke out for the 'boat people' and my godfather – an old union man – had started voting for them. Frustrated with the ongoing Labor preselection debacles in Wollongong, I had, too.

I'd met Bob Brown, leader of the Australian Greens, in 2000, at the protest of the World Economic Forum in Melbourne, an anti-corporate-power event which culminated in the solid beating of me and many others by the Victorian Police. In the context of the barricades and violence, Bob Brown's calm presence was something akin to a saintly reassurance that I was lined up on the right side.

By this stage, I'd been protesting the Tory excesses of Howard's government for years, with dwindling belief the ALP was likely to get its own shit together enough to fight back. Brown was in the thick of the action, and as the party that was defined by its participation in environmental causes, slowly registering in the world's policy consciousness, the Greens had the glow of future vision. I believed the Greens were a left-wing party; many old communists were certainly helping them out, while the Australian Democrats, who were the larger party in the Senate back then, were a present and obvious means of a centrist comparison.

When a sudden by-election in my home seat of Cunningham in 2002 provoked another murky Labor preselection skirmish, my friend Michael Organ was the Greens candidate and I devoted myself to his campaign. So did many other locals who – like Michael – came from the same working-class background that I did but were resentful and angry at Labor's aristocratic sense of entitlement to the seat. When Michael won, there were fewer Greens members at his victory party than there were people like me, cheering his victory as an affirmation of the left-wing and progressive values we no longer trusted Labor to deliver.

If I am honest with myself, voting Greens was never about voting Greens; it was about registering an electoral message of discontent with Labor. The source of that discontent was symbolised in the person of Kevin Rudd and everything that befell Labor in the wake of his leadership; the Rudd-Gillard-Rudd mess was Labor's machine eating itself, and Rudd himself personified the small-target strategy of appeal to the right that abandoned the left – what went with it, of course, was Labor's most energised base. Amongst it all, people like me – default-voting Green to seize at a moral oasis of uncompromised smug.

To be fair, Bob, and then Christine, made voting Greens an easy left-wing choice. Bob was – and remains – an activist, while Christine ran the Greens in the senate – with support from Adam Bandt in the house – as a visible, legislative left-flank. The enormous passage of progressive legislation by the Gillard government was a triumph of positive collaboration between Labor and Greens on the political left. Even when the Greens diverged from Labor on the proposal to process refugees in Malaysia and on Rudd's first attempt at an emissions trading scheme, the divergence could be explained – and I realise this position is contentious – as disagreement on the left.

But since the end of Christine, the rise of Richard Di Natale has forced me to reappraise what I thought I knew about the party I'd voted for. When soon after Di Natale's leadership was conferred, the Greens chose to vote with the Coalition to cut the part-pension, the public justifications exposed to me the ideological divide between my old-left values and the new Greens reality.

I return your attention to the house my grandfather built after the War that my family has lived in for three generations – a single asset shared by many, a house that's housed unemployed family members looking for work, family units relocating cities, university students as they've completed study and was transacted to my mother in return for her full-time care of my grandmother into old age. The lack of understanding of the interdependent economic reality of working-class families was demonstrated by the Greens' depiction of part-pensioners as some kind of property-hoarding kulaks, providing cover for Liberals who pursued the cuts entirely in line with their ideological commitment to erasing the remnants of the welfare state. Forgotten while the Greens praised themselves for a measly $15 a week increase in the pension for full-pensioners was that the part-pension was introduced by Howard as a compensation for the increased living costs of the GST.

A simple mistake? Not when the head of the Greens 'economic team' that made the decision is Senator Peter Whish-Wilson, the former merchant banker praised by the Liberal Senator Sean Edwards last year as someone who would 'would fit quite squarely in the Coalition with a lot of his positions'. As recently as 2013, Whish-Wilson was demanding a 'bigger national discussion' about penalty rates, which he described as 'outdated'.

And he's no outlier. His Greens comrade, newly-minted Milne-replacement senator Nick McKim from Tasmania, praised the Uber model of labour deregulation in his maiden speech of September 2015, suggesting Uberisation's extension to labour hire and childcare, pledging that the Greens would be 'advocating for more support, less protectionism, and the lightest possible regulatory touch from government'. And in December, Adam Bandt – Adam Bandt! – spoke in favour of a Greens/Liberal deal agreeing to ease the threshold at which multi-million dollar corporations are obliged to publicly disclose their taxation arrangements.

The result is my 'awareness sickness', my oasis of smug now sunk – and my public admission of such both an invocation to the youthful pack who attacked me online the other night, as well as, contemplating a repeat of such an outcome, my reticence in committing this personal history to print. As it's personal testimony, I can but admit to what I've seen, what I've felt, and the shifting paradigm within. I will be returning my vote to the Labor party at the next election, and not because my politics have shifted, nor my illusions traded places back to Labor from the Greens. It is a clear-eyed assessment of the reality that is the progressive achievements, however imperfect, of Labor in power and the realisation, too – that in competition amongst neoliberal sellouts with machines that are vicious and whose policies let me down, Labor is the party that I most trust to look after my ageing mum.

Chapter 5

What's Left – Progressive?

Carmen Lawrence

In politics, including in Australia, the much-overused word, 'progressive', has come to describe people's positions on a cluster of issues, the precise composition of which depends on who's doing the talking. But it appears to be used as shorthand for a vaguely left-wing way of looking at the world, based on the premise that it *is* possible to change society for the better. It's certainly not a revolutionary agenda.

Rowson[1] proposes that the progressive imagination envisages a world with 'safe and sound' ecologies; that most progressives want societies to become more equal in both opportunity and outcome. To be progressive is to place a high, in principle, value on sharing the bounties of life. According to McKnight,[2] central to being progressive today is the question of sustainability: how humans can live a good life without destroying the ecological basis for that life. He adds to the list care for the vulnerable, a commitment to the 'common good' and respect for diversity.

Crucially, being progressive is typically marked by the belief that governments have a pivotal role to play in ensuring a fair

---

1   https://www.opendemocracy.net/ourkingdom/jonathan-rowson/what-is-'progressive'.
2   D. McKnight, *Beyond Left and Right*, New Critic Lecture Series, IAS, UWA, 2007, http://www.ias.uwa.edu.au/new-critic/six/mcknight.

and sustainable production and distribution of these goods, but progressives also embrace the individual freedoms and rights that democracies claim to afford. In discussing contemporary UK politics, Roberto Unger proposed[3] that a progressive is: 'someone who wants to see society reorganised, part by part and step by step, so that ordinary men and women have a better chance to live to a larger life'. By definition, progressives understand the importance of politics in this process.

Whether the Australian Labor Party will continue to capture the majority of the votes of those who endorse any or all of these values or whether the Greens will win them over is an open question. But the signs are ominous for Labor.

In Australia, voters who might be described as 'progressive' have in recent decades voted principally for the Australian Labor Party, in smaller numbers for the Democrats and, more recently, for the Greens (although the takeover by social moderate Malcolm Turnbull might change that). The last Australian Election Studies survey showed that while there were few differences between Labor and Green voters in their preferences on economic policy and income redistribution, they differed significantly in their opinions about global warming and the treatment of asylum seekers. We found a somewhat similar patterns in our 2014 study of policy preferences:[4] Green voters were considerably less conservative than Labor voters on a measure which captured attitudes to turning back asylum seeker boats; expenditure on foreign aid;

---

3   Radio 4, 'Analysis' program. Available at: http://www.bbc.co.uk/programmes/b03hvn6n.
4   I. L. Rossen, P. D. Dunlop and C. M. Lawrence, 'Development and validation of the political MAP (Multidimensional Attitudes Paradigm),' unpublished manuscript, 2015.

increasing police numbers; harsher sentencing for drug users; and migrants' contribution to crime. And those intending to vote Green were also more likely than intending Labor voters to endorse items relating to same-sex marriage, gender roles and abortion. While Labor now presents a more reactionary position on the first of these policy groupings – particularly on the treatment of asylum seekers – it continues to embrace a progressive position on the second cluster.

Whether the hardening of Labor's position on refugee policy will see more votes bleed to the Greens, only the next election will tell, but polls suggest that inner-city seats in Sydney and Melbourne – where many progressives live – are particularly vulnerable for Labor. While the preferential, district-based voting system will continue to deliver results that favour the two major parties, strategic voting by the Coalition could see more seats go to the Greens at the expense of the more left-wing members of the ALP (who typically hold such seats). The effect could well be to shift the Labor Party even further to the right and further away from a progressive approach to key economic and social issues.

In an article on 'The Drum' following Gough Whitlam's death, Greens candidate and former adviser Robert Sims argued that 'Whitlam represented a style of visionary, conviction politics that many voters yearn for in today's age of craven politicians, opinion polls and spin doctors'. In comparing the Greens with the Labor Party of the 1970s, Sims argued that the Greens enjoy 'support from social movements and activists who want an end to business as usual' and are now more Whitlamite than modern Labor. According to this view, it is the Greens who are the beneficiaries of Whitlam's legacy and it is they who represent the modern face of progressive politics. Bob Brown has proposed that 'left' is now seen as an interchangeable word with 'progressive' and that the Greens are the only party of substance on the left side of politics.[5]

Some support for this analysis is evident in the drift toward the Greens of the well-educated, affluent and civically engaged middle class – the same type of voters who provided crucial support for the Whitlam government. It is also reflected in the policy positions they endorse.

Every election produces its own unique set of certainties about the virtues of the winners and the defects of the losers, certainties that more thoughtful consideration – and the passage of time – have often shown to be flawed. Instant, impression-based analyses of what has happened, and why, saturate the media. All the signs are that the next election will be no different. The score cards will be marked for the winners and losers and predictions made about their future prospects. In every electoral cycle, the imminent demise of the losing party (whichever it is) and creeping tide of blue (or red) – or green – across the nation will be trumpeted as unique, without precedent. Few scribes will have the humility to look back later and read what they predicted and judge whether it bears scrutiny. Most, like economists, will never have to say they're sorry.

In all of the 'horse race' commentary, it's likely that only a few will pay close attention to the serious problems masked by the sound and fury of election campaigns: the disenchantment and disengagement of Australian voters; the rot infesting the major parties; and the steady erosion of Australia's political culture. Few will reflect on the steady decline in party

---

[5] R. Simms, 'The Australian Greens and the moral middle class', 2010, http://www.auspsa.org.au/sites/default/files/the_australian_greens_and_the_moral_middle_class_robert_simms.pdf.

membership and the diminished participation by Australians in the business of shaping political values, designing policy and selecting candidates.

Yet voters themselves seem acutely aware of these problems. Much of the sentiment about politics and politicians, revealed in blogs and posts and articles, is indicative of a near universal disdain for politics as an enterprise; 'politics' has increasingly become a dirty word. To attribute 'political' motives to people is to question their honesty and integrity and their capacity to do anything other than in their own the self-interest. Many Australians now seem deeply scornful of their parliamentary representatives. This suits the agenda of those who seek to denigrate and diminish the role of government and, by definition, frustrates progressive policy objectives.

The disdain with which politics is viewed extends to the major parties which are judged to be failing our democracy. They are seen as parties in name only, having mutated into hollow corporations run by a handful of paid officials; remote from their declining membership and the rest of Australia, and ripe for the picking by special interests.

The story behind the news is that our already rudimentary political parties are withering, as power is concentrated in fewer and fewer hands – and there are no signs that this is sparking any serious effort at party reform. Whether it is the Coalition or the Labor Party, it's clear to even the most rusted-on supporters that the factions have ossified and morphed into groups in the thrall of one or two power brokers (in the case of the ALP, tightly controlled by a few union leaders), driving away members with broader interests in ideology and policy. Even the highly factionalised audience at the 2015 conference of the NSW Liberal Party fell about laughing when newly minted PM Malcolm Turnbull claimed that, unlike their rivals, the ALP, their party was not riven by factions.

As Jaensch and his colleagues reminded us in their audit of Australian political parties,[6] 'Australians don't care much for political parties': 67 per cent in their survey expressed little or no confidence in them and only 9 per cent thought that parties have high standards in the conduct of their internal affairs. A 2012 national survey of voters found there was a widespread perception that political parties were corrupt. Attitudes like these may help explain people's reluctance to become active in political parties. In her survey of organisational, including political party, membership, Crikey's Cathy Alexander reported that 'there are far more members in the RSL, the MCC and the low-profile Federation of Australian Historical Societies than in any party. There are more Scouts than Liberals, there are more Freemasons than ALP members'.[7]

Tellingly, the most recent ANU post-election survey[8] also found significant increases in voters' scepticism about whether it makes a difference which party they vote for; voters apparently find it increasingly difficult to discern any ideological distinctions. Only 56 per cent of those surveyed believed their vote made a difference, down from 70 per cent in 1996. Only 43 per cent, an all-time low for the survey series, believed it made any difference which party was in power. Perhaps this perception goes some way to explaining the rapid turnover of state governments – it becomes a matter

---

6   D. Jaensch, P. Brent and P. Bowden, 'Australian political parties in the spotlight,' *Democratic Audit of Australia,* Report No. 4, 2005, 2.
7   http://www.crikey.com.au/2013/07/18/the-partys-over-which-clubs-have-the-most-members/.
8   http://aes.anu.edu.au/publications/aes-trends.

of turn-taking, not policy merit; management credentials, not political philosophy.

These trends have been observed in many established democracies – and even some of the emerging ones. The erosion of trust in politicians and political elites is commonplace, as is greater public scepticism about these elites and their pronouncements. More alarming is that, in some places, these feelings now appear to be moving to encompass democratic regimes and institutions themselves. While these symptoms of decline are not unique to Australia, we do seem to be unusual in failing to devote serious attention to them. Neither our governments nor our political parties, with the possible exception of the Greens, appear overly concerned.

In response to similar, but much smaller scale, problems to those identified in Australia, several Scandinavian governments, with the support of all the major political groupings, undertook a systematic analysis of what was causing the recent democratic decline in their part of the world. They attempted to diagnose the flaws in their democracies and to recommend appropriate remedies. One of the reports to the Norwegian parliament concluded that 'democracy – fundamentally understood as representative democracy, a formal decision-making system employing election by a majority and directly elected bodies – is in decline. The political purchasing power of the voter ballot has been diminished'.

The report's authors were effectively arguing that the power of voters in the chain of governance had been lessened. However, their research also showed it was not that people's values had changed, but rather that politics had changed. Voters remained interested in political issues, but had come to believe that the decision-making power of their elected representatives was in decline; that governments had abdicated important areas of responsibility – primarily to corporations and financial markets – and could no longer exercise as much influence as they once had.

These beliefs are supported by the evidence:[9] not only have many of the tasks previously reserved for governments been shifted to organisations not answerable to voters, but politicians themselves publicly denigrate the capacity of governments to deliver effective policy outcomes. One of the contributing causes to this shift is the growing political influence of those for whom government is, at best, a necessary evil; the political players who have captured power but, without any sense of irony, are committed to an avowedly small or anti-government agenda. This process of 'depoliticisation' sometimes takes the form of handing over responsibility for contentious issues to 'independent' bodies and presenting them as purely technical matters, allowing politicians to avoid any serious censure for policy failure. Or it may take the form of a handover of political decision making to the market, rejecting the need for public deliberation at all. The rash of privatisations and public asset sales in many advanced liberal democracies from the 1980s onward is illustrative of the pervasive conviction that the private sector is invariably more efficient in allocating resources than the public sector. As a result, the boundaries of the state have been markedly reconfigured – and shrunk.

The authors of the Norwegian report also agreed that voters were not deluded in their belief that the scope of political power had contracted. They observed that the large economic

---

9   C. Hay, *Why We Hate Politics,* Polity Press, Cambridge, 2007.

actors, including multinational corporations were often, as a result of globalisation, more powerful than governments, and not infrequently threatened that they would move capital, production, headquarters or jobs out of the country if policy settings (including taxation) were not to their liking. Globalisation has arguably shifted power from elected representatives to major corporations and institutions – such as the EU, the World Trade Organization, the International Monetary Fund and various international agreements – and moved important issues beyond the reach of national democratic politics and accountability. These players constrain the range of actions governments are prepared to take – or can take – to redistribute wealth and protect the environment. Just ask the Greeks.

There is also a fairly widespread consensus in the academic literature that globalisation 'undermines, subverts, or sets limits on democracy'.[10] As Scholte[11] has argued, 'globalization has undermined conventional liberal democracy, with its focus on national self-determination through a territorial state'. Hay's[12] analysis gives greater weight to the impact of the international diffusion of neoliberalism more generally, with its largely unchallenged prescriptions for a technical set of devices for managing a national economy: privatisation; the contracting out of public services; the displacement of policymaking from the political realm to independent authorities; and the privileging of multinational trade interests

---

10 Ronaldo Munck, 'A new "great transformation"?,' *Annals*, 581, May, 2002: 13.
11 J. A. Scholte, *Globalization: A Critical Introduction*, Macmillan, London, 2000, 261.
12 Hay, *Why We Hate Politics*.

ahead of national priorities. As Hay puts it, this represents a rolling back of political deliberation and a rolling forward of the purview and influence of the market. He argues that this process has served to depoliticise policymaking, accelerating political disengagement and disenfranchisement. These factors have all contributed to people's increasing apathy toward conventional politics; people believe that power has migrated elsewhere and that the constraints imposed by these more powerful, vested interests are likely to swamp any other considerations, no matter what political parties promise before the election.

The absence of a serious, coherent discussion about any of these forces from Australia's political players is striking. Indeed there appears to be collusion between the two major parties to ignore what's happening, although there are some recent signs that the implicit agreement may be breaking down, perhaps because more Australians are publicly worrying that governments' authority is being usurped by the big international economic players. The recent sceptical responses to the claimed benefits of the Trans-Pacific Partnership agreement and the China–Australia Free Trade Agreement are indicative of this concern, particularly about Australian standards relating to labour rights, food safety and environmental protection. And although Labor has, of late, been more equivocal about the benefits of these agreements, it has yet to prove that this is more than oppositional posturing; it's one of the reasons why more and more progressives are eyeing off the Greens.

Australian surveys regularly show that a significant portion of voters worry about the power wielded by multinational corporations and see significant risks, especially for job security, in opening up the economy to foreign competition.[13] The rent-seeking behaviour of large international companies, their purchase of influence through election funding and lobbying and their extreme resistance to paying their fair share of tax, are the focus of particular unease. It appears that Australians are much more wary than their political representatives about the benefits of global and regional integration.[14]

The privileging of corporate interests over community and environmental concerns is also generating increasing resistance from those who do not see the outcomes of these conflicts as inevitable. That such strong community organisations have developed to campaign against the unfettered expansion of the gas and coal industries into agricultural land in New South Wales, Queensland and into pristine, Indigenous lands in the Kimberley shows that many people are unconvinced by claims that such developments are imperative for our economic security. And people notice that their elected representatives, governments and the instruments of government routinely put community interests last. The 'light touch' and self-regulation now typical of many state (and increasingly, Commonwealth) regimes is symptomatic of the retreat of government and shrivelling of the political sphere – and a failure of the Labor Party to provide an alternative, progressive, voice.

It seems that for today's Labor Party the neoliberal economic agenda has 'became more than a set of economic policies; it

---

13 M. Pusey and N. Turnbull, 'Have Australians embraced economic reform?,' in *Australian Social Attitudes*, eds Ian Marsh, G. Meagher, R. Gibson, D. Denemark and M. Western, UNSW Press, Sydney, 2005.

14 I. Marsh, G. Meagher and S. Wilson, 'Are Australians open to globalization?,' in *Australian Social Attitudes*, eds Ian Marsh, G. Meagher, R. Gibson, D. Denemark and M. Western, UNSW Press, Sydney, 2005.

gradually evolved into a deep commitment to the underlying principles and philosophy of economic liberalism, and an inability to imagine any other way of governing'.[15] The failure of Labor to question this dogma, indeed its willingness to provide the kinder face of neoliberalism is, in my view, one of the reasons for its decline in influence and legitimacy. Labor's political leaders have failed to articulate policies that can be seen to promote an improved quality of life and to foster the public good – goals central to a progressive agenda. Nor have they expended any serious intellectual effort in exploring alternative economic models, which allow for a proper weight to be given to social and environmental interests. To many observers, Labor appears bereft of either a positive vision for the country or a viable strategy to achieve it; they have little to say about 'the necessary and productive tension between individual and collective purposes'.[16]

This, of course, is not unique to Labor or to Australia; left-of-centre parties everywhere have succumbed to the sirens' song of the end of history, the inevitability of the status quo – and are suffering the consequences. Giving up the power to craft alternative policies, a focus on creating the right impression has come to dominate the public voices of the major parties. Here in Australia, Labor has been too clever for its own good, often embracing simplistic, lowest common denominator policies, emulating the worst of the conservative agenda – its asylum seeker policy being the most egregious example. In

---

15 D. McKnight, 'The renewal of social democracy,' in *State of the Nation: Essays for Robert Manne*, ed G. Tavan, Black Inc, Melbourne, 2013, 52.

16 M. Lilla, 'The truth about our Libertarian age,' *New Republic*, June 17, 2014. http://www.newrepublic.com/article/118043/our-libertarian-age-dogma-democracy-dogma-decline.

trying to accommodate all points on the ideological compass, the Party ends up losing its reason for existence. People seem to understand that to conduct politics without its 'essential, principled moral nature', as one commentator put it, is to engage in bad politics. At the very least, it is politics conducted in bad faith.

The allegiances that people feel to political parties in Australia are continuing to fray. This represents a loss of the easy vote and more people are open to being persuaded; they are less fixed in their views. On the left, the Greens are attracting new voters and perhaps, more importantly, activists. The ALP is not. This decline is most evident among the young, the better-educated and the more politically aware. Progressives are moving. They are clearly worried about the direction in which Australia is headed but doubt whether Labor can provide an analysis and understanding of what may be done. They want at least to hear a debate on issues such as the role of government, population and immigration, rising inequality, reconciliation with our Indigenous people, simultaneous underemployment and overwork, human rights and international citizenship, models of economic growth, and the priority which should be given to environmental improvement and protection. Only those parties who understand this and can craft a credible vision of a 'good society' – one which places economic decisions in the wider social and environmental content – will motivate and galvanise progressive voters to support them. With its current factionalised structure, narrow base and short-term focus, it's hard to see Labor rising to the challenge.

Chapter 6

We're Not There Yet: Labor's Past, Present and Future as a Party of Government

Andrew Giles

Modern Australia's story is in many ways the story of the Australian Labor Party. It's a story of contests between progress and reaction; with progress prevailing – driven by the Labor party, and through the actions of Labor governments.

Since Federation, it has been Labor that has driven the social and economic changes that have built our nation, from establishing the age pension to founding the National Disability Insurance Scheme.

But Labor members today aren't curators of a museum of social democracy, concerned only to memorialise past glories. Paul Keating put it this way: 'We are steeped in our history and we're proud of it… But the paradox is, obsessed with our history as we are, we are still the party that divines the future. We employ that history to shape the future'.

We remain in the business of making, and unmaking, social and economic conditions, of redistributing power and opportunity. Our past is a foundation, not a finished work. Far from it: as we are becoming a less equal society.

So, today, Labor's concern must be to reshape Australia's social compact for the times in which we live. This is to be done by restating the case for Labor as the movement for change, and the party of government, which will shape Australia's future progress just as much as it has our past.

Labor and Australian Progress

Either side of the start of the twentieth century, Australian Labor's forebears made two critical decisions. First, to recognise that economic justice could not be secured through action in workplaces alone, and that it was necessary to pursue a parliamentary path. Subsequently, to move beyond a policy in the parliament of providing support to liberal governments in return for policy concessions to seek to form Labor governments in our own right. Both decisions have stood the test of time.

While critics, including Vladimir Lenin, derided early Labor's approach, we remember how it saw Australia emerge from Federation as the world's social laboratory. It enabled the scope of Ben Chifley's ambitions for our movement, as striving not simply for extra wages but rather to bring 'something better to the people, better standards of living, greater happiness'.

From the governments led by Andrew Fisher to those of Julia Gillard and Kevin Rudd, the Labor agenda has written our history; it is Labor initiatives that have informed and expanded what it means to be Australian. Universal healthcare may well be the exemplar of the progress and reaction dynamic, of how political contest has defined our social compact and the practical limits of political reaction.

These governments have looked to Party platforms to guide their actions. Policies developed democratically by the Party, presented to the people and enacted through legislative and administrative decisions.

The role of the wider Party in framing the scope of government action deserves greater appreciation, including within Labor. It can be a vital counterweight to the voices of entrenched interests and rent seekers in our politics (as well as to deepening alienation), if we can continue to locate important decisions close to people affected by them.

Think about the great Conference debates around opening up the economy in the 1980s, and the legitimacy this conferred on complex and challenging decisions. Or about how Gough Whitlam made the case for modernising Labor and a modern Australia through the forums of an initially sceptical Party.

Perhaps the return to more open deliberations of the 2015 Conference, in contrast to its stage-managed and recent sanitised predecessors, might be a step forward. It's noteworthy that so much of the commentary focused on the manner in which we managed our disagreements. There's surely something to think further about here – if it's important to instil more respect and civility into politics, then within the party that conducts its business in the open would seem the obvious place to start.

The link between the party processes and being explicitly, and unambiguously, a party of government is vital. Involvement in Labor isn't akin to participating in a book club, it's setting a template to shape the circumstances in which we live.

In this regard, while much has already been written on the significance of the Rudd and Gillard governments, too little attention has been paid to the consequences of the manner in which government was formed after the 2010 election. Lost in other criticisms is the gulf between the propositions put before the election, and the constraints the establishment of government placed on implementing these. This is quite separate from frustration courtesy of a resistant Senate.

The compromises made to form government were effectively exploited by Tony Abbott and the then Opposition. The very real achievements of the administrations led by Julia Gillard and Kevin Rudd were obscured by (amongst other things, of course) this attack on legitimacy, which we have struggled to confront, as it requires asking difficult questions of ourselves as well.

We can start to do so by emphasising our commitment to continue to be a party of government; which follows directly from our internal democratic commitments. An open and inclusive policy development process is the input that should be followed by a wider democratic conversation at the time government is formed. Voters should be placed to appreciate the choice before them, and its import for their lives, if the decision they make is to be a meaningful one, or indeed one they choose to make at all.

Today, changes in the economy and in particular in the world of work amplify the importance of role of government to people. Notwithstanding predictions of the coming irrelevance of the nation-state, at a time of increasing inequality and insecurity the role of the state in moderating imbalances of power is as critical as ever.

Challenges to Labor

Mr Lenin wasn't alone in challenging Australian Labor's approach last century. In facing up to today's political challenges, we should be wary of the assumption they are an entirely new phenomenon.

The progressive side of Australian politics has always been heavily contested. Deakinite Liberals, a wide variety of revolutionary socialists including the Australian Communist Party, Lang Labor, the Australia Party and the Australian Democrats all sought – unsuccessfully – to claim this mantle. Not forgetting the split in the 1950s that led to the formation of the Democratic Labor Party (DLP).

But in the Greens Party, we do face the most significant challenge for the attention, and loyalty, of progressive voters in more than a century.

It's a challenge Labor has to take seriously. If we don't, we face the prospect of losing our claim to be a party of government. And everything that comes with it, including our sense of the Platform as a template for government. This is an existential challenge. But one we can answer, on our terms. Because, actually, it's about us, not them. Voters aren't leaving Labor because they've been won over by an alternative proposition. Instead, they have been expressing their frustrations with the Party – demonstrated most obviously with respect to the issue of asylum.

Labor supporters are putting us on notice, but far from walking away people are seeking to re-engage with the Party. Indeed, our membership is on the rise, drawn by the promise of having a say, most obviously through selecting our parliamentary leaders. Today we have a third more members than prior to the 2013 election.

This new generation of activists is united in a sense that three things (still) matter: that national government remains an important force for good in people's lives; formal politics can still give people a meaningful say in how their society operates; and the Labor Party is the place where a diverse range of people can come together to shape our common future for the better.

Under new leader Richard Di Natale, the Greens are trying to fudge the decision Labor took in the early 1900s. They want to play support in return for concessions, while seeking to supplant Labor as the progressive party of government in Australia. Having their cake, and eating it, too. All the while failing to grapple with critical questions around the role of government.

There's a democratic legitimacy issue here, too. In an organisation that is almost completely opaque as the Greens Party is, there's a capacity to be supremely agile in responding to changed circumstances – but no capacity to really engage people in a deep, transformative political conversation.

For me, rebuilding trust in politics boils down to rejecting cynicism. And the (re)positioning of the Greens is as cynical as it gets. It's a calculation based on exploiting dissatisfaction. It is all about presenting to a section of Labor supporters as the other side of a difficult choice that Labor, as a party of government, has made; and rejecting the critical importance of making such choices, instead of facing up to the responsibility of leading debate on them and their consequences.

But it would be a mistake to locate the threat to Labor, and to Labor's purpose, as being presented solely in the form of the Greens Party.

We must also confront a more profound challenge to democratic politics, and look to its causes rather than simply the symptoms. If there's a political crisis in western democracies, it's really a crisis of faith. Faith that our political institutions can deliver meaningful change, and that people can engage in these institutions to help in making those changes.

The implied bargain that underpinned societies like ours was founded on an understanding that growth would continue to support increased living standards. Lately, people are less confident that this is the case and have voted, or rather not voted, with their feet. There's a clear trend of political – and civic, for that matter – disengagement – when it comes to voting and enrolling to vote.

Sadly, this is most pronounced amongst many who have most at stake. We have troubling research from the Lowy Institute demonstrating that young Australians are not only switched off from political action, they have little interest in democracy at all. According to the 2015 Lowy Poll, only 49 per cent of 18–29 year old voters showed any preference for democracy.

It's not just the young. We have parties whose membership is less and less representative of the wider community and an electorate that is, albeit more slowly, moving in the same direction. In the US, we can look to the logical conclusion of this – a politics which largely ignores the interests of the economically insecure, who have opted out of involvement or been actively excluded. This has begun to change in recent times, but it is a slow process.

This opting out is born of a frustration which is readily understandable. People feel remote from decisions that shape their lives because they *are* remote from them. Think about the significance to everyday life of technocratic determinations via systems of 'double delegation' on matters like interest rates and of international trade agreements negotiated in secret.

Across the developed world, we are seeing a growth in populist politics. What these insurgent movements have in common is a rejection of formal politics as it has been practised, expressed through a deep cynicism about all involved in it. Offering easy answers to mobilise insecurity. This is true of Donald Trump, of Marine Le Pen and the Front National, of UKIP, of Beppe Grillo's Five Star movement and many other reactionary forces, Clive Palmer included. There's also, of course, been an emergent populism of the left, especially in response to European austerity.

I don't suggest for a moment that there aren't good reasons to react. A global economic crisis which grew out of unrestrained greed, and which in many countries was exacerbated by austerity, is something we should all be angry about. The question is: how should we express our anger? Put another way: is reaction really the best vision of the future the centre-left in Australia can put forward?

In my view, we should respond by remaking Labor's social democratic case, heeding two lessons from recent political history. First, reformist politics must be founded on hope – a prospect that the world can be changed for the better, that progress hasn't come to an end. But this isn't enough.

The insurgent wave that powered Podemos, Syriza and the rest of the European anti-austerity left is foundering because protest alone can't sustain a movement for change. The posture of Marlon Brando in *The Wild One* ('what are you rebelling against? What have you got?') is attractive, sure, but it's empty. It's politics for the dinner party, not government.

A critique is a necessary but insufficient basis for seeking to correct abuses and gross imbalances of power. So we must focus our attention not simply on railing against the excesses and injustices of the present, but on a program – a Labor program – for government founded in a realistic optimism.

Again, there's much to be angry about. This anger is an energy that can't be allowed to dissipate. It should be founding an alternative, and this should be the core work of our next progressive government. A response to record postwar levels of inequality that applies the lessons drawn from Labor's experience to our present challenges, and that reminds us of the moral purpose at the core of Labor's reason for being.

We shouldn't be afraid to ask 'how much is enough?' of those who profited at our collective expense, such as the owners of the 600 of our largest companies which paid no income tax last year. Or, more to the point, of those struggling to get by on Newstart; those children likely to be locked out of early childhood education; of Indigenous Australians; of retail workers relying on penalty rates and too many others not seeing the benefits of a record period of economic growth. Those whose concerns are too often too far from the centre of the progressive political conversation.

Looking Beyond 'Progressive'

In writing about the prospects of a progressive government for Australia, we can't forget these people – those for whom the character of the government matters most.

The term 'progressive' is too often a 'Humpty Dumpty' word in politics: it's whatever you want it to mean. Clearly, it's not a synonym for being left wing. It's a side step around a class analysis, too often. This enables it to function both as a label claimed by neoliberals like Malcolm Turnbull and David Cameron, and a rallying cry for populists to rebel against. Of course, Labor hasn't been an unambiguously 'progressive movement', and some say this is a label we should reject.

In a recent speech to the Fabian Society, Nick Dyrenfurth expanded on this: 'Labor has never been a straightforwardly "progressive" party, at least by the current meaning of the term. Standing against the commodification of people and place, and preserving time-honoured institutions and traditions, is both progressive and conservative, and an inherently Labor ideal'.

He's half right. There has always has been resistance to a progressive attitude within Labor and we have stood (and will continue to stand) against commodification of human beings and the places in which they live. But it's a stretch, to say the very least, to suggest that caring about people and their relationships makes cleaving to tradition an 'ideal' of the movement.

My understanding of the Labor approach sees this very differently. Our Party is in the business of making and unmaking social and economic relations. As we should be. To ensure equality between people where existing structures deny this.

This isn't a hard strand to discern in our story. Our progressive reshaping of social relationships – from opening up the franchise to striving for equality in how we recognise loving relationships – sits alongside our concern to offer economic security to all. As it must.

Progressivism separated from other distributive agendas presents a feeding ground for a populism born of resentment. Weirdly, the feeding is not only attended to by populist demagogues and regulars on the Australian's opinion page, but by some in Labor. These are the figures who have failed to heed the lesson Gough Whitlam bravely taught in the 1960s: that economic justice and social progress go hand in hand and are to be secured through opening up political space in Labor to all on the centre-left.

There's no doubt that many who are economically insecure look to more stable times, and it's clear that some have been receptive to attempts to separate their concerns from those of an inner-city 'elite' whose lives are remote from theirs. And that there are plenty seeking to exploit this insecurity, for their own reasons. Mostly, they constitute a real elite: the one per cent who are increasingly dominating our political conversation just as they increase their share of our economy.

This means we must work harder to sustain the political movement that has been concerned to simultaneously break down social and economic barriers to equality since 1891: the Australian Labor Party. Australia's next progressive government has to be fought for. To win the argument that delivers it, we must better explain both what's at stake and what difference we can make.

What's At Stake Today

We live in a world where the richest 62 people have as much wealth as the poorest half of the world's population.

In Australia, the land of the fair go, the wealthiest 20 per cent of households account for 61 per cent of total household net worth. The poorest 20 per cent accounted for 1 per cent. The wealthiest 20 per cent of households have a net worth 68 times as high as the least wealthy 20 per cent. This inequality is growing.

Ben Chifley's 'light on the hill' is the essential imagining of a good society for Australian Labor. I interpret this in the modern context as a more equal society, not simply a 'fair' one. It's an important distinction, between fairness and equality.

Just ask that notable progressive, our present Prime Minister. At the 2015 Economic and Social Outlook Conference, Malcolm Turnbull spoke about 'a nation that is as fair as it is open to opportunity'. This is in almost the same breath as he boosts the disruptors of our economic order and as he waters down the social wage, undermines universal healthcare, restricts access to quality education, attacks workplace rights and unions amongst other critical drivers of equality and indeed the prospect of social mobility.

Fairness is in the eye of the beholder, while equality is not negotiable. We should be brave in making this plain, as my friend and colleague Senator Jenny McAllister challenged: 'I'd like to see us start to think more deeply about what level of inequality we think is acceptable, and start to speak more directly about our belief that a more equal society is a better society'.

Progressives should assert this as a moral imperative: a more equal society is a better society. But pursuing equality is also a practical and prudent course to take. The IMF and OECD have advised that inequality is a brake on economic growth. For social democrats who have been struggling to balance our redistributive instincts with productive concerns, this emerging consensus has the prospect of changing the game. So, let's put doing the right thing at the centre of our struggle, knowing also that it will bring wider economic benefits.

It's been suggested that social democracy's time has come and gone, not least by the likes of Mr Turnbull and Senator Di Natale. Well, they would say that, wouldn't they? For this progressive, nothing could be further from the truth. Let's go back to first principles, in place of their determinism, and remember that, in the words of Columbia University academic, Sheri Berman: 'Social democracy was built on a belief in the primacy of politics and communitarianism – that is, on a conviction that political forces rather than economic ones could and should be the driving forces of history and that the "needs" or "good" of society must be protected and nurtured'.

This conviction certainly retains its moral force – especially in this age of rent seeking – and we now have a strong evidence base to deploy against those who say we can't fight 'progress'.

We can; remembering that political inequality is intrinsically linked to economic inequality. This recognition is central to Senator Bernie Sanders' understanding of America today, and also, I believe, to the appeal of his campaign to so many. It has also been central to the Australian labour movement's purpose, and so explains why Senator Sanders' supporters have more to be angry about than equivalent Australians. We have built institutions, and supported relationships, which have redistributed power in our society to a greater extent than in the United States.

Why Labor? And How?

In describing Australian history post-Federation as Labor's story, I'm not simply claiming the mantle for my side of politics. Rather, I'm seeking to emphasise the struggle that drives change, and where it should be located.

We can't see societal changes for the good simply as inevitable – because they aren't. The jury came in some time ago in that regard. Thomas Piketty has changed our understanding of economic inequality, while social injustices both persist (see marriage equality) and are being exacerbated.

Similarly, our sense of the possibilities of the future can't be defensive, or founded in reaction. Malcolm Turnbull cannot be allowed to define Labor's approach to seizing the opportunities of this century, or confronting its challenges. That's our job, on the terms of the people we represent.

Today, as in the late nineteenth century, only Labor is concerned to build a bridge between a response to social and economic inequality on the one hand, and political inequality on the other. And only Labor recognises how fundamentally connected these challenges are. We can, however, better place ourselves to meet them.

The structures and the culture of the ALP matter. Our continued capacity to involve and engage people in decision-making is fundamental to our claim to be not just Australia's next progressive government but to carry on as a party of government.

So we must recognise that, today, the Party isn't everything it should be. For all the talk of Party reform, too little attention has been paid to repairing our representative deficit. To strive for political equality in the wider community whilst ignoring imbalances of power within Labor is a nonsense. A priority has to be to open up our Party to give more people – and a more representative group of people – more of a say in Labor's future.

And with this, more power in shaping the circumstances in which they live their lives and the country in which their children will grow up. This isn't simply a question of structures, although how formal power is mediated in the party is obviously important if we are to continue to hold together hope for a better future and trust in the capacity of politics.

The next stage of Labor's project must be grounded in and shaped by Australian's lived experience. This is how we can best respond to the challenges of now (insecurity and inequality) and the emerging challenges of the next decade (how we work, how we live, and how we see ourselves).

We shouldn't take comfort in the past, that's for conservatives. But we must continue to have regard to it, and the lessons it offers. Not least, that politics matters and that together we can write the future, rather than have it wash over us.

There's still a 'light on the hill', and it's still burning brightly as good a symbol of hope and the positive role of government as anyone could wish for. It's as potent as we look beyond today's challenges as when imagining postwar reconstruction.

The point of all this is, of course, not simply to understand our circumstances – it's to change them. To open up social, political and economic space to all of us. To strive for a real 'sharing society', in which everyone has a meaningful say about the direction of his or her life.

This is the work of Australia's next progressive government, and it is the responsibility of the Australian Labor Party.

Chapter 7

Which Way for a Progressive Voter in 2016?

Scott Ludlam

Taking on the question of identifying the true home of progressive electoral politics in Australia – Labor or the Greens – runs the immediate risk of disappearing down one or the other partisan rabbit holes, and staying down there. That might be mildly interesting for people who've already made up their minds and are just looking for a bit of affirmation, but won't do much to slow the breakup of the Antarctic ice sheet or get refugee children off the prison islands.

We've both got our angry stereotypes of the other, so let's quickly get them out of the way. See if you can guess which is which:

Party 1: a strident and delusional protest party of dreamy-eyed hippies and bitter trots who promise solar-powered unicorns on every street corner while working to abolish the productive industries that would pay for them;

Party 2: a broken and compromised rolling civil war of union factions and ambitious neoliberal spivs, well into its twilight, whose internal contradictions and loathing average out to produce deep mediocrity rocked by occasional outbreaks of public self-harm.

It's a fortunate thing that both of these stereotypes are bullshit, and you will be pleased to know that there are good people of good heart in both the Australian Greens and the ALP working late into the night against the odds to try and make the world a kinder and less tragic place. The obvious question which then arises; ('ffs can you people please just set your partisan differences aside and work together for the good of the planet and its people?') is a pretty reasonable one.

That actually happens more often than it might look, at the fine-grained level of negotiating Senate motions or collaborating on inquiries, to campaigns like the Perth Freight Link or the way Greens regional groups allocate preference recommendations. In my time in the Senate I've worked with Labor MPs on issues as diverse as enabling legislation for the National Broadband Network, infrastructure funding, housing affordability schemes and nuclear weapons abolition, and I like to think that collectively the outcomes were better than anyone would have achieved alone. Those are the days where you raise a late night glass in the office long after the rest of the country has switched off and figure this is what people elected you to actually do. Those are good days.

The exemplar is a story that Christine Milne would tell better than I. After some adept negotiations in the wake of election 2010's indeterminate result, Christine's proposal for a Multi-Party Climate Change Committee wrote the template for world-leading climate legislation that wrapped everything from biodiversity conservation, carbon farming, low-income protection, tax bracket reform, industry support and clean energy investment into a carbon price package. Nobody got everything they wanted, but through that process at least the Parliament was operating across party lines to deliver something deeply important.

Labor supporters rest heavily on the foundational achievements of the Whitlam era or the soft-focus golden age of Hawke and Keating, but there are accomplishments closer to home that deserve acknowledgement, despite the vandalism some of them suffered in subsequent years. The National Broadband Network was the real deal – a big picture structural reform; nation building in the original sense. The Gonski reforms, attempting to deliver education funding to children our country otherwise threatens to leave behind. The Living Longer Living Better aged-care package. The National Disability Insurance Scheme – brought forward by none other than Bill Shorten – attempting to throw a vital safety net under the people who need it the most. These are big, important national reforms that should be credited to the people and the party who made them happen.

But here's the thing: puffed up in the aftermath of the carbon price rollback, Tony Abbott set his sights on gutting the Renewable Energy Target and crashing the clean energy sector for good. Instead of telling him to jam it, the Labor leadership came up with the genius strategy of meeting him half way. With Labor helping Abbott set the agenda on what degree of attack on clean energy companies they would be happy to accommodate, the Parliamentary debate was over before it even started. Polite applause all round.

Here's another: After a six-year campaign to hold it back, I had to watch Labor sitting on the opposite side of the chamber with George Brandis and Eric Abetz to pass mandatory data retention into law for every device, every man, woman and child in the country. It felt like swallowing broken glass, because I still believe that campaign was winnable. We had seven of the eight cross-benchers with us that night, and if we'd had

Labor's twenty five Senators, that piece of counterproductive authoritarian garbage would not now be law.

Here's another: After condemning John Howard for targeting Northern Territory Aboriginal communities and cattle ranchers for a national radioactive waste dump during the 2007 election, Labor promptly changed sides and started gunning hard for the Muckaty mob as soon as they won government. It took seven years of dignified resistance by local Aboriginal families supported by seasoned anti-nuclear campaigners around the country, two years of Parliamentary blocking tactics and sharp legal intervention in the Federal Court to kill off that unforgivable attack.

Another: While Tony Abbott and Scott Morrison might have perfected the art of using desperate refugee families for domestic political effect, it was Kevin Rudd who reintroduced indefinite imprisonment on offshore black sites as a method for deterring future arrivals of terrified families evacuating war zones. Rudd may be gone, but the policy lives on in the clammy hands of the stridently incompetent Peter Dutton. Labor MPs still expect a warm welcome and an open mic at refugee rights events, as though the rest of us should just let that appalling lapse go through to the keeper. Some things are hard to forget and impossible to forgive, at least while people are still killing themselves behind razor wire.

Rolling the worst elements of the Northern Territory Intervention forward another ten years. Handing ASIO the power to hack and modify an unlimited number of network-connected devices off the back of a single authorisation. Citizenship revocation laws borrowed from George Orwell's nightmares. Uranium mines. The ability to prosecute and jail journalists for merely disclosing the existence of certain kinds of ASIO operation. A blank cheque for our next wave of military misadventures in Iraq and Syria. Promoting massive expansions in coal mining, gas fracking and offshore gas extraction while positioning as a party of climate change action.

There are more. Many more, but you get the point. In large part, most of those strands of Tony Abbott's short but malignant tenure that we're stuck with in black-letter law are only there because of the enfeebled state of the Labor Party, and its inability to stand up as a party of progressive opposition when it actually counted.

It is not the job of the Australian Greens to provide political cover for these repetitive unforced errors. Where common ground exists – and there's plenty – we work together and we get good stuff done. But when Labor in Government goes after the tertiary education sector as they did in 2013, we will link arms with student organisers and tertiary education unions and fend off the assault. When Labor in opposition deftly changes sides and positions itself as the natural champion of tertiary education, which it is doing right now, we will respectfully decline to join them in pretending that 2013 never happened.

I've seen this phenomenon played out often enough that I feel like just calling it out for the brazen political gaslighting that it is. The Labor Party shows different faces to different constituencies and hopes that nobody compares notes. Sometimes it works. Sometimes it's a disaster. Consider the 2014 senate by-election in Western Australia. It would be hard to imagine two more different candidates than Louise Pratt and Joe Bullock. A woman who spent her career as an outspoken advocate for LGBTI rights, for refugees, for climate action. A man who stood shoulder to shoulder with

Tony Abbott in university politics and has stayed aligned with Abbott on keystone issues for the remainder of his political life. The Western Australian public were asked with a straight face to accept that these two polar opposites embodied the same values because the Labor Party is a 'broad church'. It was excruciating, and it cost the ALP dearly.

What the 'broad church' phenomenon means in practice is that a handful of good-hearted Labor MPs are free to go out and campaign against the Trans-Pacific Partnership despite the fact that the ALP leadership has already decided they are going to support it when push comes to shove. The church is broad enough to cultivate climate change campaigners to join the ALP, while throwing the full weight of state institutions behind Adani's attempts to disembowel the Galilee Basin coalfields. It is a church that did everything it could to block marriage equality when it was in government, only to succumb to a series of revelatory changes of heart from the safety of opposition.

It's not so much that the Labor Party routinely attempts to walk both sides of the street; it is that the rest of us are apparently meant to pretend that it *just isn't happening*.

When I say that there are people of good heart working hard inside the Labor Party, people I trust and count as friends, I mean it, and I presume things would be a lot worse if they weren't there. But the net effect of working for 'change from within' is this endless sequence of compromises and stumbles that has left people with very little idea of what the modern Labor party actually stands for. I am sure there are legitimate reasons why you'd go into the Labor Party and try and resuscitate it from within, but ultimately, these efforts seem futile by definition. 'Change from within' may have merit if the platform just needed tweaking around the edges. But a party in thrall to the coal industry in the age of climate change, that sent its soul to reside with children in offshore concentration camps, is not in need of a minor tweak. It needs to work out who it actually is.

The deepest problem with the 'change from within' strategy is that to a jaded party strategist, a vote 1 marked next to the ALP candidate by a voter desperate for something better from Labor is indistinguishable from a number 1 endorsing the sad status quo. Every electoral success on the back of a 'slightly less awful than Tony Abbott' policy platform makes it that much less likely that the platform will meaningfully change.

A Labor Government signed Australia up to the Framework Convention on Climate Change in 1992, and yet they are still backing unregulated fossil fuel exports. Cowed by the force of the Abbott/Morrison assault, Labor fatally compromised itself on protection of refugees and now wears equal responsibility for the horrors unfolding in the camps. Given multiple opportunities to put a check on Abbott's frightening lapses into authoritarian surveillance laws and foreign military incursions, Labor blinked over and over again.

It is entirely pragmatic for Labor to adopt these policy positions if they think it will help capture some imaginary political 'centre' as defined by the collapsing influence of the *Daily Telegraph* or a tiny handful of talkback radio hosts. But they can hardly expect progressive movements to keep pretending it isn't happening, or imagine that this serial surrender qualifies as leadership. For Labor campaigners baffled by the rise of the Greens or offended by the idea that the centre of gravity for progressive politics long-ago swung away from the grinding internal contradictions of the Labor

Party, I respectfully draw your attention to this dismal record. Various left factions may be willing to be crushed over and over again on matters of valiant principle, but the rest of us have run out of patience.

Until recently, Labor had slowed the rise of the Greens and other parties by deliberately obfuscating peoples' understanding of Australia's preferential system, and using fear of conservative governments to label smaller parties a wasted vote. Their success allowed Labor to campaign on major national issues with undeserved credibility as sole agents of change. But that credibility will continue to erode in the interconnected world, where friends and family are the most trusted news source and Labor's contradictions and capitulations are just a few mouse clicks away.

The way forward for the Greens is much clearer. All of our policy positions emerge from four pillars that were set down as the foundation of our party nearly three decades ago. If they haven't already come across them by the time they join, new Greens members are introduced to the concepts of Ecological Sustainability, Participatory Democracy, Social Justice and Peace and Nonviolence. Internal debates are as fiery and well informed as I imagine occur in any party, but they are at least focused on how to enact those core philosophies in the real world. The principles stand uncontested, and that's a key reason why we've continued to grow as a political movement while other minor parties have fallen apart.

The situation is always more complex than the angry stereotypes allow, and it would be foolish to pronounce on the demise of an institution as complicated and storied as the Australian Labor Party. The blunt facts are, in the immediate future neither party will hold an absolute majority in either house of Parliament, as increasing numbers of Australians throw their allegiance to minor parties and independents or opt out of the electoral process entirely.

Where goodwill and common cause allow, the urgency of our challenges demand we all work together for the good of the planet and its people. If the Labor Party resolves some of the conflicts that have it handcuffed to the wrong side of arguments of fundamental importance, they know they have a powerful ally in the green movement. But increasing numbers of people have given up hope of this ever happening, and this is beginning to show on electoral maps as new generations of voters enter the field and older generations run out of patience. Time's up.

Chapter 8

'Australia the Beautiful':
A Dangerous Myth

David Mejia-Canales

It is not the bad qualities, but the good qualities of these alien races that make them so dangerous to us. It is their inexhaustible energy, their power of applying themselves to new tasks, their endurance and low standard of living that make them such competitors.
Alfred Deakin, 12 September 1901
(Prime Minister 1903–10)

The Arrival

I arrived in Australia in late May of 1989; my first memory of arriving in this country was how vast it felt and how crisp the late autumn air was, particularly since we were so underdressed. I arrived as a refugee from the Salvadoran civil war. My old home was slowly being devastated by death and chaos; by ceasefire a fifth of the population would be murdered. It's no surprise that in comparison it felt as if I had arrived in a new Eden. This was Australia the beautiful.

I'm not sure when you actually stop being a refugee. Under law there is a point where you cross the threshold from persona non grata to citizen, but a legal definition is too blunt a tool to use to encapsulate the experience. Furthermore, using a strict legal definition can never really even begin to describe or address the multi-generational trauma that follows war. I didn't even begin self-identifying as a refugee until being a refugee in Australia was something you did not want to be. If the personal is political then I chose this label as my one-man protest to reclaim an identity that was being demonised by government rhetoric for political gain.

When my family first arrived, with all of our remaining worldly possessions in cardboard boxes, government agencies saw us as people that needed intensive resettlement, care and assistance. The government itself saw us as a welcome addition to the country. That's what it felt like to me, and that's what I need to believe for my own comfort. The promise of boundless plains to share can't be rhetoric alone because to admit that it may be would feel like peeking behind the curtain to find that the Wizard of Oz was just an angry and scared old white man.

My whole family was housed in the Migrant Enterprise Hostel in the outer South Eastern suburbs of Melbourne. Adults were provided with English language classes, information sessions on dealing with government agencies and support through the practicalities and technicalities of living in a foreign country. As kids, my siblings and I were supported through the school enrolment process, we were given toys and clothes for the Melbourne winter. The idea behind all of this support was simple: you're new here so we'll get you on your feet.

I used to hold the hostel as proof that we are a nation of the 'fair go' that welcomed those that come beyond the seas with boundless plains to share and that our current policies of mandatory detention for asylum seekers are just an aberration and a deviation from our true nature. I think I can also point to the hostel as the start of my gravitation towards the Labor Party. We did come to Australia and were living in this peculiar building on the other side of the world under the administration of a Labor Government after all. Who wouldn't gravitate towards someone promising freedom from death in a war?

Detention centre or not, the Migrant Hostel was a wonderful place for a child. If the Tower of Babel did exist, it would have been in Springvale. At the hostel, you had a multitude of people who wouldn't choose to live together. In fact, none of us would have even have had the opportunity to meet. I had never seen an Asian person before, or anyone from the Subcontinent and definitely had never met a black person. Now not only was I living next to them, underneath and on top of them, we were all playing a part in probably the most formative and transformative experience of our lives.

It wasn't until I was researching this essay that I found out that the Migrant Hostel I upheld as a model of 'Australia the Beautiful' was actually converted into a detention centre only some months before we arrived. This conversion happened under a Labor Government.

I don't believe that we were in detention ourselves because we were allowed to move freely in the community. I need to believe that I was not a detainee; it's the foundation myth I must hold to. I am living proof of the bounty this lucky country can expect to reap if it treats its asylum seekers with kindness. The idea that I may have been a child in detention, or at least a child living in a detention centre wounds me. Replacing my foundation myth of a generous Australia with a xenophobic one strikes at something that is so fundamental to my identity.

The media may repeat ad nauseam the largely empty platitudes of Australia being the 'lucky country', but for me as a boy it felt like the lucky country. This is why any thought to the contrary is so painful. The sunburnt country was so vast as to feel almost borderless, the generosity of my new home felt limitless and the safety from war it ensured was priceless. While we were incredibly homesick, we were also unbelievably grateful. During moments of melancholy my parents, my mother in particular, would tell us that we always needed to be thankful to Australia for giving us opportunities that we could never have imagined.

When she could understand enough English to watch the television news, she would say that Bob Hawke was 'her prime minister' because he had brought us here. By the time Paul Keating rose to the top job, my mother would feel the same way about him whenever he sauntered onto the television. You often hear about families that have supported one political party over another for generations, maybe this is how that alignment is made. Somewhere down the line, someone felt that the government of the day did something right by them that was so monumental as to cement an undying loyalty reproduced and shared through exchanges like the ones my mother made to the television.

When you're a child your parents are like Greek gods, they're all knowing, all powerful and magnanimous and yet still capricious, prone to bias and preferences. As a kid you soak up everything your parents do or say because you don't really have much of a choice and also because they are like deities that must be obeyed, or at least placated for life to continue running smoothly. I grew up with my mother telling me to thank this country in so many ways as well as her praising Labor leaders she will never meet for giving us a better life.

How could this not have an effect on me? How could this not have an effect on my political alignment? It did then and still does today; I'm yet to meet someone whose early personal experiences haven't shaped their later politics. I'm no exception, although my example of being a refugee is probably a lot more acute than most. As a refugee, now a citizen, I am acutely aware that the success of my integration and contribution to Australian society is a combination of personal fortitude, administrative fairness, luck and bountiful kindness from all manner of people. Too many to ever thank or even count.

However, despite how it pains me to admit it, Australia is not and maybe never was as welcoming as I once thought; neither was the political party I aligned myself with. This is devastating because it flies in the face of everything I've experienced and believed about Australia as a young man. I'm under no illusion that this country is perfect. The way we have treated (and still treat) First Peoples is a glaring example of our shortcomings.

'Australia the Beautiful' is becoming more a myth than a truth. As I've got older, I've begun to question the perception I have of my country and even my power to change it – not because I've let it decay or left it behind, but because every day I feel like Australia has left me.

Learning to Clean Toilets

> *The objection I have to multiculturalism is that multiculturalism is in effect saying that it is impossible to have an Australian ethos, that it is impossible to have a common Australian culture. So we have to pretend that we are a federation of cultures and that we've got a bit from every part of the world. I think that is hopeless.*
> John Howard, January 1989,
> (Prime Minister: 1996–2007)

Multiculturalism as a celebrated government policy is still only a couple of generations old; especially when you consider that we have spent more time living under the White Australia policy rather than free of it. This means that we are still bit players in the great multiculturalism experiment.

I know all of this logically but because I'm emotionally invested in 'Australia the beautiful and welcoming' I believe that she has always existed and was actively hunted by our leaders for their own political advantage. Because I am the product of an Australia that opened its arms to refugees and saw them as future Australians, I will staunchly defend multiculturalism's success. Having said this, it took me a long time to pinpoint why politicians attacking multiculturalism were repugnant to me and that's because it felt like an attack on me personally. I remember watching Pauline Hanson give her first speech to Parliament, that infamous bit of prose that warned of the perils of multiculturalism, and thinking to myself: 'who is going to be left to clean your toilets?'

Despite growing up in a household where my parents were actually, or at least seemingly, quite apathetic at the administration of government in Australia – despite my mother constantly heaping praise on whatever government policy allowed us to live here safely – I inhaled any and all political news and commentary. It's only later in life that I have acknowledged a need to be kinder to my parents' total lack of interest in everyday Australian politics. I was very young during the Salvadoran Civil War, I do remember martial law and the power blackouts, but my lived experience of it is fuzzy and that's largely because of my parents' protection. My parents did not take part in political demonstrations or other manifestations of political life in El Salvador because those that did often went 'missing'. It's not until later in life that I have really understood that their being actually or seemingly apathetic to politics in El Salvador was for our survival and not due to a lack of commitment. This extinguishing of desire to be involved in politics never left them I guess and maybe that just saved us from experiencing worse tragedies in war. Perversely, their political apathy allowed me to develop a voracious appetite for all things political.

The first federal election I took an active interest in was the 1996 contest between Paul Keating and John Howard. Having become a full citizen of the Commonwealth some five years earlier I felt a sense of duty to inform myself about the election and the issues surrounding it. In truth, taxation reform and Howard's brand of conservative values did not interest me in the slightest; I was more interested in whether his well-known views against immigration would poison the well for me and my family.

I remember tuning in to a current affairs show the morning after Howard trumped Keating and I heard one commentator state that: 'The Liberals have now come to power and people will find that the sky hasn't fallen in'. Frightened, I rushed outside to look up at the sky to make sure that it wasn't collapsing. I had never heard that phrase before and I was scared that in Australia, like in the country of my birth, upheavals always followed an election. The sky was blue and still in its rightful place, like it has been after every prime ministerial changeover.

This peaceful transition from one person to the other using nothing but the combined weaponry of hundreds of thousands of Australian Electoral Commission pencils was what progress looked like to our family. This is what freedom was, this was civilisation, and this is how you do fairness. In El Salvador, the outcome of an election was not the end of a national conversation but the beginning; the end would come when whoever got control of the army would take over. I remember thinking to myself that Australia was the greatest country in the world because the sky was still there, it was still blue and it was not rearranging. This is where I wanted to live because democracy was alive here. I love the country in which I was born, always will; but this Commonwealth was to me the perfect place to grow up because everyday people could influence the political process and be confident in the process unlike where I was born. I once overheard my parents talk about electoral fraud in El Salvador because apparently some distant relatives had voted in an election just after the war had ended. This alone is not cause for concern, what was concerning is that these relatives had been long dead before election day.

I tried to pass this zeal for politics to my parents with very little result. 'They're all the same' they would say, 'be thankful for what you've got'. I wish I had the maturity back then to understand that political apathy was how my parents did political involvement. However, around the 2001 election I had a very interesting exchange with my father. He told me that he would be voting for Howard because of his economic credentials and his attitudes towards immigration.

While I've always known that my father is a deeply conservative man, I just always assumed that he would vote for the Labor Party because after all their party was responsible for our refuge when they were in government so I just assumed he would vote for that party and not for the man who was actively against multiculturalism. I erroneously thought that as working-class immigrants we were all destined to be Labor-leaning, at least for the foreseeable future. While I saw my family as the epitome of the working class, my father had other aspirations. I think to my father Labor represented the workers, the proletariat, the many which is what we did not come to this country to be. We came to this country to flourish, ergo it's the Liberal Party that deserved his vote. I do think the Liberal Party owns the language of opportunity and entrepreneurism better than any other; at least they did it well enough to woo my father.

Despite my father's aspiration both then and now, to many people we will always just be working-class immigrants or worse still: the aspirational classes. My immigrant working-class background is something that I am extremely proud of. It has entrenched in me an impeccable work ethic. As an immigrant, I learnt early on that if you want anything, anything at all, you have to work extremely hard. There were so many people that had very low expectations of a refugee from El Salvador growing up in the suburbs of outer Melbourne; but growing up as an immigrant in one of Melbourne's most disadvantaged communities was responsible for shaping the work ethic that has seen me defy a multitude of soft expectations. Nothing that I have or have had was gifted or bequeathed to me, it was all earned through hard work and dedication and I genuinely believe that this fighting spirit and drive to never be recumbent is due to my working-class background. What's more Australian than valuing hard work, dedication and zeal?

My parents also had very strong work ethics; in fact, both were professionals in their past life. Despite my father's training and my mother's previous work experience, in Australia it meant nothing. They couldn't even speak a word of English let alone work in their respective fields. When we arrived, my mother became a stay-home parent and my father worked in the now defunct Nylex Plastics factory assembling car parts. He would come home smelling of all sorts of acrid chemicals, always with burns to his hands. I will never forget that smell of burning plastic mixed with superglue and sweat. His clothes were always covered in that smell even when clean. The smell seeped from his marrow.

The only concept I had of Nylex Plastics was the large Nylex branded clock I would see from the windows of the train pulling into Richmond station. I always assumed that's where my dad went to work every morning at 3 am. I remember being incredibly proud of him working in the city centre like all the other white people. I was so proud that he was already working in the city like the people on television, despite not being able to speak more than five words of English. I was devastated when I found out that the Nylex factory was actually in the industrial suburbs of Melbourne's east and the clock was just a clever bit of product advertisement.

My parents would take my brother and me to '*la cleaner*' with them under the guise of learning the value of a hard day's work but also because the work was punishing and many hands made it easier.

I would try and deflect with any excuse to avoid going, to no avail. I didn't have to go often but the times I did go I was surprised at the speed at which my parents worked, always in a really uncomfortable silence. My parents may have wanted company to help them in the gruelling task at hand but cleaning warehouses, offices and printing presses taught me the high admission price my parents paid for our safety.

While (I imagine) most children and young adults are taught how to carry out domestic chores with a slack tutorial by a parent so their child learns some basic life skills, my father taught me how to clean a floor by cleaning the floor of a shopping centre. I learnt how to clean toilets by cleaning them in an office block. I learnt how to vacuum by vacuuming a warehouse. I'm proud of this because it taught me the value of hard work and the value of *my* own work. If the Liberals owned the language of opportunity and enterprise and wooed my father that way then the Labor Party wooed me with its language of fairness, hard work and mateship. I guess this is why I found it hard to believe my Father defected to support the Liberals, because we had cleaned other people's toilets together.

I remember once cleaning the offices of a multinational health company when I asked my mother if this is what they had come to Australia for. I asked her if my father's anger, which often manifested itself in numerous beatings for us all, was because in Australia he was earning a living cleaning an office and in El Salvador he would have been the boss. I could tell the question shattered her but also gave her some sort of perverse comfort because it showed her that I acknowledged the incredible sacrifice my parents had made so that we could prosper. As an adult, I have never had to work in a factory or in the manufacturing industry, partly because my parents held the bottom of the ladder making it easier for me to climb. Yet, because of my background and my story, I definitely identify with the working class, even if that identity doesn't relate to my life today. While I may be well educated, well travelled and well remunerated I've also cleaned plenty of public toilets.

As a lawyer working in academia, I resent the amount of time I spend in an office, but that's not because I'm cleaning it. I'm acutely aware that this role reversal came about through sacrifice and hard work and not entitlement. I may not ever work in a factory, at least for the foreseeable future but I certainly relate to those that do, regardless how many rungs of the ladder I climb.

I sometimes joke with close friends that it's hard to find a Salvadorian immigrant that isn't (or wasn't) a cleaner. While I hate that stereotype (it promotes the bigotry of soft expectations), both my parents worked several casual cleaning jobs from time to time cleaning offices in industrial parks or factories and shops. Much like any reclaimed language or stereotype, I feel I can joke about being a migrant. I find that self-deprecation in particular makes people feel okay to ask questions or talk about race and class issues; however woe befall anyone who uses the Latino cleaner stereotype to laugh *at* me and not with me. Self-deprecation, what's more Australian than that?

The Labor Party

> *This is a fundamental test of our social goals and our national will: our ability to say to ourselves and the rest of the world that Australia is a first rate social democracy, that we are what we should be – truly the land of the fair go and the better chance.*
> Prime Minister Paul Keating, 10 December 1992
> (Prime Minister 1991–96)

It was because I learnt to clean toilets by cleaning other people's toilets and because I flourished with free education and free healthcare that aligning myself with the self-professed party of the workers felt natural. In fact, as a lifelong progressive it almost felt expected. At the time I aligned myself to Labor, Kim Beazley was its leader and while I had no warm feelings for him, it was the party's values that I connected with. Even though the decision to align myself with Labor felt easy, it wasn't without challenge.

The elevation of Kevin Rudd to the leadership with Julia Gillard as deputy was refreshing, particularly after 11 years of Howard's strident conservatism. That feeling magnified a thousand fold when the Labor Party came to office. Rudd competently steered the nation through the 2008 Global Financial Crisis, he closed the offshore detention camps and he apologised to our First Nations Peoples for the stolen generation.

Behind the scenes, chaos was taking hold in the Rudd Government, the history of which has been repeated and examined ad nauseam. For my part, I maintained my loyalty through Gillard's premiership and I became a member of the party in 2010. It was no coincidence that at this time I also began working for a Labor-aligned law firm where joining the party while not required, was gently encouraged and definitely welcome. I felt that I could forgive Gillard's unexplainable and silly opposition to same-sex marriage and her administration continuing the Northern Territory Intervention in Aboriginal communities started under Howard, albeit under the sinister-sounding name of *Stronger Futures*.

I felt that the party and its values were more important than the leader, I also think I was extremely forgiving of Gillard's many mistakes because I genuinely liked her after having met her when she toured my law school. That same forgiveness did not extend to Rudd's second iteration as leader. Interestingly, my mother's appreciation for whatever Labor leader happened to be Prime Minister had also run thin. She would refer to Rudd as 'that man', her words thick with venom. 'Have you seen what *that* man has done to *La Julia*?' I think that my separation from Labor gradually over time would not surprise Labor strategists but it certainly wouldn't please them. I was then an urban twenty-something, recent postgraduate living in inner Melbourne. My demographic were probably seen as collateral damage in the great Labor Civil War of 2007–13; but not my mother. My mother was a working-class woman with a seemingly undying loyalty for 'the party that brought us here'. If Labor could lose my mother, and people like her, then as far as I'm concerned it's a sure sign that they're in trouble.

It was Rudd II's 2013 revised policies on immigration, refugees and asylum seekers that finally saw me sever ties with the party and led my mother to ask me: 'who do I vote for now?'. I'm aware that a Labor government first introduced mandatory detention but it was under the Liberals that it became deliberately crueller so as to be a deterrent much later. In fact, it was Labor under Rudd that closed the offshore detention camps and it seemed for a while that compassion would be reintroduced to how we dealt with asylum seekers and refugees; at least that was before the Labor leadership wars. Postbellum Labor was different, postbellum Labor was more interested in burning its own house rather than burning the 'light on the hill'. I cut up my membership card.

I know that I was not the only one dismayed that the party that has given Australia great economic and social reforms was now playing an unwinnable game with the Liberals just for a chance to hold on to government. Labor deserved to lose the election particularly as it blatantly used asylum seekers as pawns. I refuse to say that I left the Labor Party, the Labor Party left me. Whether it's because of its behaviour towards itself while in government or its failure to be any sort of opposition once out of government it appears to me that I'm not the only one abandoning that ship.

The Labor Party has also betrayed Australian progressives in two ways: they were too concerned with fighting each other than governing this country, and they're so intent on being a Liberal Party Lite that they are happy to vacate progressive politics. It appears to me that Labor is progressive only when compared with the Liberals. What Labor is offering progressive Australians like me is a reprieve from the Liberal Party, not a remedy. This vacation of Labor from the left – in fact I would go so far as to say that it is a dereliction of their duty to provide a forward thinking, socially focused agenda – has left progressives with three choices: disengage completely, support micro parties or support the Greens.

The Australian Greens

From now on, any asylum-seeker who arrives in Australia by boat will have no chance of being settled in Australia as refugees
Kevin Rudd, 19 July 2013
(Prime Minister: 2007–10, 2013)

I first became aware of the Australian Greens through Bob Brown around the Tampa affair, when John Howard deployed Australian combat troops to intercept the *MV Tampa* from offloading refugees to the Australian mainland it had rescued at sea. As a senator for Tasmania, I always just assumed that they were exclusively a Tasmanian party, and it was a fair assumption to make.

I started considering supporting the Greens at the 2007 election, after Adam Bandt became my local member of parliament. Labor's Lindsay Tanner before him was very popular but given his retirement, as well as his crucial role in the Rudd–Gillard wars, my attention began to wander elsewhere. The Greens seemed to be putting forward the kind of ideas I wanted my elected representative to espouse: legalising same-sex marriage, health and education spending reform, a strong social safety net, sound environment policy and most importantly for me, the humane treatment of asylum seekers.

After deserting Labor in 2013, I joined the Greens. Publicly as a protest against Labor, though in the secrecy of the voting booth, I voted for the Greens in 2013 while still being a Labor member. It was my silent, secret protest against everything Labor now stood for. The Greens made me feel better about my progressive politics and they were and have become even more of a real threat to Labor. Supporting them gave me the feel good factor of knifing Labor in the front. Despite this, my alliance and allegiance to the Greens gives me some concerns, not just about the party but about progressive politics in Australia broadly.

It's true that in Richard Di Natale they have the only leader of a major political party in Australia that has (and has ever had) a non-English speaking background; yet the parliamentary seats it occupies and the policies it espouses feel at time too idealistic, impractical and geared to appeal to urban, twenty-something undergraduates. Even though demographically speaking I am no longer working class, that's my background. Being working class has made me so I often default to seeing things through the lens of my background; my family's background. If people talk about having 'the sniff test' or the 'pub test' to determine the veracity of something then when it comes to politics I feel I use something that I'm going to start calling 'the parent's test': 'would my working-class parent's benefit from this policy?'.

I want to be clear that I don't think the Greens policies need a major overhaul per se but they do need challenging. A competition of ideas is how better ideas are devised and better policies implemented. The Greens are the only left-leaning progressive party in the ring and while this is better than no progressives in the fight, it's dangerous. A party without competition becomes lazy, sloppy and then entitled. A progressive party without competition becomes the Labor party of 2010. A competition of ideas will not only benefit progressives but our politics as a whole. A strong, clear and well-explained progressive counterpoint to conservative thinking gives us all choice but not only that it gives us hope.

Labor is no longer representative of the left, even if they still would like to claim they are. They are chasing a Liberal Party to a middle that keeps on shifting to the right. To say that the Labor Party is a credible choice for progressives is a complete lie. My Labor-aligned friends disagree and point to a suite of achievements of parliaments past and a smattering of left tinted policies of today: Gonski funding, teaching children to code or making entrepreneurism visas available. Worthy policies as they may be, they're safe. Labor's policies are not revolutionary; they're not even evolutionary. Compare Labor under Bill Shorten to Whitlam's Labor at its high-water mark. Claiming the Labor Party is a viable option for progressives because if elected they would legislate to teach coding in schools is like me passing myself off as a doctor because I can apply a bandage. Labor may have good people but it seems to me they're lacking in imagination.

When I jumped ship from Labor to the Greens, I did so without looking back. Deep down I felt that in time I would return to Labor if or when they could stand up for progressive social policy with tenacity and fearlessness. I don't know how long I expected my absence to be, but the person that ensured that absence would be a lot longer was Bill Shorten.

I first met Bill Shorten at a reception at Victorian Government House, hosted by His Excellency the Governor for World AIDS Day in 2013. I approached Mr Shorten to congratulate him on being elected leader of the party. I shook his hand and made the smallest of small talk with him. He seemed so incredibly disinterested in what I had to say which totally compounded his total lack of charm. Not only that but he was appearing to scan the room looking for someone much more important than me to speak with. The photo I took with him speaks volumes; if he could have stood any further away from me, he would have been out of the frame. No sooner than the photo was taken, he turned his back and began talking to someone presumably with a title a lot loftier than mine.

As I was leaving the reception, a little despondent after my interaction with Shorten I bumped into Christine Milne, then leader of the Greens. She was in a frightful hurry, needing to catch a plane back to Canberra. I asked her for a photograph and despite her haste, she was more than happy to oblige. She asked me questions about my life and what had brought me to that event; the photo I took with her also speaks volumes. In it, she is giving me a great big hug and grinning from ear to ear. I like to think that I'm beyond emotional manipulation and can't be swayed just with a smile. My love for Labor had been long lost by then but with that bear hug Christine Milne cemented my support to the Greens and validated my joining.

I like to think that I make decisions based on reason and after a lot of analysis, and that my capacity to reason and think critically outperforms my feelings and emotions. How could I be swayed by something as simple and innocuous as a hug? Wasn't the policy and the vision more important than how I may feel for a fleeting moment at a state function taking place in a room so hot people fainted?

I often decry the notion that our politics has turned away from people that have conviction and is moving towards leaders that have charisma. It's great if the leader of a government has both, but in an era of selfies and Facebook, likeability is an important measure of respectability instead of the other way around.

I don't think that Bill Shorten's lack of charisma would matter as much if he appeared to be emotionally intelligent or have strong convictions about something, anything. I also don't think Christine Milne's charm offensive would be so charming if she didn't have sound policies that provided an actual progressive alternative. The rational side of me says that the best person to lead the government should be the most intelligent and not the most likeable. However, it is a complete fallacy to say we make our decisions based on reason and logic, we don't otherwise Australians would be the most savvy policy wonks in the world. If we were logical and reasonable, we would rake through every party's policies and discuss them on their merits. Like every other human, we make decisions based on feelings and on how someone makes us feel. Are we asking too much of our politicians, to be intelligent as well as charismatic? Possibly. Did an emotional connection to me as a fellow human being by Christine Milne win me over to the Greens? Absolutely.

The Australian Equality Party

> *The Marriage Act is appropriate in its current form, that is recognising that marriage is between a man and a woman*
> Julia Gillard, 30 June 2010
> (Prime Minister: 2010–13)

In early 2015, I was looking to elevate my political involvement and start campaigning for a candidate for the next federal election. I joined the Australian Equality Party and took a hiatus from the Greens. This move wasn't so much ideological but rather practical and self-interested as I wanted to be involved as closely as I could to a candidate's campaign and involvement in campaigns for the Greens seemed incredibly crowded with very young adults more concerned with being a staffer in Canberra than effecting change.

The Australian Equality Party is a single-issue party whose main reason for existence is for legalising marriage equality. While they profess to be in favour of a whole suite of policies that would benefit gay, lesbian, bisexual and transgender Victorians, their campaigns and communications are exclusively targeted towards achieving marriage equality.

The Party bills itself as a new voice that will act as a reminder in Parliament that we the people own the political process. The lofty ideas do not match the reality, the Australian Equality Party is a micro party led by very kind people without any political know-how or strategy. The leader of the party is a kind man with good intentions but good intentions are not a currency you can cash in at the ballot box.

I think, if anything, the Australian Equality Party is a barometer of the current mood regarding politics in the nation. People feel that they don't have an effective choice between the two major parties and the Greens are seen by some as too radical, so this is fertile ground for any person that can muster the numbers to register a political party for their cause. I expect the Australian Equality Party will suffer the fate of the Australian Democrats but with a lot fewer runs on the board.

Keep Australia Beautiful

We have a great objective: the light on the hill, which we aim to reach by working for the betterment of mankind not only here but anywhere we may give a helping hand. If it were not for that, the Labor movement would not be worth fighting for.
Ben Chifley
Labor Party Conference, 1949
(Prime Minister 1945–1949)

It's very easy for progressives to feel anguish in our political climate, even after the arch conservative Tony Abbott has been replaced by a moderately conservative Malcolm Turnbull, making it the fifth prime ministerial changeover in almost as many years. While the language that comes from the Prime Minister and his Cabinet is a lot more measured and less prone to sloganeering, at the time of writing there hasn't been a significant change in policy to accompany the change in prime ministers and this has gone largely unchallenged. In fact, Australians as a whole feel so ambivalent towards politics and politicians that our desire for political stability may cost us if we decide a stable prime ministership is more important than scrutiny and oversight.

Are we in some sort of free-fall or careening towards despair? No, but I think we're changing as a society in a way that seems dangerous but not unavoidable. Our government is increasingly giving itself broader powers in the name of national security; it is eroding human rights protections for the most vulnerable while simultaneously seeking a seat on the United Nations Human Rights Committee. Requests for oversight of how we treat asylum seekers and refugees are shut down with the three words: 'on water matter'. Whether knowingly or not, we are trying very hard to sacrifice community harmony for something as cheap and disposable as political advantage.

It's too easy to blame politicians alone for disillusioning us from being active participants in the political process. We need to take responsibility as individuals and as a society and accept that we have either explicitly or by omission made a mutually beneficial deal with our government: they will make us prosperous if we don't question their actions and motives. Visions for the long-term future of the nation have been replaced with sound bites. We've gone from 'The Lucky Country' to 'Team Australia', and somewhere, at some time, Chifley's 'light on the hill' was snuffed out or towed back to where it came from. All the while, I can't let go of the idea of 'Australia the beautiful' because even if it isn't true, and even if it never was, I believe that it can be, but only if we want it to be.

'Australia the beautiful' must be true because my brother and sisters have all gone to university. I too have been educated by the taxpayer and in fact am the most educated member of my whole family both immediate and extended. Some of my siblings have married and are raising the next generation of Australians, some rent, some own their own home and both my parents are now retired and no longer have to clean other people's toilets. 'Australia the beautiful' exists friends, or at least it has done because I am living proof of it; my family is living proof of it and to deny that, is to deny my existence.

As a political progressive, who has moved from one party to the next to find the most perfect fit, I feel stuck, helpless and increasingly disappointed and isolated because our country is being slammed to the political right aided by a Labor Opposition that is not actually opposing. My own country increasingly disappoints me when it ratchets up its populist, cheap and nasty rhetoric on human rights, asylum seekers, the environment and particularly the xenophobic discourse on immigration.

Maybe the united, pluralistic, multinational county that welcomed my family as future Australians only existed in my mind. Maybe I created it as a salve for the wounds of the war we were fleeing. I need to believe that this country is welcoming and our current attitude to asylum seekers, human rights and government transparency is just an anomaly, an aberration in a system that largely works and has done for centuries. I need to believe that even the son of two professionals-turned-cleaners can become a lawyer and the highest educated person in his family and flourish with the help of and not in spite of the government.

I don't think the progressive cause in Australia is lost. It is fractured, not coherent, and in some cases begging for a champion; however this is where I come up empty because I don't have a simple solution to begin the repair process or maybe I just don't have the will at this moment. I dare say I'm not the only one feeling battle weary, disengaged and powerless. I take comfort in knowing that I will not feel like this forever.

Regardless of how we propose to either create or rebuild 'Australia the beautiful' I know that it has to start with one simple premise: we must never be scared of our government but rather, we have to give it plenty of reasons to be scared of us.

My parents still don't talk about politics; they only really pay attention to what's happening when they have to vote and usually by asking their children who they should vote for. They always vote, not just because it's compulsory but because I think to them it's a symbol of what's possible. Once my mother came home after having cast a vote at the same time her local member was casting his amongst a small throng of media. She was so proud that her vote was worth the same as her MP's. She even asked the local member for a photograph and she scanned the local papers to see if she had appeared in them somewhere. She said to me: 'Australia, isn't she beautiful?'

Isn't she?

Chapter 9

Burying Margaret Mead: Environment and the Labor Party

Felicity Wade

I was twenty-seven and had joined the staff of the Wilderness Society only a couple of weeks before. It had been a bumpy landing. It was late 1995, the dying days of the Keating Government and a year of forest madness. At the end of the year before, the Government had identified an extensive list of native forests to be given temporary protection from logging while proper assessments could be completed. In response, the Construction Forestry Mining and Energy Union (CFMEU) had organised a logging truck blockade of Parliament House. The environment movement had played equally hardball and the Cabinet retreated, impossibly jammed.

A tired, conflicted government botched it with ample help from the key protagonists. While the sound and fury had mostly subsided, the Wilderness Society continued to be camped out in a rogue Labor Tasmanian Senator's office in Parliament House, lobbing grenades.

I was wandering about, finding the halls of parliament both exciting and lonely. I was pretty-much ignored by my new employers, given no sense of my task or the larger strategy. Unlike most in the Wilderness Society, I had no history in either the environment movement or politics. I'd never been to a forest blockade. I saw an ad in the newspaper and applied for the job as a communications officer. I was wondering what on earth I was doing there. I was feeling nostalgic for my previous job in advertising, never mind that I had left it because I wanted to change the world. I hung around. I was irrelevant, no one stopped to include me amidst the exciting flap of daily tactics.

Then Bob Brown waltzed into town. This was before his successful run at the senate in 1996. I organised some interviews for him and was given the job of driving him to the ABC studios on Northbourne Avenue. It was the first time in three weeks that anyone had actually spoken to me. I don't remember the details, but he asked me questions about my love of the bush, where I'd come from, had me blabbing about the mistake I'd made in taking the job and reassured me that we needed people like me in the battle for Australia's environment and that my efforts to work out my place in it mattered.

It was encouragement that changed the course of my life. Twenty years later, I remain a solid Bob Brown fan.

But I am card-carrying member of the Labor Party and run the Labor Environment Action Network (LEAN). My love of the once-in-a-generation politician and activist didn't hold me to his party, even though I had a box seat in watching its emergence and establishment in Australian Federal politics.

I am a creature of the environment movement. The world outside formal politics has energy and freedom unavailable inside the system and much can be won without its constraints. I believe more than ever that ideas are only generated out of civil society – those battling in the tedium of daily politics have limited horizons and imaginations.

The Wilderness Society – my particular corner of that movement – was largely invented by Bob Brown and shares some key bits of DNA with the Greens. Brown was the Society's charismatic leader through the Franklin River campaign. When I quickly shifted out of the no-persons land of the Wilderness Society's national organisation to run the New South Wales chapter in 1996, my board was held together by Geoff and Judy Lambert, some of Bob Brown's oldest confidantes. And for at least most of the next two decades, an obsession with Tasmania's forests defined the organisation.

Inevitably, the relationship between the Greens and the Wilderness Society had to change and grow up. Rules were introduced that no decision-making person in the Society could be a member of a political party after the Queensland election in 1995. (Formally illegal in terms of freedom of association, but no one let that worry them.) The Greens backed the Liberal–National Party Coalition after they promised to block a freeway through koala habitat on the Gold Coast while the Goss Labor government negotiated a huge protected area on Cape York with the Wilderness Society. The Society had a civil war over it, and much blood was lost. This was the beginning of the discussion about whether the Greens were the political arm of the environment movement and if so, who called the shots.

But that is all very ancient history. I have a backpack full of stories of the decades, as an environment activist and my tetchy relationship with both the parties of the left, the Greens and the Labor Party. The activist straining for particular policy outcomes is inevitably in conflict with political parties whose interests are mixed up with the pursuit of power. In the end, however, I joined the Labor Party. As with anyone who joined during the last Labor Federal Government, it was not because of the inspiration it provided! Fundamentally, it was because I believe it is time for environment advocates to talk to the centre. Put another way, I am keen to bury Margaret Mead and her ubiquitous quote:

> Never doubt that a small group of thoughtful, committed citizens can change the world: indeed, it is the only thing that ever has.

This quote headed the fundraising letter I received at last tax time from one of Australia's largest environment groups. On protection of the environment, Mead is out of date. Her quote speaks to an earlier stage of the environment movement's mission.

Environmentalism has won the argument but not the institutions of our democracy. What's more, with climate change threatening life as we know it, the challenge is huge and can't be delivered by the morally fearsome few – we must speak to all sectors of society and truly build coalitions across interests. To deliver lasting and deep change we must take most of the society with us, imposition of change by minorities is brittle and breakable.

The environment movement did a great job of hectoring from the margins and dragging the goal posts way out. But now people across society recognise that we can't trash the planet. Sure, there are still powerful vested interests trying to protect their profits. And middle Australia may not particularly like smelly greenies and our austere, earnest ways. But they are on our side. We are no longer a minority group of outsiders pushing from the edge.

My thinking was that it's time for us to dump the moral superiority of vanguard politics. It is time for environment advocates to talk to the centre, rather than fighting it and alienating natural allies. We need to own our status as representatives of middle Australian values and join centrist institutions and enshrine environmental values in their heart.

So there I was entering the big, powerful institution of the ALP, feeling like Dorothy entering the Wizard's house – tentative and awed, flanked by a few powerless comrades of the brave, brainy, big-hearted variety.

We set about rebuilding LEAN – the Labor Environment Action Network – and making it a force for change in the Labor Party.

LEAN's campaign

LEAN was started as a cross-factional environment organisation within the Labor Party by former ALP President and NSW Senator, Jenny McAllister and former NSW Premier, Kristina Keneally in 2004. After a few iterations, LEAN is once again an active force and has proven the power of cultural subversions by winning its campaign to have the Party re-embrace climate leadership, adopt a 50 per cent renewable energy target by 2030, and commit to net zero emissions by 2050 with credible interim pollution reduction targets to get us from here and there.

Of course, as with any campaign, we relied on those uncontrollable external factors that fell our way. Over the first six months of 2015, the build up to the Paris Climate Meeting shifted the international discussion and Tony Abbott's strident opposition to climate action began looking crotchety and regressive. The debate over the Abbott Government's attempts to scrap or hobble the Renewable Energy Target alerted Labor to the popularity of renewable energy amongst the electorate.

But when we sat down in a room above a pub in central Melbourne in late 2014, the fear of Labor retreating on climate change was very real. The wounds of the political car-crash of carbon pricing under Rudd and Gillard were still fresh and hard-heads were arguing that silence on the issue was the best path forward. One of the first hurdles was to ignore some senior figures telling me that if I cared about climate change I would back off and leave the issue until Labor was in Government.

LEAN wanted to do three things: put climate change back in the centre of Labor's offering by winning policy change on renewable energy targets and economy-wide pollution targets; embed within the Party the idea that near complete decarbonisation of the economy was possible; and change the narrative so it wasn't a greenie imperative but core Labor business.

That meeting of a scraggly bunch of Labor members developed a campaign platform and frame. The frame included arguments about why Labor needed to make climate change a conviction issue, not a tactical one. We were on strong ground in making the point that the electorate wanted to see Labor showing that it believed in something after the mess of the Rudd–Gillard years. We were careful to frame the imperative in terms of Labor's key concerns, with climate change as a threat to equity, safety and prosperity; and the solution as an opportunity for economic growth, innovation and job creation. We also foregrounded the need to deliver transitions that provided protection for impacted communities as important Labor business.

Our policy prescriptions were grounded in the work of ClimateWorks, a climate policy group at Monash University chaired by former Labor Deputy Premier of Victoria, John Thwaites. 'One of ours' is a powerful legitimacy enhancer in the Labor Party, especially when it comes to green issues. ClimateWorks had released a report in September 2014 that modelled a path for the Australian economy to reach net zero emissions by 2050. The report provided a straightforward narrative about what it would take to deliver the changes needed. From it, we pulled the timeline for deployment of renewable energy and we established our central call for a transformation of the energy sector. To deliver this, we identified that Labor needed to create one ministry for climate change and energy to stop contradictions in the sphere and a comprehensive approach to carbon sequestration through land use.

In the end, our campaign failed to solidly engage the Party in the detail of paths to decarbonisation instead coalescing around the two headline policy asks: a policy of 50 per cent renewable energy by 2030; and adoption of the carbon pollution reduction targets proposed by the Climate Change Authority, which we short-handed to 50 per cent by 2030. The campaign was titled 50/50. Its target was the 2015 National Conference of the ALP to be held in July 2015. Held once every Federal term of Parliament, the National Conference debates and establishes the policy platform of the Federal Labor Party.

When it came to strategy, our path to influence the Party was defined by our limited tools. LEAN is one of a number of internal Labor 'ginger' groups, communities of interest around particular issues that seek to push for policy change. Other such groups, most notably Labor for Refugees and Rainbow Labor were much better connected. They could rely on building a community of powerful figures who were prepared to stand up for the issue in the Party's traditional decision-making elites.

LEAN does not attract the ambitious or the powerful, or their acolytes. Our issue is too tricky and politically fraught – a wholesale restructure of the economy is not bite-sized. What's more, it explicitly requires conflict with some of the Party's strongest vested interests.

As for the union leadership, most did not answer our calls. Those who did meet LEAN patted us on the head and sent us on our way. The union and Party elite's interest in groups of organised rank and file members is understandably small – a disempowered membership has fed the system as long as anyone can remember. A survey of the tools at hand left us with a singular path forward – talk to the membership!

All this made for a genuine manifestation of the rank and file. In terms of strategy, LEAN had little choice but to rely on a grassroots approach. This is what makes the possibilities that LEAN began to model new and powerful.

With no access directly to the membership, the local ALP branches became our surrogate. Getting our hands on lists of local branch secretaries was our next great challenge. These had to be stolen or handed over – in the digital age version of a brown paper bag – by friendlies in state offices. We cobbled the money together to pay a freelance designer to design the materials: workers and wind turbines beneath the Southern Cross all in Labor colours of blue and red. Not a touch of green to be seen.

At state level, we held open meetings to kick start LEAN. Small groups of people would turn up and form LEAN groups. From this, we built teams of volunteers who met and built connections and skills and set about visiting the local branches of the Labor Party. LEAN volunteers would give a short presentation often followed by long debates and lots of questions. When it came time to test the membership's appetite for climate action by asking for support of our position, there was unequivocal enthusiasm.

Three hundred and seventy local branches passed motions in support of LEAN's call for adoption of 50 per cent renewable energy by 2030 and adoption of credible carbon pollution reduction targets. For a party making much of the need to reform, and to include its membership, this was a powerful demonstration of the membership's commitment. I did very little of the on-ground meetings, mostly watching from my email account as the list of local ALP branches rolled in, a catalogue of Australian places: Balranald and Geraldton, Townsville and Burnie, Mt Druitt and St Kilda. It was a testament to the broad, often slumbering – but still very much alive – community of Labor true believers across the country.

As National Conference approached, dodgy photos taken at branch meetings in support of 50/50 tumbled across social media. We had more of these photos than we got around to posting. These images, often groups of ancient stalwarts with a smiling green-shirted young LEANer, created not only a catalogue of all the plastic chairs on wooden floors in dark, 'echoey' halls that are the architecture of meetings of the Labor faithful but a testament to the diverse, ordinary, passionate people who make up the membership.

Over the next months, the state Conferences in New South Wales, Queensland, Tasmania and Western Australia supported the adoption of the Climate Change Authority's pollution reduction targets. In New South Wales, LEAN had nothing to do with this. The local branches put it to the conference themselves. Because Party Conferences at the state and Federal level are the highest policy-making forum of the Party, theoretically this meant that a large section of the Party had already committed to the pollution reduction targets.

LEAN also engaged with the party's official policy development process. The previous National Conference had established the 'National Policy Forum' with the intention of enriching and broadening the policy development discussion before National Conference. The National Policy Forum was a group of sixty people, twenty from the Federal Parliamentary party, affiliated unions and the party membership. Its members were charged with consulting across the party before meeting for two face-to-face seminars in the lead-up to the National Conference to formally propose policy changes and additions to the existing National Policy Platform.

LEAN had no representation on the Policy Forum so we just started turning up. We wrote a comprehensive submission to the Environment and Climate Change chapter as well as making suggestions to embed climate impacts and mitigation across portfolios. Many of our suggestions were adopted. We headed off some worrying proposed changes to Labor's nuclear policy, strengthened the commitment to environmental law reform and included acknowledgement of the scientific consensus of the need for developed nations to deliver net zero emissions by mid century. Needless to say, the National Policy Forum did not support our proposal for inclusion of our renewable energy target or specific pollution reduction targets. It was however, an important context – with most of the party's key players in the room – to prosecute our argument.

As the campaign strengthened in the branches, LEAN talked with people across the Party. A number of trips to Canberra were arranged with fairly open invitations for anyone actively involved in LEAN to join us to visit Labor MPs. Democratising access is another of my bugbears and allowing ordinary members to front up to their politicians and talk to them about the campaign was a small victory. One evening, Shadow Climate Change Minister Mark Butler hosted LEAN drinks in Parliament House and a broad array of Labor MPs turned up. After myself and leader Bill Shorten had spoken to the crowd Joel Fitzgibbon jumped up – not a natural ally of environmentalists – to assure us that his and Gary Gray's attendance were not as spies but as those who recognised we had to get along and sort out these issues cooperatively in the Party.

A couple of months out from the Conference the internally powerful Construction, Forestry, Mining and Energy Union (CFMEU) responded to our campaign with an open letter to all Federal Labor MPs and the union leadership. It expressed its opposition to our call for 50 per cent renewable energy by 2030. Shifting energy generation away from coal-fired power to cleaner sources will have deep structural impacts on the CFMEU membership and the industries they work in. The CFMEU, under the leadership of National President Tony Maher had been remarkably progressive on the issue, recognising the inevitable threat to his members and responding to try and ensure workers were protected in the transition.

The CFMEU had supported the climate package of the former Labor Federal Government and embedded themselves in the negotiations, ensuring their interests were well defended while also allowing the reforms to occur.

This was a moment when the campaign nearly derailed. We had no structural power; CFMEU had loads. We wrote an open letter back stating our opposing view on the costs to consumers and workers that the transition would impose as well as the larger imperative that modernising our energy system presented to the economy. We minnows had no choice but to stand our ground. Luckily, we were backed by a huge swathe of rank and file members and their branches.

At a meeting of the national Left a couple of weeks before conference, I stood to outline LEAN's proposal. As we were still negotiating with the CFMEU, no one was supporting us – overt opposition to the CFMEU is not a common habit of the Left of the Labor Party. As I was speaking I saw CFMEU National Secretary Michael O'Connor raise his hand for the floor after me and was nervous. O'Connor said he wanted the room to know that the CFMEU knew climate change was happening and was committed to responding, that they had some differences of view with LEAN that we were working to resolve but thanking us for showing respect and not calling them rednecks. Having come up against the CFMEU over decades in the forest debate, that exchange most powerfully illustrated the value of being 'inside'. The ability to resolve the conflict came only from environmental concern being an organised and legitimate stakeholder within the Party. In return for support of the 50 per cent aim, the CFMEU was able to negotiate strong undertakings from the Party to protect its members. The resolution on the floor of Conference that committed Labor to 50 per cent renewable energy by 2030 included a commitment to establish an agency to redeploy affected workers and structural adjustment strategies and investment for impacted communities.

Resolution 214R was put to the Conference by Bill Shorten and seconded by Tony Maher. It was passed unanimously.

And that's the happy ending: at the 2015 National Conference in Melbourne in July Bill Shorten proclaimed climate action a key differentiator with the Coalition Government, adopted a 50 per cent renewable energy target for 2030 and included in the Policy Platform a commitment to credible pollution reduction targets before the next election. As the *Sydney Morning Herald* put it: 'The Shorten approach follows a strong and well-coordinated campaign inside the ALP by a group calling itself the Environment Action Network and backing a "50/50" campaign in favour of 50 per cent renewable energy by 2030'.

A large block of LEAN lime T-shirts whooped and hollered from the floor, causing Tony Maher to comment from the lectern that it was like looking being at a swimming carnival – green and red before him. Shadow Environment Minister and newly-elected National President Mark Butler, who was a consistent supporter of LEAN, generously acknowledged the campaign across the weekend:

> In my nearly 30 years in the Party, I have not seen an organising effort on a policy issue like LEAN has delivered. It was phenomenal.
>
> It was not always a comfortable relationship for a Shadow Minister to have a strident and well-organised lobby group keeping the pressure on, but this campaign was important. It gave Bill, I, and the rest shadow

cabinet the assurance that the Party was behind us as we stepped out to lead on climate change.

Senior Right figure and Shadow Finance Minister, Tony Burke said:

> It's the most effective grass roots effort I've seen within the ALP. The leadership consulted widely to work out what needed to be done and then campaigned relentlessly in every Party unit to push Labor's commitment as far as possible. They campaigned hard at the grassroots while also enhancing a strong relationship with the party's leadership.
>
> I've never seen anything like it. I don't quite know how they did it but I do know our environment policy is the strongest we've ever had and LEAN had its fingerprints over every page.

In November 2015, just before the Paris Climate Change Conference leader Bill Shorten formally delivered the second part of our campaign with a Labor commitment to delivering net zero emissions by 2050 and adoption of at least 45 per cent pollution reduction (on 2005 levels) by 2030. Climate change policy is now central to Labor's differentiation with the Turnbull Coalition. Bill Shorten attended the Paris Conference and consistently talks of climate action's role in delivering economic opportunities and a modern, dynamic Australia.

LEAN demonstrated that the membership could be organised to force change on the parliamentary leadership. We proved too that the membership care about the environment. However, one good campaign does not a reformed party make. This is the bigger challenge.

Labor Needs to Work out Integrating the Environment

Labor's history on environmental reform is pretty good. Labor is the party that saved the Franklin, the Daintree and Kakadu. Labor is the party that introduced environmental impact assessments and put environmental considerations in the mix of all planning and land use decisions. Labor is the only party that in government has delivered significant environmental outcomes. This sets it apart from all.

However, it is my contention that Labor's environmental legacy has been delivered by 'the great men of history' (and I don't use the gendered term by mistake). Labor's environmental outcomes have relied on powerful individuals within the parliamentary party spending personal political capital to deliver. Bob Hawke protected the Franklin River, Graham Richardson protected the rainforests of the Wet Tropics and Tony Burke delivered the world's largest marine park system.

The last NSW Labor Government illustrates this. Premier Bob Carr and Environment Minister Bob Debus were a dynamic duo, one from the Right and one from the Left. These two men, as key players in the NSW cabinet, mandated great environmental outcomes – a million hectares of wilderness were protected, the world's first emissions trading scheme established and the native forest industry was restructured. Their exit from Parliament however led to a fallow time for environmental issues with no continuity embedded in the institutional arrangements of cabinet or caucus. The last term of NSW Labor was deeply stinky and deeply brown.

My fear is that this model has worked for protection of iconic places but may be inadequate to deliver the changes the climate crisis demands. To shift an economy against the wishes of some of the world's largest vested interests will require considerable political leadership and some existential commitment. Deeper roots are essential if the party is to respond confidently to the challenge.

There are three factors of production – labour, capital, and the resources out of which things are made (called 'land' in the original classical formulation). The Labor Party was born in a time when the conflict between labour and capital was the main game in town. The third factor of production was a neutral actor to be happily exploited. This of course has changed fundamentally with the earth making pretty powerful noises about its conflict with capital's exploitation. The Labor Party has failed to modernise to include this. And with life as we know it under threat from climate change, this isn't good enough.

As US President Obama said at the United Nations Climate Change Summit in September 2014, 'For all the immediate challenges that we gather to address this week – terrorism, instability, inequality, disease – there's one issue that will define the contours of this century more dramatically than any other, and that is the urgent and growing threat of a changing climate'.

To be a modern social democratic party, Labor must embed a response to this challenge. Recently I heard Labor giant Barry Jones discussing the importance of climate change action to Labor's future. He catalogued a long list of 'things beginning with C' that Labor needs to grapple with in order to deliver this: 'coal, cities, cars, consumption, concrete and contraception' were among his list. This points to the big philosophical nature of the challenge of truly embedding an environment sensibility in the heart of Labor. It goes to some fundamental issues in our current political economy.

It also reveals that climate change is not just another of the band of 'socially progressive issues' that mark so much of modern elite politics. Rampant inequality and climate change are fundamentally the economic issues of our century. A proper response to these is a different beast to the 'progressive' politics I see pedalled so often by both parties of the left. I hate the word progressive. I want it buried with Margaret Mead. It mostly describes a flaccid politics that appeals to socially progressive, post-materialist elites without fundamentally challenging the neoliberal hegemony. It explains why the Greens lost three per cent of their primary vote when Malcolm Turnbull became Prime Minister. I want a more robust politics than the grab bag of social issues it usually denotes. I want a politics that addresses the disparity, ugliness and planetary challenge of globalised capitalism.

It is also interesting that the centrality of environment issues is already felt in the dynamics of Labor Governments. Bob Debus, a veteran of state and Federal Labor cabinets made the observation to me recently that, 'The schism down the centre of the Party these days is not left and right, it is brown and green. The great debates around the cabinet table in my experience divide on this fault line'.

The key question becomes, can Labor modernise to include this deeply twenty-first century imperative? Labor has a history of morphing and modernising. But old habits and structures are entrenched and the necessary adjustment to Labor's core mission is not going to happen lightly.

You hear the odd lament that the Party missed the moment in the early 1980s when it could have bought environmentalism in, perhaps affiliated environment groups like unions. While this is probably fantasy considering the limitations of much labourist thinking, it points to that moment when Labor's failure to respond made it complicit in the creation of the Greens. Now that was a strategic blunder that has been creating huge effort on the left flank ever since! And with the percentage of 18–25 year olds voting Green heading towards 30 the pain is only set to continue.

Another impact of the rise of the Greens is that the Labor Party has lost a whole generation of politically active types for whom the environment is a key motivator. They have joined the Greens and their environmental activism has been sorely missed. The lack of connections between the environment sector and the Labor Party remains shocking. There are very few personal friendships. This is tactically baffling to me as an environmentalist and as a Labor person. It would seem to reflect a lack of long-term strategic thinking from both sides. My clear commitment to environment outcomes was a source of distrust in the Party. It is the distrust of two cultures meeting who know nothing of each other except for unsubstantiated claims the others are cannibals. But Labor is no more a monolith than any other group of humans and the dearth of environmentalists has mattered to the Party's ability to respond to the environmental imperative. The lack of connection has also limited the environment movement's ability to deliver lasting, audacious outcomes. Often the environment movement actively limits progress on its issues with its naivety and arrogance. It's refusal to run a long-range game, to work with allies and to learn the lessons of history limits its impact. Much of this could be improved with better relationships delivering a deeper understanding of the dynamics and imperatives of governing.

Don't get me wrong there are large barriers to entry for the idealistic and the activist. There is plenty to dislike in the

Labor Party and real cultural barriers to getting involved in its decision-making, the most obvious being the distasteful nature of the factions. The factions are led by oligarchs, whose power is based largely on their ability to remain in these arid places, operating on loyalties and enmities born in student politics. I don't have a critique of factions per se. In a large institution, people inevitably form into groups in order to assert power and leadership around shared ideas. And this system still manages to produce some good, smart politicians. But beyond that gracious acknowledgement of the notion of factions, today's factions are pretty ugly. While they might nourish those who grew up in them, it is nonsensical that a person who joined the Party later in life would submit to the factions. With few real ideological differences, they are little more than power-hungry friendship groups. So does this mean – unless you go to university with these characters and are acculturated to the factions – the best one can hope for is to be a loyal branch member? This is a problem for the Party. Especially, as Barry Jones eloquently put it, pre-selection today is primarily 'a reward for factional fidelity'.

The Hope of the Membership

But there is great hope. And I believe reason to try and realise this hope. As with any political party, Labor includes two parties. There are those involved in the wheeling and dealing, the careerists and factional players. And then there is membership, numerically much greater, the good souls who join because they genuinely want to make Australia a better place. Labor is full of such people. Getting inside it is a warmer experience than the media face would suggest. It is thick with the salt of the earth, people who believe in their country, equity and decency.

And at least as many are ex-members of the ALP – people who joined to make a difference and found paths to do this difficult to locate. My osteopath for instance explains she joined the Labor Party when it delivered the first female Prime Minister, thinking it was time to pitch in. She attended one or two dull branch meetings and gave up.

But those members who battle on are the people who joined LEAN and went out to visit branches. John Christoforou is a 57-year-old accountant and small business advisor on the NSW Central Coast who jokes, 'I care so much for the environment I joined the Labor Party'. He visited every branch in the Federal seat of Robertson. John Gain is a retired carpenter who travelled the length and breadth of New South Wales talking to regional branches and in his quiet way backed with steely commitment convinced them of this issue's importance. David Mason is a former senior human rights bureaucrat and winner of the Public Service Medal who in league with his environment activist kids not only presented tirelessly to branches but also wrote many of our serious policy submissions and runs our Twitter account. (There is no better place to keep up with Labor-related environment news!) Louise Crawford is a Victorian actor in her early 40s who joined the Party to change the world and stop climate change. She managed the branch visit program across her state.

According to the 2011 Review of the Labor Party written by John Faulkner, Steve Bracks and Bob Carr, Labor still has 900 local branches. These meet each month in draughty halls. They turn up because they believe in democracy and the social-democratic ideal. They turn up because they believe in Labor and its promise of a fairer country. They are the great, untapped resource. Australia has no other political network like it!

LEAN was a wobbly, imperfect attempt to shift the fundamentals by aggregating the power of the branches and the membership. One branch member, in the Federal seat of Kooyong, explained to me recently about how hard it was to run a branch and how disempowered they mostly felt but how LEAN's visit, the enthusiasm and passion of its presenter and the promise of working together across the Party was energising – 'it was like a pipe that suddenly had water gushing through it or a wire that once again had electricity'.

As the early attempts at democratising in the Party have shown, the Iron Law of Oligarchy is alive and well. The Iron Law of Oligarchy explains that in any complex organisation power coalesces in the leadership. Democratisation does not necessarily change outcomes or re-make the Party. The great experiment of community pre-selections in New South Wales, where candidates were chosen by a ballot equally weighted for local ALP members and local community members, universally delivered the factional pick. This is not proof of the factions' ability to pick stellar candidates but a reflection of the lack of invigorated alternative relationships and networks in the Party to support and promote leaders. Someone argued to me recently that democratisation was a good thing as it would keep factional power in place but ensure they can't bowl up complete duds as candidates – this is a weak offer indeed!

The only answer to re-invigorating the Party is to once again build participatory democracy; an alive and agitating membership. This won't come from the never-ending rounds of rules debates alone. These are the domain of insiders, and more specifically insiders for whom the system has failed. Nothing is more alienating for 'normal', good-hearted party members than an embittered insider 'rabbiting on' about rules.

Instead, reform must be grounded in things we passionately believe in.

I believe that serious organising of the membership could force change. I'm unsure whether LEAN will survive, there are huge pressures on a voluntary group which, in reflection of my thoughts above, is not 'owned' or supported by either the Party or the environment movement. But the promise is there.

It is my dream that LEAN builds ways for serious activists, wanting real change to deliver on John Button's promise – to change the Labor Party and change Australia. That is, not only deliver environmental commitment but a model for more fundamental reform by rebuilding a community of empowered and active members.

I believe Labor can do things the Greens can't. To change the fundamentals of our future requires we take the majority of people with us. Labor is still the party that is overtly interested in the economic interests of ordinary Australians and can bring the centre with them, leading and compromising to deliver deep and lasting change. Australia is not just us inner-city wankers. It is a melting pot of people doing their thing, getting by. The 'paradise of dissent' is still deep in the Australian psyche but it's not going to be delivered by an elite or a minority. The broad middle of Australia is open to fairness. And it wants its kids to live in a safe and healthy environment. Our challenge is to deliver a politics that speaks to the values and imaginations of middle Australia.

Labor at its best is magnificent. Sometimes you catch it within the union movement – that whiff of passionate commitment to fairness, the hatred of the accumulation of capital at the expense of ordinary people trying to look after their loved ones. I heard it echo recently at an event reflecting on the work and philosophy of Gough Whitlam – the depth of thought, effort, and institutional strength that lies latent in a hundred years of people straining for justice and a better society. It is a deep well. And of course, the membership that is defined by people of decency who believe taking the centre with us to deliver equity and fairness is a historic mission. It is in all our interests to try and revive Labor's tired and sometimes obscured heart.

Chapter 10

Why Progressives Should be Pro-Growth[1]

Andrew Leigh

One of the dividing lines between Labor and the Greens is our attitude to economic growth. Labor's policy platform is unequivocal:

> Labor is a party of economic growth. We reject the arguments of those who do not believe in economic growth.[2]

By contrast, the Greens platform reads:

> The pursuit of continuous material-based economic growth is incompatible with the planets finite resources. In order to provide for the needs of present and future generations, economic management should

---

1 This is an edited version of a speech delivered at the Ginninderra Labor Club on 18 May 2011. My title borrows from Gene Sperling, *The Pro-Growth Progressive: An Economic Strategy for Shared Prosperity*, Simon & Schuster, New York, 2006. Thanks to Jennifer Rayner for valuable comments on an earlier draft.
2 ALP National Platform, Chapter 2.

prioritise improving the quality of life rather than the production and consumption of material output.³

This sceptical attitude to economic growth can also be seen in the speeches of Greens representatives. Richard Di Natale claims that there is a belief that GDP and the stock market are all that matter.⁴ Lee Rhiannon argues that economic growth is not the solution to women's empowerment.⁵ Scott Ludlam has compared continuous economic growth with cancer.⁶

Attitudes to economic growth are as good an issue as any to define the policy difference between Labor and the Greens. In part, this reflects the difference between a party of government and a party of protest. But it runs deeper. A party that compares economic growth to cancer is one that deliberately places itself outside the important economic debates that Australia faces.

True progressives should never shy away from making the case that economic growth matters.

---

3   Greens Policy Platform, Economic Principle 2.
4   'Every generation has its fashion and we are cursed by the belief that narrow economic measures such as Australia's GDP and the performance of the stock market are all that matters', Richard Di Natale, first speech, Australian Senate, 16 August 2011.
5   'So the assumption that increased economic activity will help everyone is highly problematic. Put simply, the problems women face are not only economic, they are complex and require careful, participatory solutions that are more than simply an increase in economic activity.' Lee Rhiannon, debate on International Aid (Promoting Gender Equality) Bill 2015, Australian Senate, 5 March 2015.
6   'When our economy fails to grow we call it a recession; but an entity that knows only blind growth we call a cancer.' Scott Ludlam, first speech, Australian Senate, 16 September 2008.

Why Growth Matters

As Australians, we're used to economic growth. Yet it is easy to forget how unusual growth is in human history.

Go back a few centuries to the Victorian era and the average person was no better of off than the average caveman.[7] There were a lucky few who enjoyed tea in china cups, but the true living standards of 1800 were better captured by Charles Dickens than Jane Austen.

Indeed, economic historian Greg Clark makes the point that on some measures, the vast mass of the world's population were *worse off* in 1800 than their ancestors of 100,000 BC. Victorians were shorter – reflecting their poor diet and exposure to disease in childhood.

In 1800, life expectancy was around 30–35 years, pretty much what it had been on the savannah. And citizens of 1800 probably worked longer hours than cavemen. From the Stone Age to the Renaissance, most people ate around 2000 calories a day, compared with the 3000 calories a day that we consume. In fact, most of us would find it difficult to get by on 2000 calories a day, because our bodies are significantly bigger than those of our ancestors.

There's something slightly shocking about the thought that our ancestors – just seven generations ago – experienced stone-age living conditions. For them, it was normal to go to bed hungry. Everyone knew someone who had lost a baby in childbirth – sometimes with the loss of the mother too. Illness was normal and uncontrollable. Life for most was, as Thomas Hobbes famously put it, 'nasty, brutish and short'.

---

7 Gregory Clark, *A Farewell to Alms: A Brief Economic History of the World*, Princeton University Press, Princeton, 2007.

There was simplicity in a world without economic growth. An artisan would engrave his prices on the stone wall of his workshop, knowing that his son would be charging the same. Living standards for most people were low, and there was no expectation that your children would enjoy anything better.

Then – beginning in a little island off the coast of Europe – something changed. With the Industrial Revolution, people began to experience rising living standards. Average income tripled from 70 cents per person per day in 1800 to $2.30 by 1900. In the twentieth century, average incomes rose tenfold to $22 per person per day.[8]

That transformation had immediate effects on people's health. A person born in 1900 could expect to live to 40. By 2000, babies born in a developed nation could expect to live into their 70s. Today, Australian life expectancy is 80 for men and 84 for women. Economic growth is the central reason why Australian life expectancy is twice as long as at the time of Federation.

People don't just live longer – we live healthier. A survey of elderly veterans in the United States found that in 1910, nearly all were suffering from digestive disorders.[9] By the end of the twentieth century, just one-fifth suffered from the same health problems. Another study looks at direct measures of health, such as the ability to perform light housework, or the number of days each year that illness confines a person to bed. The authors conclude that the self-reported health of men

---

8 Arnold Kling and Nick Schultz, *From Poverty to Prosperity: Intangible Assets, Hidden Liabilities, and the Lasting Triumph Over Scarcity*, Encounter Books, New York, 2009, 26.

9 Dora L. Costa, 'Health, income, and retirement: Evidence from nineteenth-century America,' *The Journal of Economic History* 55(2) (1995): 374–375.

aged in their early-70s today is similar to the levels recorded for men aged in their early-60s three decades ago.[10]

Underpinning economic growth has been a massive rise in productivity. Workers today create more value in an hour than their great-grandparents did in a day. A century ago, it took 1700 hours of work to buy a year's food supply for a family. Working a typical week, that's 10 months' labour. Today, a family's food supply takes a month and a half of work.

That's true of other products too. Since the late-nineteenth century, the number of working hours to buy various products has dropped dramatically. It used to take 260 hours of work to buy a bicycle – now it takes 7 hours. It used to take 2 hours of work to buy a dozen oranges – now it takes 6 minutes. Not surprisingly, that's meant an increase in the number of leisure hours: from 2 hours a day in the late-nineteenth century to 6 hours a day now.

The Easterlin Paradox Debunked

If you had to name one central fact to characterise the past two centuries, it would be income growth. It has made us healthier and allowed us to enjoy more leisure. It has lengthened our lives and allowed us to be more generous.

Yet some now argue that economic growth has gone too far. In *Growth Fetish*, Clive Hamilton argued that once a society has developed to the point at which the majority of people live reasonably comfortably, the pursuit of growth is pointless and

---

10 David Cutler, Jeffrey Liebman and Seamus Smyth, 'How fast should the social security retirement age rise?,' NBER Retirement Research Center Working Paper NB04-05, National Bureau of Economic Research, Cambridge, MA, 2007.

should be curtailed. Internationally, books like Tim Jackson's *Prosperity Without Growth* have become bestsellers.

At the core of many of the anti-growth arguments was the contention that once incomes reach a certain threshold, more money doesn't buy more happiness. The person most closely associated with this idea is Richard Easterlin, who wrote a famous article in 1974 that looked at the relationship between GDP and happiness across nine countries. Easterlin found that there was no statistically significant relationship, and concluded that across countries, money didn't buy happiness. The relationship became known as the 'Easterlin Paradox'. His article has since been cited nearly 2000 times, and has become one of the most famous ideas in the social sciences.

In 2008, a pair of economists at the University of Pennsylvania – Betsey Stevenson and Justin Wolfers – decided to revisit the Easterlin Paradox.[11] But rather than using data for just nine countries, they exploited the fact that we now have more happiness surveys. A lot more.

In 2006, Gallup surveyed people in 132 countries about their life satisfaction. As the chart below shows, the relationship between satisfaction and log GDP is almost perfectly linear. There is no evidence of satiation. If anything, money seems to buy more satisfaction as you get richer. When we move from nine countries to 132 countries, the Easterlin Paradox simply doesn't hold up.

---

11 Betsey Stevenson and Justin Wolfers, 'Economic growth and happiness: Reassessing the Easterlin Paradox', *Brookings Papers on Economic Activity*, 2008. See also work by Angus Deaton and Alan Krueger, which reaches the same conclusion.

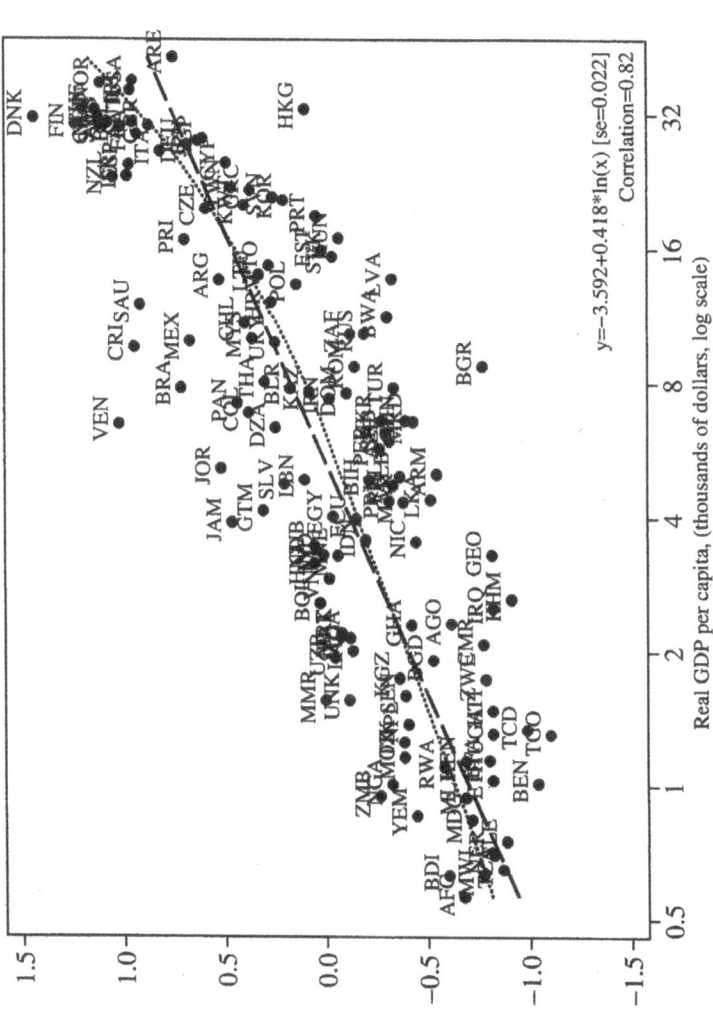

Figure 1: Life satisfaction and income (source: Betsey Stevenson and Justin Wolfers)

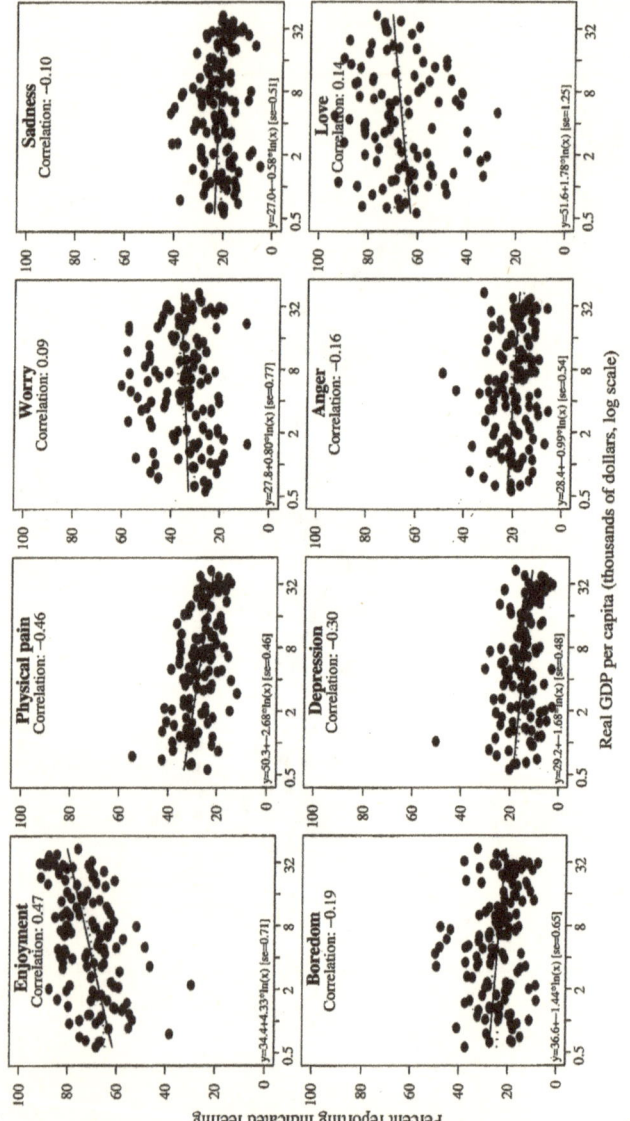

Figure 2: Emotions and income (source: Betsey Stevenson and Justin Wolfers)

Interestingly, money doesn't just buy more happiness. In countries with higher levels of GDP per capita, people are more likely to say that they experienced enjoyment, and more likely to say that they were pleased at having accomplished something. People in affluent nations are less likely to have experienced physical pain, loneliness, depression and boredom. Indeed, people in richer countries are more likely to tell an interviewer that they experienced love in the previous day. That's right, Paul McCartney, money *can* buy you love.

Environmental Concerns

A popular belief is that economic growth and environmental damage go hand in hand. This concern comes in two forms – some people argue that we will use too many inputs, while others argue that we will produce too many outputs. Let me address each in turn.

The view that our economy will eventually use up all the stuff in the world is based on a static view about where our GDP comes from. If it were the case that all workers produced goods requiring non-renewables *and* if we never became any more efficient at producing those goods, then rising incomes and population would eventually use up all the world's resources.

But it turns out that neither of these things are true. Most workers don't produce goods from non-renewables. In fact, three-quarters of Australians work in the service sector. For detectives and doctors, barristers and baristas, the product of their jobs doesn't weigh much (leading some to dub the phenomenon 'the weightless world' of work). In fact, the entire output of the United States weighs only marginally more today than it did a century ago.[12]

---

12 Kling and Schultz, *From Poverty to Prosperity*.

Productivity too, is always increasing. Today's cars use less fuel. Our computers use less electricity. And, thanks to recycling, our paper uses fewer trees.

Our economy is also shifting from one resource base to another, a phenomenon that economist Paul Collier characterises (not very reassuringly) as 'running across ice floes'.[13] In the nineteenth century, the British government worried that it was going to run out of tall trees for the masts of ships. We will probably look back at arguments about 'peak oil' in the same way.[14]

The other environmental concern about growth is that people say it inexorably leads to more pollution. Here, the best example is urban air pollution. In the 1950s and 1960s, people became concerned that growth would inexorably choke cities like London and New York. Yet through cleaner cars, cleaner factories, and shifting industrial pollution away from the largest urban areas, we have managed to reduce urban air pollution while still enjoying economic growth.[15]

Today, our major environmental challenge is climate change. Here again, I am optimistic that we can decouple growth from carbon pollution, in the same way as we successfully did with

---

13 Paul Collier, *The Plundered Planet: Why We Must – and How We Can – Manage Nature for Global Prosperity*, Oxford University Press, Oxford, 2010, 98. Our ethical obligation with natural resources, Collier argues, is to bequeath future generations assets of equal value to the natural resources we use. We are not obliged to preserve the world as a museum, but we are 'custodians of their value'. In the mid-nineteenth century, a generation of prospectors who mined Victoria's gold and left us with Melbourne's wide streets and magnificent buildings. We look upon them more fondly than if they had sold the gold and left our generation nothing in return.

14 On peak oil, see Michael Lynch, 'Peak oil is a waste of energy,' *New York Times*, 24 August 2009.

15 Economists refer to this tendency of environmental outcomes to worsen and then improve as the 'environmental Kuznets curve'.

urban air pollution (and with the CFCs that were damaging the ozone layer). I do not believe that the best way to deal with climate change is by abandoning economic growth. Indeed, I think that growth will help us address dangerous climate change, since higher incomes will provide more resources to assist with the transition.

An Imperfect Measure

One of the curious things about economic growth is that while it closely tracks many of the things that we care about – such as health, longevity and love – it is far from being a perfect measure of wellbeing. Indeed, growth in Australia's GDP (or our GNI or GNP, if you prefer) captures some things that we would think of as bad, and fails to capture other things that most of us would regard as good.

Robert Kennedy put this best in a speech at the University of Kansas, less than three months before he was tragically shot:[16]

> Our Gross National Product... counts air pollution and cigarette advertising, and ambulances to clear our highways of carnage. It counts special locks for our doors and the jails for the people who break them. It counts the destruction of the redwood and the loss of our natural wonder in chaotic sprawl. It counts napalm and counts nuclear warheads and armored cars for the police to fight the riots in our cities. It counts Whitman's rifle and Speck's knife, and the television programs which glorify violence in order to sell toys to our children. Yet the gross national product does not allow for the health of our children, the quality of their education or the joy

---

16 Remarks of Robert F. Kennedy at the University of Kansas, March 18, 1968.

of their play. It does not include the beauty of our poetry or the strength of our marriages, the intelligence of our public debate or the integrity of our public officials.

More recently, Australian economist John Quiggin argues that there are three things wrong with GDP as a measure of a nation's economic wellbeing: 'it's Gross (doesn't net out depreciation of physical or natural capital), Domestic (doesn't net out income paid overseas) and a Product (takes no account of labour input)'.[17] A number of economists have argued that we should instead be tracking Net National Disposable Income per Capita.

But either of these measures has the problem that it's just an average. Suppose you're in a café with 25 people when a member of the BRW 200 Rich List drops by for a latte. If we just look at averages, the average wealth per person in the café is now at least $10 million – even although no-one has gotten wealthier.

The same problem occurs if economic growth goes only to the richest. In Australia, recent decades have seen an increase in inequality, but everyone's incomes have gone up. According the OECD, the past quarter-century has seen incomes for the richest tenth grow by an average of 4.5 percent per year. For the poorest tenth of Australian households, incomes grew at 3.0 percent per year.

Australia's experience contrasts with the United States, where incomes for the bottom tenth have barely budged in a generation. But it does highlight the importance of talking about both growth and inequality. Or perhaps we should focus more on median incomes, just as we do with median house prices.

---

17 John Quiggin, 'Is happiness gross?,' 7 August 2006, www.johnquiggin.com.

Just as median house prices are unaffected by the doubling of millionaires' house values, so a measure of median incomes would be unaffected by the doubling of millionaires' incomes.

Boosting Growth

By now, you've probably guessed my secret: I think growth is good. As Winston Churchill said of democracy, it's not perfect – merely better than all the alternatives. The challenge now is to find the set of policies that are best for promoting economic growth.

In the long run, the key to boosting growth is raising productivity – producing more with the same set of inputs. During the 1980s and 1990s, tariff cuts, competition policy and enterprise bargaining were among the underpinnings of productivity growth, but what is the answer to the modern productivity puzzle?

In my view, the best productivity policy we can pursue today is to improve our education system. Raising the skill level of the workforce is essential if we are to adapt to changes in the labour market.

We need to raise *quantity* of education – boost the average number of years of schooling that each person receives. That means encouraging young people to complete high school, undertake vocational training and go to university.

We also need raise the *quality* of Australian education. Since the 1960s, the performance of Australian 14 and 15 year olds on literacy and numeracy tests has failed to rise, and may even have fallen somewhat.[18] One possible reason for this is that

---

18 Andrew Leigh and Chris Ryan, 'Long-run trends in school productivity: Evidence from Australia, *Education Finance and Policy*, 6(1) (2011): 105–135.

the academic aptitude of new teachers has fallen.[19] Policies to boost teacher effectiveness are vital to Australia's future growth prospects.[20]

Getting education right isn't just good for our economy – it's also great social policy. A first-rate education is the best antipoverty vaccine we've yet devised.

Education is also good for civic activism.[21] A bit more school, some vocational education or a few years at university are all factors that help make you more likely to join organisations, volunteer at the local sports club, or donate money to a worthy cause. Admittedly, the past few years have seen Australia become better educated but more disconnected – yet the decline in community engagement would probably have been worse still if educational attainment had stagnated.[22]

Another crucial element to the productivity puzzle is technology. As recently as the early-1900s, American jurist Oliver Wendell Holmes quipped that if all the medicines in the world were dumped into the ocean, it would be better for humanity and worse for the fish.[23] A century on, medical advances have vanquished diseases like smallpox, polio and

---

19 Andrew Leigh and Chris Ryan, 'How and why has teacher quality changed in Australia?,' *Australian Economic Review* 41(2) (2008): 141–59.
20 For more discussion of this issue, see Andrew Leigh, 'Robots, remuneration and restructuring: How do technology and inequality shape one another, and what we should do about it?,' Melville Lecture, Australian National University, 16 November 2015, www.andrewleigh.com.
21 John F. Helliwell and Robert D. Putnam, 'Education and social capital,' *Eastern Economic Journal*, 33(1) (2007): 1–19
22 On the decline in community life, see Andrew Leigh, *Disconnected*, New South Books, Sydney, 2010.
23 Quoted in Robert Guest, *The Shackled Continent: Power, Corruption, and African Lives*, Smithsonian Books, Washington, 2004, 200.

tuberculosis from the developed world. Our emergency departments are considerably better at saving critically injured patients. And in mental health, we are steadily doing better at diagnosing and treating mental illness as soon as it appears. Ensuring that Australia has the right technological infrastructure and incentives to innovate is vital to raising productivity.

Conclusion

There's an old joke that goes:

> Q: How many conservative economists does it take to change a light bulb?
> A: None. The darkness will cause the light bulb to change by itself.

My main argument here has been that economic growth tends to benefit all Australians. But you should not mistake my belief in the benefits of growth with complacency about the need for government to help build a better Australia. Unlike the conservative economist in the joke, I do not believe that markets can solve all problems. Government has an important role to play in providing public investments and managing risks. But it should also promote pro-growth policies, since growth tends to raise wellbeing.

A central policy difference between my political party and the Greens is that Labor recognises the value of growth. Far from regarding growth as a cancer, we recognise that it has the potential to make us happier, and it need not leave us with a dirtier environment. Indeed, the example of the past shows that we can use the resources from growth to improve our natural surroundings. Sometimes the changes come in unexpected ways. In the early-twentieth century, some Londoners worried that there would soon be so many horses plying the streets that the manure would become unmanageable. With the advent of the motor car, worries about exhaust fumes quickly replaced concerns about horse manure.

Globally, Australia's geographic position could hardly be better. At the start of the Asian Century, our proximity to fast-growing nations such as China, Malaysia, Vietnam and Korea will prove vital not only for goods trade, but also because it will allow us to plug in to global growth in other ways as well. Thousands of foreign-born students now study in our universities, while many Australian-born students take the chance to complete all or part of their education in an Asian university.

Great fundamentals place the onus on us to do something special. With the right policies and effective leadership, we can lay the foundations for continued productivity growth, ensuring that future generations enjoy steady improvements in living standards. We can make schools and hospitals work even better, providing the building blocks of a happy and healthy life. We can improve trust in politics, engaging with voters about the trade-offs that are at the heart of decision-making. We can continue to close the gaps between Indigenous and non-Indigenous Australians, applying hard-headed analysis to find out what works, and what does not. Through trade, aid and diplomacy, we can help improve the lives of many in our region. Unlike those in the Greens, I am confident that economic growth will be part of Australia's continued success.

Chapter 11

Making Progressive Government Happen

Adam Bandt

In Germany, they call it a 'grand coalition'. No party ends up with a majority in their own right after an election, so their versions of Labor and Liberal join together to form government. In 2016 as this book about green/red relationships goes to print, the world's fourth largest economy is governed by the equivalent of a Labor/Liberal alliance, a grand coalition with the parties together holding 80 per cent of the seats in Parliament. The role of opposition is taken by the Greens and the Left parties.

Joint government by supposed political enemies (the social democrats and the conservatives) is no mere aberration in Germany. In fact, it may be fast becoming the norm. Between 2006 to 2015, a grand coalition was in place for six of those ten years. For much of this last decade, alternative coalition arrangements would have been possible involving the Greens, the Left party and the SPD (the Labor equivalent), but the parties chose otherwise.

Germany is an instructive example for those interested in the relationship between the Greens and 'social democratic' parties at a national level in Australia. Though the first (small 'g') green party began in Australia in 1972, the (capital 'G')

Greens started life in Germany in 1980 and in 1998 they became part of a national coalition government with the Labor equivalent (SPD). Instead of being seen as some dysfunctional aberration, power-sharing governments in Germany are viewed as normal and potentially productive. Indeed, the Greens/SPD government in the late 1990s put in place a world-leading 'energy transition', which on a good day now sees Germany generate over three-quarters of its electricity from renewables. Even after Angela Merkel's conservatives took government with the help of a small free market party in the mid 2000s, and even though the current grand coalition seems to be taking its foot off the accelerator, this energy transition has endured as official government policy.

Because of the energy transition the Greens drove in a green/red government, the world's fourth largest economy under a conservative leader generated 78 per cent of its electricity from renewables on a July day in 2015, with its annual average now above 30 per cent. Amazing. In fact, the persistence of these Greens/SPD reforms under subsequent conservative German governments offers hope for those who believe greater cooperation between Greens and Labor in Australia can deliver lasting change. But the German experience suggests something else might happen: Labor may choose to work with the Liberals instead. And my experiences of sharing power in the Australian parliament from 2010–13, which will be considered in more detail in this chapter, suggest Labor may in fact prefer to jump to the right in response to the growing Greens.

Readers may note that I have put 'social democratic' in quotation marks when referring to the ALP. I am mindful of Julia Gillard's strong statement in a 2013 speech while Prime

Minister in the power-sharing parliament that 'I'm not the leader of a party called the Progressive Party, I'm not the leader of a party called the Moderate Party, I'm not the leader of a party even called the Social Democratic Party. I am leader of the party called the Labor Party – deliberately because that is where we come from, that is what we believe in, that is who we are'. Former Treasurer and now Labor Treasury spokesperson, Chris Bowen, claims in his *Hearts & Minds: A Blueprint for Modern Labor* that liberalism is in fact the defining feature of the ALP:

> Vladimir Lenin said in 1913 that 'The Australian labour Party does not even call itself a socialist party. Actually, it is a liberal-bourgeois party, while the liberals in Australia are really conservatives'. Lenin was right (well, about this question, anyway). Labor is, as Lenin implied, the true liberal party in Australia.

So Labor is not socialist or social democratic or progressive, it is just labour, which is really liberal.

With some in Labor increasingly willing to jettison any baggage supposedly associated with even social democracy, I suggest the Greens could now properly be termed Australia's social democratic party, but we can leave that fight for another day. It is clear though that the Greens are now the only party in Parliament that won't shirk terms like 'progressive' because we are anchored in the values that define our party's charter: social justice, ecological sustainability, grassroots democracy, and peace and non-violence. Labor engages in ever-more frequent soul-searching about what they stand for, but that is not something that troubles our party. The Greens' question at this moment in time is a different one, namely how to change the world in accordance with our values and policies. For progressive politics in Australia more broadly, much may hang on how each party resolves these questions.

In the long term, the Greens are aiming for government in our own right. In the words of former leader Bob Brown, we're not there to keep the bastards honest, we're there to replace them. That is how we'll best implement progressive change. Given that after a handful of federal elections around two to three times as many people now routinely vote for us as for the Nationals, and our vote sits at a quarter to a third of the vote achieved by Labor and Liberal, it is not too difficult to imagine a trajectory that has us soon polling the same as the two old parties. However, an increase in our overall vote doesn't automatically imply more seats or more power in Parliament and even the most optimistic of us knows it won't be a quick trip from one seat in the House of Representatives to 76, the number needed for majority government. So what might the next ten or so years look like?

The next decade will matter. Climate scientists have told us we're in the 'critical decade', where decisions we make now may determine whether we can stop runaway climate change. The collapse of the biosphere as we know it, the scientists tell us, is only a matter of time unless we change our ways. In Australia, that means more fires more often, worse droughts and floods, more deaths and a massive threat to our way of life. This country has an added responsibility to act swiftly; being the world's largest per capita polluter and an exporter of about six times as much coal as we burn at home. Inequality also continues to grow and some basic elements of our social compact, like public health care, public education and welfare,

are under threat as government revenues collapse and the old political parties fear a sensible debate about securing the country's revenue base.

Progressives have a strong and proud tradition of prioritising reason over force, democracy over authoritarianism. But we can also sometimes think there is infinite time to act, to hone our arguments and gather more data, to debate amongst ourselves how best to address a problem. As Bob Brown also says, progressives often feel burdened by doubt because we are smart enough to realise we may not know all the answers, while the right has no such qualms and just gets on with it and acts. Progressives (in and outside the Greens, in social movements and in parliaments) need a plan for the next 10 years. Yes, we need to plan for the longer term as well, but a progressive route map and timetable for the short to medium term is vital. Without it, Australia may wake up in a decade to find we're living in a hollowed-out uneducated quarry, lonely in a hot world.

This chapter argues that for the Greens to implement the important parts of our platform in the timeframe imposed by the climate crisis, we should aim at a minimum to get back into balance of power in *both* houses of Parliament and keep alive the prospect of green/red cooperation, but that in such a situation Labor will have an important choice to make and may opt for conservatism instead of progressive government.

A couple of caveats before we begin. This chapter focuses on the relationship between Labor and the Greens at the national level. My colleagues in Tasmania and the Australian Capital Territory are far better placed to discuss the experiences in and out of government in their jurisdiction, and our MPs in other Parliaments have their own stories to tell. Also, this piece is attempting to take a step back from the battles and exigencies of Parliament and the way MPs vote on any particular issue to tackle some deeper questions.

The Greens are in the House

In the next decade, there are likely to be four federal elections. What is our party's trajectory over this period? In the last four elections, we have grown from 2 to 10 Senators. The Greens are now in our third decade of representation in the Senate and we have seen other Senate-focused parties – most notably the Australian Democrats – come and go. During our time there, we have seen the issues we have advanced (such as climate change and marriage equality) moved from the fringes to centre stage, with other parties also moving from rejection of our ideas to their embrace. We are now established as Australia's third political force.

It is vital that people vote to re-elect all our Senators and then elect more, because that is essential to driving progressive change and protecting hard-won gains from destructive governments. Even if our vote continues to rise at the same rate over the next four elections, though, no-one expects another five-fold increase in the number of Senators simply because of the math of the Senate voting system. But in any event, one fact is indisputable: while our presence in the Senate over many years helped the Greens grow and saw a big increase in votes and Senate seats, the best outcomes for the climate and for implementing Greens policies have been achieved because we broke through in to the House, with shared balance of power in *both* chambers.

In 2010, the people of Melbourne elected a Greens MP for the first time. Very quickly, we found ourselves right in the middle of Parliament, with our House vote essential to the formation of government. We made history by winning in Melbourne and entering the lower house at a general election. But Melbourne also sent a powerful signal to the rest of the country. Seats would start changing hands on the basis of who stood for the strongest action on climate change or marriage equality, who offered the most compassionate and practical approach to refugees and who had the best plan to secure revenue to fund social services. For an election where the old parties ran as far away as possible from compassion, equality and climate action, it was fitting that neither of them won.

So after sitting down with Julia Gillard, whom history will rate more highly than the reception she received while in power, I co-signed an agreement that made a number of things happen. We put a price on pollution. $10 billion was set aside to grow the Australian clean energy industry. A $3 billion authority was established for early stage renewable energy projects. Children were able to get Medicare funded dental services. Democracy and transparency were also advanced, with a new independent Parliamentary Budget Office established to allow non-government MPs to get policies costed and cross-benchers were able to ask questions during Question Time. Private members' concerns were debated and voted on, which meant even more was achieved by the Greens, from increasing protections for firefighters with cancer to strengthening the rights of the Territories to legislate for their own affairs to advancing the marriage equality debate.

We didn't get everything we wanted. We tried unsuccessfully to get Labor to adopt a more progressive position on a number of matters, including refugees, marriage equality, the mining tax and industrial relations. And history shows that some (but by no means all) of the advances we did achieve were torn down by a ferocious troika of Tony Abbott, Rupert Murdoch and Australia's fossil fuel lobby. Nonetheless, the gains that we, Labor and some independents made were groundbreaking. And they made a difference, with pollution in the electricity generation sector plunging, and they continue to drive change, with billions of dollars financing renewable energy. Much of our legacy still remains. And critically, *little of it was in Labor or Liberal platforms before the election, with only the Greens advocating for strong action.* To put this another way, had we not won that single seat in the house of government, the re-elected Labor government's response to global warming would have been a 'climate assembly' of 150 people picked randomly from the phone book, brought together for a talkfest, for that was their election platform.

For all their years in parliament and their achievements there, the Australian Democrats were never in balance of power in the lower house (or indeed there at all) and never struck written deals with any other party. Governments will negotiate their way through the Senate (with varying degrees of success) but they need to get themselves into government in the first place. History suggests that Labor and Liberal like being in government and that they're often prepared to do a lot to be there. And until we Greens form government in our own right, shared power in the lower house can work because it gives us far greater opportunity to implement our vision than being in the Senate alone.

Constitutionally, there are differences in what the two chambers of Parliament can do. Also, if a Senator wants reform in area A, then unless that Senator is prepared to 'cross-trade' by passing unrelated government bill B in return for the desired gain A, then they must simply hope that the government will bowl up something that relates to issue A so that their power can be exercised. But what if the government doesn't care about Senator's issue A and never bowls up a bill? Or if the government is prepared to do a quarter of what the Senator wants on issue A, but no more? This point raises important questions about how real climate action can be achieved, in particular. As we have seen, the Greens secured the best climate action when in shared House balance of power, better than in sole Senate balance of power when we were forced to be responsive to the government's agenda. Is there any reason to think things will be different in the future for those of us who want real climate action?

As well as growing in the Senate, a strong Greens presence in the House is a *sine qua non* of taking real political action on climate change and inequality in Australia. The Greens are not in parliament just to make up the numbers. We are not a ginger group trying to force another party to change its position. We are not a faction of any other party. Nor are we there only to secure a handful of concessions while other parties get to implement their agendas. So we need to be in the House, especially because the House leads to government, providing an opportunity to exercise power in a very different and important way compared with being in the Senate alone. Until we govern in our own right, we must get ready to be in balance of power in *both* houses, not just one.

Labor's First Complaint (or 'Parties Own Voters, Don't They?')

As mathematics affects our rate of growth in the Senate and as the Greens need to expand in the house of government, both to better reflect the will of the Australian people and for our own growth as a political party, the lack of proportional representation in the House of Representatives leaves us no option other than to grow our presence by defeating someone else who wants a particular seat, which may well be a Labor MP or candidate. This will obviously be a point of conflict between Greens and Labor.

Labor sometimes complains that the growth of the Greens in the lower house is solely at the expense of 'good' Labor MPs. But no political party or MP owns a seat. The people do and the people of that electorate can vote for whoever they damn well choose. This 'taking for granted' of voters, where Labor arrogantly believes it can shift to the right as much as it wants but that people must still vote for it, reflects much of what is wrong with politics. Also, Labor's complaint is no longer borne out by the evidence, with the Greens at state level now winning seats formerly held by the Coalition. And if Labor is so concerned about the fate of these 'good' MPs, surely they can move them into other 'safe' seats to replace some of the dead wood in their ranks. And will it really make a difference anyway, given that after decades of 'good' Labor MPs supposedly fighting on the inside of their party, Labor still has fundamentally conservative positions on many issues that matter? Perhaps most persuasively, if recent history suggests that one Greens MP in the lower house can have a far more catalysing effect on changing Labor's position than had a Labor MP been elected in that seat, surely the progressive cause will be aided by having more than one.

In any event, if Labor really believes their complaint valid, they would do well to take a farsighted approach and support a system of proportional representation, which would allow progressive parties and independents to jointly expand their parliamentary representation at the expense of the conservatives. A 'one vote one value' system would also see Greens voters receive their fair share of parliamentarians, with 10 to 15 MPs in the House instead of a solitary one. (Here we need to underscore the difference with Germany's voting system, which will affect how Labor and the Greens can relate here at home.) But even sticking with the electoral system we've got, minority parliaments are becoming more likely and Labor will need to work out what to do about it. The old parties may try to mask their structural decline through a weighted voting system (that saw Tony Abbott's Coalition in 2013 get 46 per cent of the vote but 60 per cent of the seats), but things are changing. From the time that Menzies was first elected to when John Howard took the helm there were usually no cross-benchers in the House and on the rare occasions some broke through, the number never passed two. During the Howard and Rudd (Mk 1) eras, each Parliament averaged just under three cross-benchers. But in 2010 the number was six and in 2013 about a quarter of the population chose not to vote for Labor or the Coalition and five crossbenchers were elected, a resounding rejection of any idea that the alleged tumult of a minority Parliament had turned people off new parties and independents.

The crossbenchers are coming.

After 2010, Should Greens and Labor Cooperate or Compete?

After the experience of the 2010 parliament, the question of how the Greens and Labor (and indeed independents) relate to each other is no longer a minor debating point. The fate of governments will hinge on it. In the aftermath of Tony Abbott's sweeping victory in 2013, some have even claimed that there should be no further agreements between Labor and the Greens.

Tony Abbott was no Angela Merkel or David Cameron, each a conservative leader accepting the reality of climate change and willing (certainly in theory, and sometimes in practice) to back renewable energy and pollution cuts. Abbott's campaign was premised on rolling back what the Greens had achieved in minority parliament. Progressive forces thus needed to hold the Senate in 2013 to keep the climate gains we had made in 2010. With the Liberals accepting the public offer of Labor MP Michael Danby for him to preference the Liberals (under Tony Abbott!!) ahead of the Greens in his seat of Melbourne Ports, in return for the Liberals preferencing Labor ahead of me in my neighboring seat of Melbourne, a joint Liberal/Labor deal to force the Greens out of the House of Representatives, we needed to make history (again!) by winning the seat of Melbourne in our own right.

For the Greens coming out of a shared power Parliament, 2013 was a tale of two elections. In Melbourne, our vote went up by more than 18 per cent on the previous election's results. This was reflected in surrounding seats like Batman and Wills, where we bucked the national trend and lifted our vote. Across the country, however, the Senate vote collapsed, dropping 34 per cent, with a similar national drop in our House vote outside of greater Melbourne. Had the Greens vote increased in the rest of the country in the same proportion as in Melbourne, there could well be at least two extra Greens from Qld and NSW sitting in the Senate, possibly more, and Greens voters' preferences may have tipped the balance against minor conservative parties in other tight races. Speculating on Senate results is a dangerous sport with many moving parts, but if the Greens got the results in the rest of the country that we did in Melbourne, then in the 2013 Parliament the Greens and Labor may have been able to block any climate repeal bills proposed by the Abbott government, setting the scene for an enduring climate legacy akin to that achieved in Germany.

Instead, outside of Melbourne the Greens' national vote slumped and the Abbott government was delivered enough conservative Senators to repeal the price on pollution (though strong campaigning did keep the Clean Energy Finance Corporation, the Australian Renewable Energy Agency and the Climate Change Authority). Of course, much more was going on to shape the 2013 election result beyond the Greens' own campaign, not least of which was Labor's internal turmoil overshadowing much of the election year. Critically too, once the anti-carbon pricem campaign built up a head of steam, Labor ran away from talking about climate change at all and desperately tried to change topics, which was a huge blunder. But the brutal reality remains that the failure to run an effective progressive campaign outside of Melbourne in 2013 may have played a role in costing the country the carbon price, especially when the swing in Melbourne shows us what might have been delivered elsewhere. Given the high stakes for climate change action and the progressive agenda generally, we must understand why. Part of the explanation, I argue, lies in the question of how the Greens relate to Labor and progressive voters. And we need to thrash this out if we are to avoid repeating our failures.

Three factors distinguished the Melbourne campaign from that run elsewhere. First, it was people-powered. On the weekend before the election, for example, 584 supporters knocked on over 10,000 doors. We reached out to over 60,000 voters directly during the whole campaign. And this wasn't me doing it as a paid MP, it was an amazing collection of people from all walks of life, Greens members and non-members, getting involved in politics in every way conceivable. This 'Melbourne model' of campaigning is now being rolled out elsewhere in the Greens. Secondly, we addressed head-on one of the biggest fears of progressive voters in 2010: Tony Abbott. We made it perfectly clear that not only would we not support him in the event of a minority parliament, but that we would be the real opposition to him. Unlike Labor, who would vote with him to keep refugees in detention and turn back boats, or for measly five per cent pollution cuts, we would stand up to him. Sadly, this was not a prominent feature of the national campaign. (We did get a chance to remedy this when some lost ballots in Western Australia allowed a rerun of an election for the Senate where it was declared that we had lost a seat. Faced with repeating the national campaign or instead adopting a people-powered campaign with a strong candidate and a focus on taking the fight up to Tony Abbott, we did the latter and achieved an incredible result.)

Thirdly, and especially relevant to the questions being explored in this book, we were proud of the agreement with Labor. Instead of disowning it, we reminded people in Melbourne of the powerful things they had achieved by voting Greens. Further, this addressed one of the most powerful objections people sometimes raise to voting Greens, namely that as a newer party we won't be able to achieve anything: here was demonstrable proof of precisely the opposite. Moreover, we were able to achieve it by holding true to our values, an indication of how politics ought to be. Many progressive voters see the likes of Tony Abbott as the greater threat to the values we hold dear and were thus pleased to see Greens and Labor cooperating; disavowing the agreement would have sent a confusing message to those voters whose main goal in 2013 was to stop Tony Abbott. (After the 2013 election, when we did in fact stand up to Tony Abbott and played a key role in helping to stop his agenda in the Senate, our vote recovered in the polls.) When the then Prime Minister, Tony Abbott, and former Victorian Premier, Jeff Kennett, feel compelled to weigh in to condemn you and announce the Liberals would be preferencing the Greens last, you know you're having an impact. Instead of distancing ourselves from the arrangement reached with Labor, in Melbourne we owned it and the change it drove for the country and the progressive agenda.

Some have argued that the Greens' result at the 2013 election suggests the arrangement with Labor is why our vote collapsed. From this they draw the conclusion we should be wary of future agreements with Labor. However, if there were to be a reaction to the agreement with Labor, surely that would have been felt most strongly in the seat that required the agreement with Labor in the first place: my seat. After all, the only reason an agreement with Labor was reached in the first place was because of the situation in the House of Representatives. Without the seat of Melbourne going Green, there would be no agreement (and no carbon price). There is simply no empirical evidence to suggest that progressive lower house MPs who signed written agreements for a minority government suffered electorally as a result. There is plenty of evidence to the contrary.

One lesson we can draw from the 2013 spike in the Melbourne area and slump elsewhere is that at a national level, many progressive voters actively want the Greens and Labor to share power to achieve progressive outcomes, including by striking agreements to form government where appropriate. And this is part of the reason why we should be aiming to do it again as a means of making progressive change happen, if – and it's a big if – Labor is up for it. And only if – again, a big only if – any deal is good enough, because we Greens would be better to stand alone than sign up to something substandard. We should always be prepared to walk away from a bad deal, because power for its own sake is no power at all.

Further, working with Labor only happens to the extent necessary to achieve progressive social change. It is a question of tactics and strategy, not a question of identity or power at all costs. We must fiercely retain our independence. There are thus very strong arguments against going into a formal coalition with Labor the way the Nationals have with the Liberals. For the Nationals the trappings of power come at the cost of being able to exercise it. An agriculture minister who can't stop a coal mine on farm land in his electorate; MPs who routinely vote against the right of farmers to lock the gate against mining and fracking on their land; a party opposing any push to wind back the powers of the supermarket duopoly. *Ad hoc* arrangements about how we will vote on particular matters in particular parliaments are appropriate and can ensure stability (as we agreed in 2010, promising in writing to vote to ensure confidence and supply) but although it would fall to our party to make any such decision if and when it arose in the future, it is fair to say that none of us is currently clamouring to give up our separate identity under the banner of a 'coalition'. And unlike the protectionist arrangement ensuring sitting National MPs aren't challenged by Liberals (and vice versa), elections in particular will of necessity be a time of ferocious competition between all parties, including between Greens and Labor, as discussed above.

Competition at election time so we can grow, cooperation during power-sharing Parliaments if we can make change.

Labor's Second Complaint (or 'Why Red/Blue may be Next Year's Fashion Colours')

I spoke above of the ferocity with which the Labor/Greens/independent arrangement was attacked by the conservatives. Perhaps less remarked upon, and certainly less analysed, is Labor's internal conflict over having to work with the Greens. Most commentary on Labor's 'killing season' and the return to Rudd before the 2013 election has focused on the personalities and the machinations. However, it is relevant that Kevin Rudd's efforts at carbon pollution reduction involved choosing to negotiate with the Liberals instead of the Greens to develop the Carbon Pollution Reduction Scheme ('CPRS') (better known as the 'continue polluting regardless scheme'), which would have driven negligible pollution cuts in Australia and made it virtually impossible to increase ambition as the science demanded. By contrast, because we were now in the House, Julia Gillard chose to work with the Greens and to formalise that arrangement, including – and I underline this – by doing things that would have an impact on Australia's fossil fuel sector. For this Julia Gillard deserves praise, but that's not how some of her colleagues saw it.

Many in Labor's right wing became increasingly furious. Two things stuck in their craw: that Labor would formalise an agreement for government with the Greens; and that this would involve hurting coal. Labor should not be working with the Greens and others on progressive issues, they argued, because it would not be well received amongst the party's apparently conservative voters. The implied next step was fairly clear: that if Julia Gillard had to be removed or written deals reneged upon (such as the agreement with independent Andrew Wilkie over pokies reform) to reassert conservatism, then so be it.

A substantial section of the Labor Party would rather side with the Liberals than with the Greens, just as they routinely do in Parliament. This isn't simply about particular personalities in the Labor party: it goes to structural conflicts within Labor. On a whole swathe of key issues that help define the Australian political landscape – fossil fuels, the mining sector, refugees, debt, national security, levels of government spending, neoliberal economics in general – most Liberal and Labor MPs agree and regularly vote together in Parliament. To be sure, there remain important differences between the old parties. But the points of agreement are strong. Draw Liberal and Labor on a Venn diagram and much of the two circles overlap. Rather than break away and chart a course for the new, many of Labor's powerful would rather stay on the same page as the Liberals and have ever-diminishingly small squabbles over the old.

Some within Labor are confronting this issue head on. Victorian Labor Premier Daniel Andrews went out of his way during the 2014 election campaign to announce that he would not strike any deals with the Greens in the event of a minority parliament. Chris Bowen, in his same 'blueprint' for Labor referred to earlier, writes that 'Labor and the Greens are not different shades on the same continuum; we are different parties that believe in different things' and that there should be no further agreements for government between the two parties. I suspect a polemic against the Greens written from the backbench in the immediate aftermath of a failed leadership challenge might not end up being the considered view of a Labor Party that can sniff the treasury benches in a future hung Parliament. Nonetheless, it shows the issue for Labor is not just a *tactical* question about how to relate to the Greens at any given moment in time, but rather a *fundamental philosophical and existential* question about what their party believes in.

So, what does this boil down to? It is not the Greens that have to choose between Labor or the Coalition. It is Labor that has to choose between the Coalition or the Greens. And if the world's fourth largest economy can routinely be governed by grand coalitions, it's not much of a stretch to imagine a 'red/blue' alliance here either. It is a side-effect and not an aim of our growth, but the rise of the Greens will increase the pressure on Labor to decide where it stands.

What to Do When Everyone Else Loves Coal

Labor's slow creeping over to the Liberal/National position on social, environmental and economic matters serves to highlight how truly different the Greens are. Former Prime Minister Tony Abbott said coal was 'good for humanity'; new Prime Minister Malcolm Turnbull and his ministers likewise declared a strong moral case for coal. During debate in the Senate, Coalition Senators proudly wore hi-vis vests embroidered with the logo 'Australians for Coal'. And infamously, a gloating cabal of ministers – including the Minister called the Minister for the Environment, Greg Hunt – hugged each other in the chamber upon the world's first ever repeal of a price on pollution. Meanwhile, Labor's current resources spokesperson, Gary Gray, was an executive for massive fossil fuel company Woodside. Labor's last long-serving energy and resources minister, the Left's Martin Ferguson, left his post to head-up the peak fossil fuel lobby group APPEA, the self-described 'voice of Australia's oil and gas industry'. And even the Labor Left's former climate change minister Greg Combet, who worked with us to achieve many good things in the minority Parliament, now says 'I have always been a fossil fuels man' and spruiks for one of Australia's big fossil-fuel based electricity companies, encouraging coal-seam gas.

However, activists know there is something significant about Labor that doesn't apply to the Liberals. Many in Labor consider it a party of the left and there are strong connections with many unions and community groups. Labor has internal groups who want greater action on climate change. Labor still wants to appeal to a constituency that is progressive, rational and therefore in favour of taking the kind of climate action the science requires. As such, Labor is at least partly conflicted and open to some form of pressure from below. At the moment, the campaigns run to change Labor's position appear to be having some success. And the pressure points that do exist – for example, in the numerous Greens/Labor marginal seats that exist around the country – give opportunities for civil society to push for Labor to take a better position. There are more places for campaigners and the public to push Labor on, say, climate change than there are the Liberals. And the number of these pressure points looks set to increase.

Labor may be in the thrall of the fossil fuel sector, but they are also capable of being pressured to take a different position in the way that the Liberals currently don't seem to be. The Greens' job is not to be this 'pressure group'. But we have always understood that successful change won't come through Parliament alone, rather only through strong social movements working together with Parliamentarians. As such, the Greens have a unique capacity to push in the same direction as broader civil society, including by providing political 'pressure points' in lower house seats. When to this is added those in Labor who want their party to adopt more progressive positions, there is an array of forces capable of making real change. Given the political economy of Australia, it is difficult to discern what the corresponding strategy would be with the Liberals, a party that seeks to electorally pander to climate denialists while shilling for the fossil fuel sector.

Whilst some might wish to entertain the thought of advancing Greens policies by striking a deal with the Liberals, we forget salient lessons from the 2010 and 2013 elections at our peril. Many progressive people are moving from Labor to the Greens precisely *because* Labor too often sides with the Liberals. Further, many progressive people actively want Labor and Greens to cooperate where policies coincide. We can and should speculate on what the Greens might do if a more enlightened Liberal party started a bidding war with Labor on climate change policy, but when even Malcolm Turnbull is happy to go to global climate talks in Paris to advocate Tony Abbott's policy, that day seems far away. While the 2010 arrangement had its flaws, it is difficult to imagine this level of climate ambition being negotiated with the Liberals. Provided Labor doesn't choose red/blue, then green/red is the best of the scenarios for tackling climate change and inequality until the Greens can govern in our own right.

Does that mean the Greens can just be taken for granted by Labor? No, it doesn't. For when Antony Green's chamber graphic on election night shows a healthy dose of Greens sitting in the middle of Parliament, the message we'd send would be loud and clear. We may aim to strike an agreement with Labor for stable, effective and progressive government, but if Chris Bowen's mantra that 'We must govern alone, or not at all' prevails and Labor refuses to deal, then all bets are off and don't count the Greens in either column on questions of confidence and supply. If Labor seriously wants to turn down government with us, then send Labor back for further discussions with their soul mates in the Liberals. And we Greens too will then have an obligation to speak to everyone again. If that fails, then all things being equal, that sounds to me like a great basis to go back to the people and seek another electoral mandate. We should be unafraid to fight a new election called because Labor wouldn't accept a reasonable proposal from the Greens for stable, effective and progressive government. For fundamental to the argument of the anti-Green forces within Labor is an assumption that the Greens have 'nowhere else to go' other than to support Labor. It's the same contempt with which they have treated Labor voters for many years. But those voters have found somewhere else to go. And it hasn't yet dawned on these Labor heavies that the Greens are not a faction of the Labor Party and will not fall into line whenever the going gets tough.

Progressive Government Needs a Plan

Some may protest that this approach is going too far and that the Greens should aim only at growing our presence in Parliament and eschew arrangements with others. Such is the lack of fundamental commitment of Labor to the things we believe in (or even that the public wants, such as politicians that aren't corrupt, as the New South Wales experience reminds us), they may argue, that we ought to maintain a very great distance. To them I say three things: first, we're different parties and will remain so, because working with someone should never mean joining or becoming them; secondly, yes, we should always be prepared to stand alone; but thirdly, what is the alternative strategy to get the climate action we need in the time the science demands? Ultimately, a government will have to do something in the next decade, and I am gravely worried that without Greens in (even shared) power, it just won't happen. I'll happily jump straight to 76 seats in the House of Representatives, but given that even the Liberals struggle to do this more than once in a blue moon without leaning on the Nationals, something needs to happen in the meantime. Disagree with the strategy, but given the urgency it's time to start laying alternative theories of change on the table.

What might future green/red power sharing look like, if Labor comes to the party? Should we repeat the 2010 agreement or do something else? Maybe. Maybe not. Everything should be on the table, from taking ministries to staying on the cross bench, from detailed policy changes to parliamentary reform, from guaranteeing supply sight unseen to wanting to help craft Budgets. These are decisions that will have to be made by the parties at the time, depending on the circumstances, and we should not be wedded in advance to any particular kind of agreement.

However, if we accept that government is one of the few places left that can make the big changes needed in the time the climate science requires, then we are obliged to work backwards from that goal and ask how best to get there. In Germany, the Greens drove a plan that combined industry support, national energy independence, community-led renewables, jobs and climate change, got the social democrats on board, got into government and explicitly asked the public to help pay for and support this energy transition. And, by and large, the plan endures. It is time we worked out how to do the same here too.

Chapter 12

Labor, the Greens and the Union Movement

Shaun Wilson

The union movement may have a decisive impact on the battle for the progressive vote in Australian politics. That battle is between the Australian Labor Party (ALP) which, like all mainstream social-democratic parties, faces electoral decline, and the Australian Greens who are likely to make further parliamentary breakthroughs in coming years as well as broadening their appeal. I argue that the union movement is central to the reshaping of the progressive political landscape, and that it is a mistake to see declining union membership, industrial weakness, and troubles over corruption as signs that unions are irrelevant to national politics. Forces inside and outside Labor will continue to identify the vulnerabilities of the union movement as reasons to reduce union influence on Labor. This strategy, however, is now complicated by the strength of the Greens and the potential for alliances between the union movement and this third political force.

I begin by considering the political-economic and sociological conditions that have given rise to a weakened union movement, a declining ALP, and an emergent Greens. Three scenarios identify the stakes involved in the shifting relationships between these three forces. The first involves

Labor severing union links in search of a new centre-left identity and electorate. The second considers the possibilities and pitfalls of a deepening alliance between unions and the Greens, effectively transforming the latter into Australia's equivalent of Canada's New Democratic Party. The third considers a reconstructed relationship between the independent union movement and a Labor Party committed to ensuring an ongoing but perhaps different place for unions in the ALP and to policies that make it easier for unions to organise workers and bargain collectively. These scenarios are merely intended as heuristic – as guides to the forces at play and to the limits of reform strategies that at face value seem obvious and sensible. The overarching framework of the chapter implies a competitive relationship between the two political parties that is, given the way electoral opportunities emerge and political bargains are struck in Australian politics, a reasonable starting point. Such a framework commits us to *one way* of seeing the relationship between the Labor Party and the Greens that should not ignore the opportunities for political cooperation in forming governments and defeating extreme Coalition policies.

Labor and the Greens: The Current Situation

Australia's political system is reaching a turning point where there are two viable political forces on the centre-left of politics, and a large and united liberal-conservative Coalition. Although Malcolm Turnbull's ascendancy to the leadership of the Coalition may trigger divisions between liberals and conservatives on the political right, this possibility should not distract from the fact that the Coalition is a large and united electoral force polling around 45 per cent of the national vote, while Labor is polling 30–35 per cent and the Greens 10–15 per cent. A generation ago, Labor's vote rarely fell much below 40 per cent, even in a heavy election defeat, and the only challenger on the centre-left was the Australian Democrats that had emerged out of severe partisan divides following Whitlam's sacking. Until recently, critics dismissed the Greens as likely to go the way of the Democrats – they would either remain small or offer a temporary 'third choice' in a system resistant to new entrants, at least in the House of Representatives. This thinking is now outdated. The Greens – a stable gathering of ex-Labor leftists, ex-Democrats, middle-class progressives, environmentalists, and members of the not-so-new social movements – has proved more electorally durable than the Democrats on any number of measures, the most important of these lower-house representation federally and in the state parliaments of New South Wales, Victoria and Tasmania. Moreover, a sense of the stability of the Greens political presence is given by the rising numbers of voters who *identify* as Greens, an achievement that eluded the Democrats.

Two triggers made the Greens an electoral force: the inability of the Democrats to recover from infighting after supporting the GST in 1999, and successful Greens opposition to the Tampa politics of 2001, which the crafty wedge-politician, John Howard, used to produce a new majority in November that year. No doubt, a succession of capable leaders (most notably Bob Brown), internal stability, and the skilful use of organisational resources have supported this rise. Underneath, a slower-moving story helps explain their electoral durability. Australia now has a largely de-industrialised economy if the state of traditional manufacturing industries is a guide, which has in turn diminished the share of unionised workers in blue-collar jobs – Labor's traditional base. The nation now has three vast and multicultural urban centres with post-industrial service economies in which education, skills and housing have become key commodities. These cities are socially diverse, loosely organised around an individualistic and consumption-driven culture, and are divided by economic inequalities in almost every respect. Such diverse, unequal and even fragmented urban realities have provided the backdrop for the Greens to expand on their electorate of committed environmentalists to include the cosmopolitan and socially-liberal voters of the inner cities who either work in government, in Australia's patchwork and underfunded welfare state, or in the more liberal professional occupations.

The Greens electorate is a middle-class electorate of relative opportunity – and Greens are happy to tell pollsters this fact. In the Australian Election Study of 2013, 66 per cent of Greens voters identified as middle class, more than even the Liberals (57 per cent) and sharply more than Labor voters (45 per cent).[1] Given ongoing shifts in urban geography, the inner-cities of Sydney and Melbourne are likely to become bastions of Green politics, with Labor's decline in the inner-cities outpacing that experienced in the so-called aspirational outer-suburbs. It appears that the middle-class progressive voters of the 'Whitlam coalition' forged in the 1970s are the ones who have most deserted the ALP.

Where does this situation leave Labor? Criticising the ALP for its failings is a national pastime even though on a range of measures Labor remains one of the world's most electorally successful social-democratic parties, and its efforts at

---

[1] Clive Bean, Ian McAllister, Juliet Pietsch and Rachel Gibson, *Australian Election Study, 2013*, datafile, Australian Data Archive, 2014.

defending a modified 'wage-earners' welfare state' (Castles's term) since the 1980s have left Australia as the most social-democratic of the Anglo-democracies. Similarly, Labor's commitment to multiculturalism helped transform the nation's cities, achieving a blend of diversity and social integration that other nations only aspire to. Moreover, the ALP remains the party of choice for wage-earners on low-to-middle incomes.[2]

Despite continuing support for Labor among these voters, the Party's share of the national vote – down from 44 per cent in 1993 to 33 per cent in 2013 – has eroded steadily as socio-economic change has gathered pace. Not surprisingly, the declining share of unionised voters has been a significant factor in this decline.[3] But, by the late 1990s, other forces would further drive apart the coalition of voters that produced the Whitlam and Hawke Governments. The wedge politics of the Howard years – focused on boat arrivals in Australia's north – aimed at dividing up this Labor coalition forever. The ALP reached the limits of its liberal multiculturalism when it abandoned the rights of asylum seekers in a desperate attempt to hold onto older-Anglo and blue-collar voters threatened by the insecurities that an 'open door' asylum policy apparently represented. From then on, Labor appeared to its own progressive voters as lacking conviction, only capable of producing disappointing compromises that satisfied no-one. At the same time, for an older and culturally-insecure

---

[2] Shaun Ratcliff and Shaun Wilson, 'Rural conservative, inner-city elites, and suburban aspirationals: Geographic variation in income voting in Australia,' paper, Australian Political Studies Association Conference, University of Canberra, September 2015.

[3] Andrew Leigh, 'How do unionists vote? Estimating the causal impact of union membership on voting behaviour from 1966 to 2004,' *Australian Journal of Political Science* 41(4) (2006): 537–552.

population, the ALP no longer symbolised 'old Labor' that was 'for the workers' – it was, in the eyes of this electorate, a party committed to the multicultural reinvention of nation.

When Labor regained the political ascendancy, however briefly, it became the party of the increasingly ambitious reformer Kevin Rudd and the stoic and sensible feminist, Julia Gillard. Its agenda was still recognisably nation-building and social-democratic, less focused on market reforms than the Hawke-Keating governments, and more focused on improvements in Australia's welfare state. The *Fair Work Act*, increases in superannuation and pensions, the Gonski reforms to school education, the National Disability Insurance Scheme, and attempts at progressive taxation reforms all illustrate these ambitions. It was thus especially disappointing that the Government's braver, more energetic reform efforts either stalled or became mired in controversy, failing to contribute to Labor's credibility as the party capable of progressive reform.

Despite their successful campaigning in 2007, unions were much less important to day-to-day policymaking than during the Hawke–Keating years.[4] This does not mean that voters were left unaware of the relationship between Labor and the unions, especially after Opposition leader Tony Abbott revived the 'faceless men' metaphor to condemn union influence on Labor's decision to install Julia Gillard as Prime Minister in 2010. Indeed, the Coalition continues to campaign relentlessly over union influence on Labor. Political events have painfully reinforced this narrative, especially instances of corruption in

---

4 David Peetz, 'Are Australian trade unions part of the solution, or part of the problem?,' *Australian Review of Public Affairs*, February 2015, http://www.australianreview.net/digest/2015/02/peetz.html.

NSW Labor politics and misdeeds highlighted by the Royal Commission into Trade Union Governance and Corruption.

Not surprisingly, these crises have emboldened Labor Party reformers. Figures including Kevin Rudd, Carmen Lawrence, John Faulkner and (most ferociously) Rodney Cavalier have all pointed to the corrosive impact of factional overlaps between the ALP and unions on both the internal workings of the Party and its policies.[5] Their common purpose is to turn Labor into a social-democratic party proper, or even a social-liberal party, but not to remain a labour party rooted in historical-institutional connections to the union movement. Such a reformed party would not necessarily follow the 'New Labour' formula of Tony Blair; it would emerge out of the sober recognition that the union movement can no longer produce the electoral base necessary for Labor to win government and a recognition that new mechanisms are vital to any 'democratic opening' that would broaden that base.

Some of these calls are based on bitter lessons from a life in politics, and others from a particular reading of the zeitgeist. Isolated to an Australian context, they search for uniquely Australian failures and look to Australian solutions. But similar dilemmas face all Anglo labour parties and, indeed, the established social-democratic parties of Europe, suggesting that the problems for the mainstream centre-left are greater than those generated by the party-union relationship in Australia. Indeed, some national union movements continue to maintain membership even where their political allies have

---

[5] Gabrielle Chan, 'Labor elders back reforms aimed at diluting union and factional power,' *The Guardian*, 22 July 2015, http://www.theguardian.com/australia-news/2015/jul/22/labor-elders-back-reforms-aimed-at-diluting-union-and-factional-power.

lost voter support. In fact, no major social-democratic party in an advanced democracy has scored above 40 per cent of the vote in a national election since the Spanish Socialists under Zapatero in 2008 and Kevin Rudd's Labor Party in 2007. Germany's Social Democrats look incapable of expanding their support beyond 25 per cent and even the once-mighty Swedish Social Democrats now barely manage 30 per cent in elections.

The twin forces of social fragmentation and economic polarisation have driven the rapid transformation of politics in democracies, especially where access to political representation for parties of discontent is made easier by proportional voting. The shifting pattern of political representation looks similar across diverse contexts: increasing support for parties to the left of the mainstream social-democratic party, a loss of support for the established parties of the centre-left and rising support for populist right parties opposing immigration and hostile to the Islamic religion. However, single-member systems have also begun to represent these differences, albeit via different mechanisms: strong regional or local concentrations of support based on distinct social profiles. Canada's New Democratic Party is important as a social-democratic, union-based party to the left of the Canadian Liberals, with strong regional representation. Scotland has left Labour for the Nationalists who now dominate Scottish politics as well as Scotland's representation in Westminster. These broader trends suggest that prospects for the Greens will continue to rise, mostly at the expense of Labor's parliamentary representation in the inner-metropolitan areas of Australia's east-coast capitals.

Established two-party systems are destabilised by new entrants and the growing dependence of major parties on coalitions with minor parties. Rivalries are particularly apparent in majoritarian systems like Australia's where parties compete over *actual electorates* instead of a share of the national vote. Such antagonisms are sharply in evidence in inner-Sydney and Melbourne between Labor and the Greens, but they are balanced by an awareness on both sides of the need for cooperation. Such cooperation has emerged across many rounds of preference negotiations for the House of Representatives and the Senate and in the States. The Greens have twice cooperated with Labor in government in Tasmania and, critically, in the minority ALP government of Julia Gillard between 2010 and 2013. Given that Labor's best recent election performance in 2007 yielded just 83 seats out of 150 from a primary vote of 43 per cent that does not seem achievable in 2016, it seems sensible to anticipate future coalitions between Labor and the Greens to form government.

The State of the Union Movement and Why it Matters to Politics

Given their declining representation of workers, the spotlight on union governance and corruption, and calls for Labor to dissolve ties to their long-time allies, it seems a distraction to devote much attention to the role of unions in the future of Australian social democracy. Surely, the central role played by working-class actors capable of striking over wages and conditions and turning out *en masse* for Labor is being replaced by new and different forms of expression and contention – by diffuse, kaleidoscopic activism generated by social-media, by the interests and constituencies generated by an ageing population dependent on a larger welfare state, and by more voters having direct voice in candidate selection in

Labor politics. So two questions must be asked: are there good reasons to believe that unions will continue to play a central role in these transitions?; and, will unions remain valuable allies in the political system? I argue that the answer to both questions is yes.

Union decline, it is argued, is an inexorable reality of individualised, affluent societies – wage-earners are sufficiently convinced of their own personal efficacy and confident in the prospect of their own economic mobility to see unions as redundant and membership pointless. However, the 'individual' decision to join a union is in fact conditioned by complex background institutional forces, particularly by favourable legal and bargaining frameworks and well-organised workplaces that structure these decisions.[6] Australia's staged deregulation and decentralisation of its labour market – a process that involved unions via the Accord at least in its initial phases – undermined traditional protections for union representation. Closed shop arrangements, for example, were eradicated by conservative state governments in the 1990s,[7] and vast privatisations and outsourcing have reduced and transformed the role of the public sector. In response, unions invested heavily in organising to sustain networks of activists and members in workplaces across the country capable of recruiting and representing wage-earner interests in decentralised bargaining. Coupled with unfavourable shifts in the sectoral composition of work and the diffusion of aggressively managerial cultures throughout workplaces, organising initiatives by unions have faced a daunting task.

---

6   Margaret Levi, 'Organizing power: The prospects for an American labor movement,' *Perspectives on Politics* 1(1) (2003): 45–68.
7   David Peetz, *Unions in a Contrary World: The Future of the Australian Trade Union Movement*, Cambridge University Press, Melbourne, 1998.

Not surprisingly, membership has fallen to alarmingly low levels (just 15 per cent in 2015) and is now lower than all other Anglo-democracies except for the United States. OECD (2015a) statistics show that union decline has been faster in Australia than anywhere else outside Eastern Europe. This decline is a conundrum to which I return later on.

Declining union density, though an important and troubling trend, is not a complete indicator of union vitality and influence. For one, unions have successfully turned their attention in these troubled times to a form of 'political organising' vaguely reminiscent of the early period of the Federation that produced Australia's wage-earners' welfare state. Union strength in the workplace in the first decade of the twentieth century had been seriously weakened by the long recession of the 1890s, and union activists had turned to politics to make gains, recognising the power of law to shift the rules of the game.[8]

Much more recently, the Your Rights at Work campaign of 2007 emerged as genuine political activism that benefited and surprised both Labor's leadership and reticent trade union leaders as it helped to sweep from office one of Australia's most successful conservative governments. Analysis of the 2007 federal election results suggests that the seats targeted by unions swung significantly more to the ALP, with the campaign probably 'making a difference' in enough seats to help build Labor's majority and to protect the ALP from defeat in 2010.[9] There is little question that the success of Your

---

8   Peter G. Macarthy, 'Labor and the living wage 1890–1910,' *Australian Journal of Politics & History* 13(1) (1967): 67–89.

9   Shaun Wilson and Benjamin Spies-Butcher, 'When labour makes a difference: Union mobilization and the 2007 federal election in Australia,' *British Journal of Industrial Relations* 49(s2) (2011): s306–s331

Rights at Work improved the union movement's ability to influence the shape of the Fair Work legislation that became the Labor Government's corrective to the aggressively anti-labour WorkChoices legislation. The campaign has spurred learning across the movement; unions played important and probably electorally significant roles in Coalition defeats in the Victorian and Queensland elections held in 2014 and 2015 respectively.

ACTU President Ged Kearney also argues that union impact remains greater than the density crisis suggests. Writing in the *Guardian* newspaper in 2015, Kearney points to the continuing high rates of collective protection offered under the Australian system.[10] Indeed, ILO reports suggest that Australia is one of a few countries to increase collective bargaining coverage against the trend towards deregulation, especially in crisis-wracked Europe.[11] If one also considers that, after taxes, Australian workers earn among the world's highest minimum wages, we get a picture of a wage-earners' welfare state that has been maintained albeit in a 'hollowed-out' form after decades of market-driven reform.[12] Unions

---

10 Ged Kearney, 'Membership figures don't tell the whole story about the union movement's value,' *The Guardian*, 7 November 2015, http://www.theguardian.com/australia-news/commentisfree/2015/nov/07/membership-figures-dont-tell-the-whole-story-about-the-union-movements-value.

11 Jelle Visser, Susan Hayter and Rosina Gammarano, 'Trends in collective bargaining coverage: Stability, erosion or decline?,' Issue Brief 1 (Labour Relations and Collective Bargaining), International Labour Office, Geneve, 2015, http://www.ilo.org/wcmsp5/groups/public/---ed_protect/---protrav/---travail/documents/publication/wcms_409422.pdf.

12 Shaun Wilson, Benjamin Spies-Butcher, Adam Stebbing, and Susan St John, 'Wage-earners' welfare after economic reform: Refurbishing,

can rightly claim to have defended workers' wages at the bottom and to have used their influence to ensure that union-influenced bargaining still protects wages and conditions for many workers.

Union density and influence can be seriously undermined by the combination of employer and state aggression to organised labour. The leading example of such a destructive impact is the United States. Such hostilities also emerged in Australia, especially during the WorkChoices years of 2005–08. But, paradoxically, the *success* of unions in politically defending the pro-labour institutions may have factored in reduced 'demand' for membership among workers. The extent of local success in this respect is clearer when we compare minimum wages and collective bargaining coverage for the five English-speaking democracies (see Table 1). Australia has the highest post-tax minimum wage of the six liberal welfare states and maintains higher levels of collective bargaining by virtue of ongoing award institutions. If *active* union membership today is driven by worker demands for basic protections – decent wages and a voice in bargaining – then Australian industrial institutions have maintained these even as union membership and influence at work have declined. One might compare the situation to France, with its high minimum wages and strongly institutionalised worker voice via the Mitterrand-era *lois Auroux*; France has very low union density, with the state effectively replacing the need for membership.

---

retrenching or hollowing out social protection in Australia and New Zealand?,' *Social Policy & Administration* 47(6) (2013): 623–646.

Table 1: Australia compared: still a wage-earners' welfare state

	After-tax minimum wage at purchasing power party (in dollars)	Collective bargaining coverage (% of workforce)	Union density (% of workforce)
Australia	9.54	60.0	15.1
Ireland	8.46	40.5	29.6
New Zealand	7.55	15.3	19.5
Canada	7.18	29.0	27.2
United Kingdom	7.06	25.6	29.5
United States	6.26	11.5	10.8

Sources: Australian Bureau of Statistics, 6333.0 – Characteristics of Employment, Australia, August 2014, , http://www.abs.gov.au/ausstats/abs@.nsf/mf/6333.0; OECD, 'Minimum wages after the crisis: Making them pay', OECD Directorate of Employment, Labour and Social Affairs, May 2015, http://www.oecd.org/social/Focus-on-Minimum-Wages-after-the-crisis-2015.pdf; OECD, OECD.Stat: Trade Union Density, accessed 21 December 2015, https://stats.oecd.org/Index.aspx?DataSetCode=UN_DEN; Jelle Visser, Susan Hayter and Rosina Gammarano, 'Trends in collective bargaining coverage: Stability, erosion or decline?', Issue Brief no. 1 (Labour Relations and Collective Bargaining), International Labour Office, Geneva, 2015, http://www.ilo.org/wcmsp5/groups/public/---ed_protect/---protrav/---travail/documents/publication/wcms_409422.pdf.

Evidence from the *Australian Survey of Social Attitudes (AuSSA) 2015* adds to understanding about how the public now understand the role of unions.[13] Voters continue to believe

---

13 Betsy Blunsdon, *Australian Survey of Social Attitudes, 2013*, Australian Data Archive, Australian National University, 2015. Sample is n=556 from the first two waves of data collection. Data here is unweighted and the older respondents are overrepresented in the sample.

that unions matter: 51 per cent of respondents agreed that 'workers need strong trade unions to protect their interests', with disagreement from only a quarter of respondents. At the same time, however, 39 per cent of respondents also believe that 'individuals can represent their own interests without the help of unions'. Women are less individualistic in their attitudes with only 35 per cent agreeing with this statement compared with 44 per cent of men. When non-members were asked about whether they would benefit *personally* from joining, just 22 per cent agreed. This result suggests most of the workforce sees no personal benefit from membership. Unpacked, such a low number may be driven by ideological opposition to unions, the job situation, or resistance to paying membership fees. But some of the failure of respondents to see benefits from membership may derive from the success of unions in ensuring basic protections of wages and voice for many *without* membership.

Survey data offers insight into how voters see unions functioning as political actors. Questions probed the two competing public images of unions today: as successful political activists (for example, in opposing WorkChoices); and as a set of closed organisations that shield misconduct among officials. In 2015, 44 per cent of respondents agreed that union corruption is a 'serious issue' (dramatically higher among older respondents) and few people trust political campaigns by unions (just 20 per cent) – a somewhat inconsistent finding given the powerful impact of the anti-WorkChoices campaign. Of course, it is difficult to interpret these findings without further context.

Australian unions have achieved remarkable successes in protecting basic entitlements and in mobilising against

Coalition governments. These successes, however, are offset by severe declines in membership that are destabilising the union movement's ability to defend its influence in the Labor Party and its role in the workplace. In no trivial way, the re-organisation of centre-left politics depends on the effectiveness of their future response – a subject to which I now turn.

Unions, Labor and the Greens: Three Scenarios for the Future

The dominant theme of this book is the apparent choice facing voters between supporting Labor and turning to the Greens as the future force on the centre-left. The two parties are institutionally and politically different creatures but will continue to appeal to overlapping constituencies. Thus the most likely prospect is that these parties will remain in a state of 'cooperative competition' over voters and electorates, with the Greens eventually prevailing in the inner-city and Labor undertaking a painful search for new outer-suburban and regional electorates to replace these losses and to preserve the Party's ability to win majorities.

What is the future role that the union movement might play in these realignments? Given that union politics, as well as Labor politics, is in a state of crisis and flux, it is reasonable to assume that the status quo will be revised. It is therefore useful to think through some scenarios that might shape the future contest – and potential for cooperation – and what role unions will play in all of this. These scenarios are not forecasts or predictions; they are intended heuristically – to make space to think over what political forces might be mobilised to determine patterns of possible future variation.

Labor Dissolves its Relationship with the Union Movement

Despite the problems that Australian unions confront, it is probably the case that antipathy towards unions from within Labor has peaked. ALP politicians are increasingly aware of the limits and pitfalls of the 'New Labour' model of Tony Blair as well as the long-term impact of policies that undermine the vitality of the union movement. Equally, there is growing respect within the Labor Party of the campaigning capacity of the union movement and its ability to make a difference at the ballot box. Moreover, few Labor politicians believe unions have too much industrial power *even if* their views about the political role of unions within the ALP are more divided.

Complicating these improvements, however, is the continuing and widespread perception that unions are inward-looking organisations dominated by backroom deals aimed at the protection of their industrial-political interests. Labor is thus damaged by association and – if the recent Royal Commission is any guide – calls inside and outside Labor for the Party to distance itself from the union movement will continue. The present relationship with unions, it would seem, is a major threat to renewing Labor's appeal.

For Labor's part, a divorce from the union movement would signal a final break from the social and industrial base that gave the Party life some 125 years ago. Central to such a divorce would be dramatic reductions in the formal role that allied unions play in the policy-making institutions of the Party, particularly the guaranteed 50 percent representation of delegates at Party conferences. Such reductions would also send a symbolic message to voters (and business) that Labor was not a 'party of the unions' (indeed, Party finances are not particularly dependent on unions[14]). A proposal by former Labor senator John Faulkner seeks to have union-appointed delegates reduced to 20 per cent of the total, with union members encouraged to join the ALP to have a say.[15]

Figures from the Party's NSW right-wing faction, such as Chris Bowen, see such reforms as part of transforming Labor into a 'social liberal' party. Bowen's description is useful because it rather uncritically embraces the 'engineered' individualism of the electorate and refashions Party institutions in that image.[16] In policy terms, Labor would emerge from a liberal makeover looking more like the American Democrats: a party wedded to markets and moderate social reforms. Such a transformation would mean that any commitment to the remaining institutions of the wage-earners' welfare state would be limited at best and the prospect of *reducing* inequality fairly bleak.

Critical to reform proposals is the need to develop a broader democratic base for the Labor Party and direct voter involvement in candidate and leader selection is one widely-discussed (and now partially implemented) mechanism for achieving this. The central merit of such reforms is the popular mobilisation of local communities – the choice of candidates with deeper roots and appeal to local ALP community members. Anthony Albanese's narrow loss in the federal Labor leadership election of 2013 (he gained 48 per cent of

---

14 Joo-Cheong Tham, *Money and Politics: The Democracy We Can't Afford*, UNSW Press, Sydney, 2010.
15 Michelle Grattan, 'Cut union representation in Labor conferences: Faulkner,' *The Conversation*, 14 Oct 2014, http://theconversation.com/cut-union-representation-in-labor-conferences-faulkner-32634.
16 Chris Bowen, *Hearts & Minds: A Blueprint for Modern Labor*, Melbourne University Publishing, Carlton, 2013.

the combined vote, but 60 per cent of the membership vote) will limit factional power over the leadership over time. But this may not produce the outcomes envisaged by reformers. Jeremy Corbyn's triumph in the British Labour Party's highly liberalised, membership-driven leadership election in 2015 suggests that open processes will not necessarily produce leaders consistent with a post-union transformation of labour politics.

On the union side of the relationship, a parallel dissatisfaction has long been evident. Many unionists, from ordinary organisers to reformist leaders at all levels, point to problems in the relationship between unions and Labor. They are critical of the role that union organisations are expected to play as stepping stones in the parliamentary careers of ALP politicians, even though this route to political life has produced some of Labor's most revered leaders. Unions have also had to endure long periods where ALP policy damaged the interests of ordinary wage-earners, with excessive thrusts in the direction of competition policy and deregulation, and there is an abiding sense that union influence on Labor policy is in fact limited.[17] A more independent union movement would have greater freedom to criticise organised politics and its constricted, uncreative policy parameters. In exercising such independence, unions could combat public misperceptions about the purpose and principles of unionism. Indeed, contrary to such perceptions, several major unions are not ALP-affiliated so any move to dramatically limit the role of unions in Labor would probably trigger more disaffiliations.

Such a 'spirit of independence' in the union movement might spur also new efforts to deal with the membership crisis,

---

17 Peetz, 'Are Australian trade unions part of the solution.'

similar to the way that workplace organising was ambitiously prioritised by the ACTU under leaders Bill Kelty and Jennie George at the end of Labor's long period in office in 1996. These efforts produced a new generation of capable union leaders. The focus would be to recruit and organise the 10 per cent of employees who are 'unrepresented', ie workers not presently in a union who would prefer to be. If such reformist energies coincided with new leaderships mainly drawn from committed activists from the shop floor, less concerned about future political careers, unions in new and critical areas of the workforce might undergo significant renewal. Still, such experimentation may have to combat an increasingly hostile organising environment, such as that evident in the United States, and involve completely new thinking.

The Potential for Union Alliances with the Greens

Weakening ties between unions and Labor carries risks for both. Unions deliver candidates, activists, and a still-substantial electoral base for the ALP – and unions have the capacity to campaign on new media platforms and in close elections with considerable effect. Unions also greatly benefit from party representation, overlapping personnel and networks, and formal consultation processes when Labor is in and out of government. Losing these kinds of influence would be a major threat to the 'power resources' of the union movement. A transformation of the relationship into one where the ALP treats unions as 'just another interest group' would thus symbolise the loss of the power of wage-earners to directly shape Australian politics.

The ongoing capacity of unions to mobilise resources for political allies creates the potential for new alliances. One obvious possibility for a deepening alliance is between unions and the Greens. The potential here becomes apparent if we follow a different reading of the zeitgeist – one that would have seemed unlikely a generation ago given the ideological conflicts between environmentalists and the industrial left. Unlike some other environmentalist parties, the Australian Greens are a distinctly left-of-centre force, not only on environmental and social issues but on policies for wage-earners, taxation and welfare. They are a product of, and an ongoing response to, a leftward drift in the political orientations of Australians under way for some time now.[18] Moreover, as a party with a good deal of continuous parliamentary representation, it is harder and harder for conservatives (or Labor) to portray the Greens as irresponsible, hell-bent on imposing an 'environmental dictatorship' on the land of farms and mines.

An alliance between unions and the Greens makes even greater sense once consideration is given to where union density remains strong – in the public sector and in the welfare sector.[19] School teachers, nurses, university lecturers and public servants have all become potential constituencies for the Greens given their commitments to the public sector, liberal multiculturalism and social justice. It is therefore not surprising one higher education union, the NTEU, supported the Greens financially in the 2013 federal election (donating

---

18 Shaun Wilson and Kerstin Hermes, 'Political values and attitudes,' in *Contemporary Politics in Australia: Theories, Practices and Issues*, ed. Rodney Smith, Ariadne Vromen and Ian Cook, Cambridge University Press, Port Melbourne, 2012, 72.

19 Peetz op. cit., 'Are Australian trade unions part of the solution.'

$1 million). But union support for the Greens already acts as a way of strengthening union political voice as well as putting pressure on the ALP. Despite differences over energy policy (etc), the Greens have benefited from substantial donations from industrial unions including the Construction Forestry Mining and Energy Union (CFMEU) and the Electrical Trades Union.

The Greens have a consolidated voter base from which to build middle-sized political influence. Around eight per cent of electors say they are 'closest' to the Greens according to the AuSSA 2015 – an achievement that eluded the Australian Democrats. The Party has effective campaigning machinery and has quickly become part of the social tapestry of areas like Sydney's Newtown and Melbourne's Fitzroy which no longer identify as Labor. Since the socio-cultural changes that have accompanied the ascendancy of the Greens are unlikely to run out anytime soon, there remains tantalising questions about what moves the Greens make to develop further as a political force.

One vision for becoming a larger political force would be to model itself on Canada's successful New Democratic Party (NDP). Despite its disappointing election showing in 2015, the NDP is a major presence in the House of Commons with strong regional support in Quebec and British Columbia. At first blush, these parties have very different histories. For one, the NDP is much older, and was effectively set up by unions. The Australian Greens do not allow any affiliations so unions cannot emerge as foundational to the organisation and policies of the Party in the same way. Another difference is that NDP rival – the Canadian Liberal Party – is a centrist, non-labour party that leaves more space to the political left in Canada that the NDP can dominate. Still, a stronger alliance with Australia's left-wing unions would offer the Greens considerable resources in their quest for parliamentary influence. Such an opportunity might emerge if a future Labor leader, desperate for government, took the risky step of divorcing the ALP from the union movement altogether, and left open space for the Greens to occupy. In this context, it is not particularly surprising that the more left-leaning NSW Greens selected Jim Casey, union leader and firefighter, to contest the otherwise middle-class electorate of Grayndler centred on Newtown and Balmain. The point here is that any effort by Labor to further undermine its relationship with the union movement comes with risks. It would shift the political opportunity structure in favour of deepening alliances between unions and Greens, especially if the latter more vigorously pursued anti-austerity politics.

As well as policy differences between unions and Greens in a range of areas, there are structural factors that limit the deepening of such an alliance beyond one of mutual convenience. The moderating impact of greater parliamentary power and the tempting search by the Greens for more middle-class voters in the political centre is one such limit. As demographic changes under way in their own strongholds leave these electorates progressively more affluent, there is some prospect that Greens parliamentarians will shift their policy positions to represent these middle-class constituencies, and avoid the challenge of confronting structural inequalities in Australian society. Moreover, in a quest to break with 'old politics', the Greens may well follow their own path to social liberalism, extending the metaphor of a 'clean environment' to a 'clean politics' that disavows 'vested interests' of all kinds over political decision-making. Indeed, such a rationalistic approach – of considering all policies 'on their merit' – is the refrain of federal Greens leader, Richard di Natale. The construction of organised politics on these terms is relevant in explaining why the NSW Greens endorsed reforms to donation laws by the O'Farrell Coalition Government that halted union donations to political parties. (The laws were struck down by the High Court). This style of politics, it must be remembered, severely undermined the Australian Democrats because its representatives convinced themselves that the 'reasonable' and 'deliberative' role of softening unpopular Coalition reforms would be respected by its enigmatic but nonetheless left-drifting electorate. It was not. Consequently, there are good reasons to think the Greens would avoid a comprehensive move to the political centre accompanied by the political 'rationalism' of the sort described here.

A Reconstructed Relationship between Unions and Labor

As the previous section makes clear, a divorce between unions and Labor carries risks for both sides too frequently omitted in discussions of reform. A corrective reading of the situation recognises that the industrial and political arms of the labour movement are too intertwined to embark on far-reaching reforms in this direction. It would equally recognise that alliances between the Greens and unions are far from unrealistic and that a general call from unions to support the Greens would boost their parliamentary vote considerably. It would further recognise that voter polarisation over future austerity programs will continue to benefit parties that disrupt 'normal politics' from both the left and right. Given gloomy prospects for the revival of mainstream social-democratic and labour parties in their present form, it is more realistic for Labor to expect greater reliance on the Greens in their efforts to win government and to identify the losses (as well as imagined benefits) that likely come with greater distance from unions.

The same reading of the times recognises that inequalities will continue to animate the demands that workers make on elected officials and continue to stimulate the need for union representation. Labor's wage-earner electorate will continue to seek protections at work – decent and real employment, opportunities for education and training, low-cost child care, and adequate pensions and superannuation. These are core commitments of a social-democratic program, to be struggled for alongside unions. The development of a more comprehensive program must travel beyond the technocratic design of policy 'packages', crafted by those far removed from constituencies who depend on social protection. It would necessarily involve ordinary ALP members, unions at all levels, and the community. The same program would also address increasing concentrations of severe disadvantage in Australia's cities[20] and in regional centres. Although disadvantaged communities are often located in areas outside the traditional heartlands and institutions of Australian social democracy, they would benefit most from a massive investment in employment, services and infrastructure.

As a revitalised party for wage-earners, Labor would also recognise that industrial laws make it difficult for unions to organise workers, and that there are benefits for workers and

---

20 Hal Pawson and Shanaka Herath, 'Dissecting and tracking socio-spatial disadvantage in urban Australia,' *Cities* 44 (2015): 73–85.

the economy if industry-wide collective bargaining became central to industrial relations. Such reforms would assist in better regulating the more 'disorganised' and unequal sectors of Australia's labour market. In shifting policies to make union membership easier, Labor would also recognise that membership is not only falling but also changing – members are more likely to work in professional employment and overall density is now higher among women.[21] Women express more collectivist and pro-union attitudes and, as women become more important as workers, workplace leaders, and breadwinners, their needs also become more important to social-democratic politics (ie equal pay, childcare, parental leave, superannuation reform, etc).

How would an acknowledgement of these realities alter how we see the essential problems in the relationship between unions and Labor? Surely, a starting point is to transform the 'union debate' from a focus on 'how much' or 'how little' influence but *what kind* of influence and what kind of relationship. A revised relationship with Labor might involve unions following the path of the Norwegian union movement in making support for the Labour Party in that country more conditional on Labour-led governments finding robust alternatives to neoliberalism.[22] And, if Australian Labor reform efforts seek to democratise the ALP in ways that end the current bloc-vote of unions at conferences,[23] then the union movement must propose ways that promote the voting power

---

21 Ibid.
22 Wolfgang Biermann and Kristine Kallset, 'Everyone on board! The Nordic Model and the Red-Red-Green Coalition—A transferable model of success?,' *Internationale Politik und Gesellschaft*, 4 (2010): 167.
23 Chan, 'Labor elders back reforms.'

of ordinary union members, especially in unions affiliated to the Labor Party (as happens with British Labour).

To conclude, whatever emerging configurations reshape the centre-left, these will be critically shaped by two factors relevant to the union movement. The first is the ability of the union movement to increase its membership and influence among workers and the second is the shifting opportunity structure that determines the relationship between unions, the Labor Party and the Greens. Progressive politics cannot sustain a political majority without keeping ordinary workers allied to its essential causes and in turn, progressive politics has diminished meaning when these interests are ignored. The most serious risk of such a narrowing of progressive politics is that ordinary workers, who do shift-work, look after the elderly, drive trucks, and serve people in supermarkets – in the ordinary jobs that keep the country going – lose the franchise in the workplace and politics that they need and deserve.

Chapter 13

Progressivism at an Industry Level: Reflections on a Successful Unaffiliated Trade Union

James Tierney

> *at the end of the day, while the political insiders may be obsessed with the union movement's relationship with Labor – or any other political party – it is really a second order issue to our members.*[1]
> Ged Kearney, ACTU President
> Former President of the nurses' union

To be a 'progressive' is a title often claimed but rarely defined. Politicians as different as Nick Clegg, Jeremy Corbyn and Hillary Clinton all claim to be progressives, presumably to avoid the pejorative title of 'liberal' (or perhaps more accurately in the case of Clegg and Clinton, 'weather vane'). Both the ALP and the Greens have claimed to be, in almost identical language, 'the force for progressive change in Australia'. While the parameters may be unclear, in a modern context, progressive politics appears to consist of socially liberal political model underpinned by research based,

---

1 Ged Kearney, 'ALP must show respect to union base', *The Australian*, October 13, 2010.

expert-driven policies. Progressives may differ in their view of capitalism and the role of government, but there is general support for reducing income inequality through an expansive social safety net, universal health care and universal access to affordable quality education. Perhaps the most salient feature of progressivism as opposed to traditional liberalism is the commitment to constant research, review and renewal of policy aims in an attempt to find pragmatic solutions, rather than basing policy around more nebulous moral or ethical arguments.

The making of a progressive government is a product of many forces. The decisions made in the ballot box are obviously central, but the influence of social movements, research organisations and lobby groups is often substantial.

In the context of political analysis and debate, however, the influence of non-political groups is largely downplayed. As political commentators and politicians themselves bemoan the perceived 'hollow core' of the Labor party or the unrealistic idealism of the Greens, one could be forgiven for thinking that progressive policy has its origins in the party room alone. Scant attention is paid to the role progressive organisations play in promoting ideas and pressing left-wing parties, sometimes unwillingly, towards a progressive agenda. To elect a truly progressive government, rather than one that is nominally left-wing, progressive social movements must be active and influential.

Like other social movements, strong, independent trade unions can help to elect a progressive government. In one sense, trade unions are by their very existence of force for progressivism, serving as a bulwark against the unequal bargaining power between employers and employees.[2] Trade unions

---

2   It is of course not a given that a trade union will support progressive policies. Conservative unions that use their delegate power to block

can also aid progressive politics through direct campaigning for progressive political parties and by providing support for broader progressive policies and initiatives. But an underappreciated aspect of trade unions' role in progressive politics is how unions can develop meaningful policy within their own industry. Strong unions build coalitions, commission or engage in research and form policies based on that research. These policies often form the focal point of enterprise bargaining and political campaigns.

Strong unions, of course, are in shorter supply than they once were. Over the last 30 years, union membership has dropped from almost half of the working population to just 15 per cent.[3] Some unions have suffered catastrophic drops in membership and density (the percentage of employed workers in an industry who are members of the union). Even among those unions free from scandal and with stable membership, many have been affected by 'institutional sclerosis' – a rigid hierarchy has formed, dedicated to ensuring factional representation within Labor party caucuses and protecting incumbents, which stifles democracy within the union, detaches the leadership from its members and diminishes the union's ability to adapt and promote change. To quote David Peetz, 'if unions were once part of a solution, then their

---

progressive policies in the Labor party is the most commonly decried example, but unions will take a protectionist stance when trade liberalisation or structural shifts in the economy are likely to adversely affect or deplete their membership.

3   Australian Bureau of Statistics, 'Trade union membership falls', 17 October, 2015, Last modified May 13, 2013. Accessed April 2, 2016, http://www.abs.gov.au/ausstats/.

decline and the problems they face in arresting that decline now constitute part of the problem itself'.[4]

The Australian Nursing and Midwifery Federation (ANMF) has largely managed to avoid these pitfalls. Its membership and density has soared during this period, and the union has been able to mobilise its increased base during successful industrial campaigns. The branch has been agile and democratic enough to support its members' interests and respond to a variety of challenges within the health sector.

The nurses' greatest success is the story of how it fought for and won legislatively mandated nurse-patient ratios in Victorian public hospitals. The process that led to the passing of the *Safe Patient Care (Nurse to Patient and Midwife to Patient Ratios) Act 2015* in Victoria is worth closer analysis. From the inception of the policy, through industrial campaigns to the lobbying of the Andrews Labor government, the 15 year history of nursing ratios in Victoria provides an excellent example of the influence that mobilised, powerful, independent trade unions can have in promoting progressive policies, and dragging the government along with them.

In recounting the nurses' progress towards promulgating nurse-patient ratios, it will be important to note the significant advantages it had over other movements in fomenting change. The nurses' advantages as a movement can be, to varying degrees, instructive to other trade unions and social movements that seek to promote a progressive agenda within their own areas of influence. First, the nurses' institutional power and resources allowed them to mobilise and negotiate from a position of strength. The nurses also maintained strong

---

4 David Peetz, 'Are Australian trade unions part of the solution, or part of the problem?', *Australian Review of Public Affairs*, February 2015.

public support, which enabled the union to frame the claims in ways that had universal resonance. The final advantage – the most contentious and the most germane to the question that enlivens this book – is the union's freedom from the constraints of the Labor party.

The Nurses' Union and Nurse-Patient Ratios

The Australian Nursing and Midwifery Federation (ANMF) is the biggest union in Australia (it overtook the Shop Distributive and Allied Employees' Association in 2012). It has over 230,000 members nationally and more than 70,000 members in Victoria. Its membership is more than 90 per cent female.[5] The membership growth of the union has been remarkable. In 1989, ANMF membership stood at 15,712. ANMF membership density in 1989 stood at 28 per cent.[6] By 2014, of the 92,891 nurses and midwives in Victoria, 70,328 were members of the union – a density of 76 per cent.[7] In a period where trade union density has collapsed across Australia, the Victorian nurses' union has increased its membership sixfold.

In addition to membership growth, the Victorian Branch has experienced 25 years of internal stability. The Branch has

---

5 Nursing and Midwifery Board of Australia, *Nurse and Midwife Registrant Data: October 2013*, Melbourne: NMBA, December 2013.

6 Australian Nursing Federation (Victorian Branch), 'Membership Figures', *Annual Report 1989–90* (internal publication, ANMF Archives, Melbourne, Victoria, 1990), 8.

7 Australian Nursing and Midwifery Federation (Victorian Branch), *ANMF Annual Report 2013–14*, (internal publication, ANMF Archives, Melbourne, Victoria, 2014), 2; Nursing and Midwifery Board of Australia, *Nurse and Midwife Registrant Data: June 2014*, Melbourne: NMBA, December 2013, 3.

only had two Secretaries in this time – Belinda Morieson and Lisa Fitzpatrick, who took over when Morieson retired – both of whom were nurses who became officers within the Branch. The current ACTU Secretary, Ged Kearney, is a former President of the Victorian Branch. While the leadership has been stable, democracy within the union has been enhanced through yearly delegates' conferences, special interest conferences and the voting power of individual members. Many key branch policies and grievances have emerged from delegates' conference discussions.

While the branch was stable from the early 1990s onwards, nurses in Victoria faced increasing pressures in their workload, and in keeping their job. Under the Kennett government, Victoria moved towards competitive market models of service deliveries and a new range of service providers from the private sector entered the public health market. Two thousand nursing positions in the public sector were eliminated. Many registered nurses were replaced by patient-care assistants, and the Kennett government encouraged providers to fill rostering gaps with agency nurses. Public health providers moved to a 'case mix' funding model, whereby providers received funding on the basis of the number of a particular type of patients they treated. It was in this fraught climate that the ANMF and the Health Services Union (HSU) sought to renew the public sector enterprise agreements that were to expire in September 2000.

For the first time, nurse-patient ratios were to feature as an issue for debate during the negotiations. A nurse-to-patient ratio is the number of patients assigned to each nurse within a given ward. Using this ratio as a measure to determine staffing is a relatively new concept in nursing. In the 1990s, American researchers, led by Linda Aitken, stopped looking purely at nurse staffing numbers at institutions and began to focus on nurse-to-patient ratios as a means for understanding patient outcomes and addressing why nurses believed themselves to be understaffed. Researchers observed that nurse-to-patient ratios were an accurate predictor of risk-adjusted patient mortality rates and incidents of 'failure to rescue'. The more patients any given nurse had to oversee within a given ward, the more patients died.

Ratios was plainly an industrial issue. Higher ratios meant greater employment for registered nurses and greater restrictions on unqualified hospital assistants performing nursing duties. It was also a professional issue – nurses suffer from one of the highest rates of burnout and stress across all professions, and greater staffing levels were shown to improve job satisfaction and retention rates. But ratios was also a policy issue of universal resonance – research clearly showed that higher staffing rates ensured a greater level of patient care and reduced the risk of avoidable fatalities and other complications on the ward. As a pragmatic (but undoubtedly expensive) policy goal, it was in everybody's interest.

The leaders of the ANMF, Morieson and Fitzpatrick, were heavily influenced by Aitken's work, and the issue of ratios was receiving increasing traction within the membership as a solution to a crisis in recruiting and retaining nurses. Members and ANMF leaders agreed to include nurse-patient ratios in the union's log of claims. During negotiations and the industrial action that followed, the ANMF framed the dispute around patient care – that proper wages for nurses and the implementation of nurse-patient ratios were essential in ensuring adequate patient care. Morieson stated:

> Nurses don't get their job satisfaction out of a glamourous lifestyle or big money. They get their job satisfaction out of being able to care for their patients properly but also able to pay their mortgage. That means you've got to have enough nurses and you've got to pay them properly. And I know that the community supports the nurses in this campaign. You can't argue against that, can you?[8]

The campaign built around patient care was progressive, evidence-based and founded in universal public concerns around health care. Improving conditions for patients had broad social resonance. The government could not rely on typical challenges to industrial action, decrying nurses as militant or greedy, because the nurses had framed their claim around an issue of fundamental importance to all Victorians.

The government unexpectedly changed hands during the dispute. In the State election in November 1999, after trailing by almost 20 points in opinion polls, the Labor Party, led by Steve Bracks, took power. After the election, the ANMF sought to hold the ALP to its pre-election promise that it would abide by 'the independent umpire's decision' and agree to private arbitration in the Australian Industrial Relations Commission. Perhaps not recognising the cost implications until it was elected; the Bracks government expressed staunch opposition to nurse-patient ratios once it took office. When negotiation between the government and the ANMF broke down, nurses voted to take industrial action, closing 1 in 5 beds in public hospitals. After a period of intense industrial action, the parties agreed to arbitration.

---

8   Belinda Morieson, conversation with author, December 23, 2009.

The arbitration was heard before Commissioner Blair, who, after hearing submissions from both sides, determined that 'those who choose to say that there is not a nursing crisis are, in the Commission's view, in a state of denial'. He found that the only way to overcome the crisis in nursing and provide high quality patient care was to implement nursing ratios in all major hospitals. By framing their industrial claims around broader concerns for public welfare, the ANMF was able to convince the Commission that ratios were in the best interests of the State. Victoria became the first place in the world to implement enforceable nurse-patient ratios.

The union has remained active in conducting research and commissioning reports to buttress its claims regarding the benefits of ratios. It has also built coalitions with other nursing bodies to increase its influence and fight for other progressive healthcare policies. The union worked with the Nurses Board of Victoria (NBV) and the Nurse Policy Unit in the Department of Health to introduce a private counselling service, available only to members. The ANMF launched a 'No Lift' campaign in public hospitals, which led to the creation of the Department of Health and Safety Victorian Nurses Back Injury Prevention Project. No Lift programs have since been adopted in all public hospitals. The Nursing and Midwifery Health Program Victoria was set up in 2006, largely as a result of the union's lobbying, to treat nurses and nursing students experiencing substance abuse and mental health problems. All of these programs were grounded in research and drawn from grievances raised by members.

Despite the proven benefit to patients, nurse-patient ratios have been called into question in each round of public service enterprise bargaining negotiations, and are a constant source of tension between nurses and their State government employer. In 2011, the union fought an intense battle with the Baillieu Coalition government over ratios. Negotiations began in October 2011. The government, the Department of Health and the Victorian Hospital Industry Association all sought to cut ratios and substitute registered nurses for low-skilled 'health assistants'. A leaked Cabinet-in-Confidence document revealed that the government's strategy was to force the union into arbitration in the Fair Work Commission, to stretch the union's resources and rely on the Commission being sympathetic to the employer's demands. The nurses initially took protected industrial action in November, but no agreement was reached. After the Commission suspended protected industrial action, the parties negotiated further, but these negotiations also broke down over nurse-patient ratios. In February 2012, the nurses took unprotected industrial action, risking substantial fines against the union and its leaders. Following further consultation with the government and the VHIA, an agreement was reached in May. The agreement retained all existing ratios and included wage increases of between 3.5 per cent and 4 per cent per annum.

The nurses sought to circumvent this constant fight over ratios by having ratios legislatively protected. In the lead-up to the 2014 Victoria State Election, the nurses lobbied the ALP to commit to passing legislation that would protect nurse-to-patient ratios as part of its election platform. Having the ratios enshrined in legislation would ensure that ratios were no longer a contested element of enterprise bargaining negotiations. The nurses were heavily involved in negotiations with Emergency Services Minister Jane Garrett and Health Minister Jill Hennessy. The Safe Patient Care (Nurse to

Patient and Midwife to Patient Ratios) Bill 2015 was passed into law by the Legislative Council on 9 October 2015. The nurses' progressive agenda had become the ALP's.

It is of note that the Greens, in particular Coleen Hartland MLC, have advocated the nurses' cause for a number of years, Coleen Hartland MLC in particular, and with greater enthusiasm than the ALP. In 2007, Victorian Greens MPs donated to an ANMF welfare fund for nurses whose pay had been docked for taking industrial action. Steve Bracks had tacitly supported the fines. The Greens also made legislatively mandated nurse-patient ratios an element of its platform in 2014. It took both parties until 2014 to support a policy that had been an industrial reality for 15 years. This is not an indictment of either party, it merely reinforces the fact that progressive policy often comes from below.

The Nurses as a Blueprint: Organisational Strength, Framing and ALP Affiliation

In assessing whether the nurses can serve as an example to other unions and social movements seeking to formulate and fight for progressive policies, it should be noted that the nurses can draw on three distinct advantages that other movements may not possess: its organisational strength, its influence in public debate, and its independence.

The first advantage is the most obvious. The Branch has more than 70,000 members and more than 75 per cent of nurses in Victoria are members. It has 500 workplace delegates, most of whom have industrial experience and are well trained in union organising principles. It has extensive branch resources, including numerous organisers, industrial officers and media staff. Most unions could only dream of that level of density and organisational strength. It also has the benefit of being able to organise a large percentage of its base around a single public sector campaign. The branch can draw on significant industrial strength during campaigns.

The second advantage relates to the nurses' ability to put their case positively in the public forum. By having a deep understanding what they are talking about, the nurses have a significant advantage in framing public debate around patient care. While few professions are as trusted as nurses (they have been ranked the most trustworthy profession in the Roy Morgan Poll of Profession Perceptions for 21 years in a row), all movements can benefit from framing their debate around an issue grounded in research and public support. A federal government debate about the future of health care will be fought in the sort of vague, plenary rhetorical area where progressive movements may flounder. The Institute of Public Affairs (IPA) and *The Australian* and the Samuel Griffith Society and Andrew Bolt and Sussan Ley may be able to confidently assert that unions are greedy and that the health sector needs less red tape, less bureaucracy, less cost and more free-market incentives. But being forced to debate specific, research-backed proposals like nurse-patient ratios is often beyond the purview of generalist commentators or politicians. The nurse's proposals have withstood criticism and proven persuasive with judicial officers and the public.

The final advantage is the most contentious – the extent to which the nurses have benefited from being an unaffiliated trade union. The ANMF is affiliated with the ACTU and Victorian Trades Hall Council, but is not affiliated with the ALP. The current Secretary, Fitzpatrick, explains that although the debate over affiliation is raised from time to time, most notably in 1998, it has never gained much traction, mainly because the members are not as a whole aligned with left-wing politics. Also, Branch Council and the leadership see little value in affiliation:

> There was a time that we thought about whether or not we should affiliate… given that many other unions are, and really, I think the decision was that we have to work with whatever government was in power.[9]

The ANMF's decision not to affiliate is not an ideological stance per se, but a pragmatic recognition that regardless of which government is in power, they will be drawn into negotiations where the parties have conflicting interests.

While each affiliated union's relationship with the ALP varies, there is no question that certain unions and their leaders prioritise their role within the ALP to the detriment of member concerns and building broader coalitions within their industry. Party elder John Faulkner decried unions within the Labor Party as 'large, faceless institutions controlled by union secretaries, who are in turn obedient to factional cartels'.[10] Rather than pushing the Labor party towards progressivism from within the party, Labor party factions oversee union elections and drag the unions away from flexible, innovative thinking, as these factions seek to influence policy and those chosen to execute it. These factional heads have no experience or relationship with the rank and file. Instead, as Barbara

---

9   Lisa Fitzpatrick, conversation with author, December 15, 2009.
10 John Faulkner, 'Public pessimism, political complacency, restoring trust, reforming labor', Address to the Light on the Hill Society, Revesby Workers' Club, Revesby NSW, October 7, 2014.

Pocock described, they become 'ghosts in the machine of unions, with voices, agendas and interests quite different from those of many members'.[11]

No leader in the nurses' union has ever held office with the ALP. All of the leaders are former nurses. With the exception of a couple of experienced industrial officers, all of the industrial-professional staff are also former nurses. No-one within the organisation has an agenda other than improving the working conditions of its members. The nurses have avoided the factional squabbles and the consequent policy inertia that often comes with ALP affiliation. They have a leadership that is wholly committed to advancing nurses' aims, and a membership with an active role in driving branch policy. Moreover, despite lacking the 'insider access' often extolled by advocates of the union–Labor relationship, or perhaps as a consequence of this independence, the nurses have forged coalitions with other peak health bodies to increase its knowledge, influence and organisational strength. The nurses, free to battle on their own terms, have thrived.

There are progressive critics on both sides of the Labor–union alliance. Some critics reject the current relationship on the basis that staunchly pro-market members of the Labor Right undermine the union movement from within the party. Other critics who see the Labor Party as the vehicle for left-wing, progressive change, the primary alternative to the Coalition, condemn the influence within the party room of socially conservative right-wing unions, which prevent the Labor Party from implementing progressive reforms, particularly on social issues such as gay marriage.

---

11 Barbara Pocock, 'Institutional sclerosis: prospects for trade union transformation', Labour and Industry, Vol. 9 , No. 1, 1998, 26.

There may be merit in both claims. But to focus on the ALP–union relationship (or to suggest, as Guy Rundle and other commentators have, that progressive unions like the ANMF, National Tertiary Education Union and Electrical Trades Union could form their own progressive bloc) is to miss the lesson of the nurses' union.[12] Where other movements obsess over electoral politics, factional alliances and their place in the progressive political landscape, the nurses have achieved progressive change at an industry level by simply getting on with it.

The union is not actively involved in electoral politics, nor does it seek to be. It is not an advocate for broader progressive political aims. It has no professed preference for the Greens or the ALP. But it can serve as a model to both unions and other social movements for the way in which it has increased democracy within its own branch and for its successful lobbying for change within the health industry based on practical, research-based policy. The story of the nurses also serves as a reminder that left-wing governments must sometimes have progressivism forced upon them.

---

12 Guy Rundle, 'Why the union movement should divorce the ALP', Crikey, April 3, 2014. Accessed April 2, 2016, http://www.crikey.com.au/2014/04/03/rundle-why-the-union-movement-should-divorce-the-alp/?wpmp_switcher=mobile&wpmp_tp=1.

Chapter 14

Does Turnbull Offer a Progressive Alternative?

Peter Van Onselen

In his 1967 memoir, *Afternoon Light*, Robert Menzies wrote: 'We took the name "Liberal" because we were determined to be a progressive party, willing to make experiments, in no sense reactionary but believing in the individual, his rights and his enterprise, and rejecting the Socialist panacea'.[1] This commentary has been used by the progressive wing of the party ever since to justify why Liberals should not allow conservatism to dominate policy and personnel. Conservatives reject the argument, pointing out that for Menzies – himself a conservative on many issues – the rejection of the socialist panacea was the more important part of the descriptor.

The elevation of Malcolm Turnbull to the prime ministership in September 2015 raised the seemingly real prospect of an embrace of progressive politics within the Liberal Party. The opinion polls had long shown that Turnbull was the preferred Liberal leader amongst Labor and non-aligned voters. But such support is no guarantee that a Turnbull prime ministership would see a change in direction for Australia's right-of-centre major party.

---

1 Robert Menzies, *Afternoon Light: Some Memories of Men and Events*, Cassell, Melbourne, 1967, 286.

If members of the parliamentary Liberal Party are asked which faction they are aligned with – the moderates or conservatives – most will tell you with a straight face that there are no factions inside the Liberal Party. Shortly after he assumed the prime ministership, Turnbull uttered similar words to the New South Wales state council of the party, receiving laughter rather than applause for having done so.[2]

One of the few parliamentary Liberals who seriously thinks about the philosophical direction of the party, the leader in the Senate, George Brandis, claims: 'It is now as commonplace to speak of the conservative and liberal (or moderate) wings of the Liberal Party as it is to speak of the socialist Left and Right factions of the ALP'.[3] Speak of, perhaps. But in reality the party remains a conservative entity, and the moderate wing of the party is at best questionably progressive on most policy fronts. This increases the degree of difficulty Turnbull will have if he tries to shift the party's philosophy too much or too quickly.

This chapter looks briefly at the history of progressive politics within the Liberal Party, to the extent that there is one, including the role of so-called 'moderates' within the state organisational divisions of the party. It also explains why the Liberal Party has always been more akin to a conservative party, rather than its name sake, finally examining the reasons

---

2   Turnbull was claiming that the Liberal Party is not run by factions. In the months that followed an all-out factional brawl erupted as the pre-selection showdowns for the 2016 election were opened.

3   For a thorough understanding of Brandis's assessment of the philosophical direction of the Liberal Party and the factional divides that exist, including this quote, see George Brandis, 'John Howard and the Australian Liberal tradition,' in *Liberals and Power: The Road Ahead*, ed. Peter van Onselen, Melbourne University Press, Carlton, 2008, 48–79.

it is unlikely Turnbull will live up to his progressive credentials. If this book is about finding a home for progressive politicking in Australia, within one of the mainstream parties, readers will get little comfort from the conclusions in this chapter.

Turnbull Observed

The elevation of Turnbull to the prime ministership raised tantalising possibilities for commentators and political scientists alike. Would he try and recast the Liberals as a more moderate political force? Could he improve the government's working relationship with the Greens, thereby helping the Coalition achieve greater policy outcomes in the Senate? The change of leadership within the Greens parliamentary party opened the door to a decoupling of the traditional Greens–Labor alliance, if the Liberals could find a way to take advantage of the change. Would Liberals and Greens consider preference agreements if common policy grounds could be found? And if Turnbull narrowed differences with Labor on some policy scripts, even occasionally outflanking Labor on the 'left', how would the opposition react?

Those of us who have closely observed Turnbull's political career – from the moment he booted out the moderate Peter King to win preselection for the Liberals in the seat of Wentworth in 2003, to his elevation to the Howard government's front-bench, to the party's leadership in opposition in late 2008 – have long wondered what kind of prime minister Turnbull would make. The tendency he showed to support progressive policy settings prior to commencing his political career (for example championing the Republic), or with his push for climate change action during his first stint as leader, is less likely to direct Turnbull's approach as prime minister now. A carefully crafted pragmatic agenda is more likely. The wilderness years Turnbull endured between leadership stints (2008–15), of a similar nature and duration to that of Howard (1989–95), taught Turnbull that to be a 'successful' Liberal leader he needs to avoid issues that risk splitting the party. With Tony Abbott's ongoing parliamentary presence, this tendency is all the more likely to dominate Turnbull's approach in 2016, notwithstanding minor adjustments in philosophical direction under his leadership. While a strong result at this year's election could see Turnbull start to 'come out of his shell', if an agenda to support such a shift isn't laid out ahead of polling day political, problems may soon follow.

The Ties that Bind

For decades non-Labor political parties have been united as much by what they oppose as what issues bind them together. Opposing socialism brought together the Free Traders and the Protectionists in 1909, because the emerging Labor Party was seen as the greater of evils. A large part of the success of Menzies in founding the Liberal Party in 1944 prior to the end of the Second World War was to re-direct that focus, to proactively appeal to the so-called forgotten people. Menzies' book, *Afternoon Light*, used similar rhetoric to re-focus the Liberal Party's ideology after he retired. However, in office Menzies was the beneficiary of what Liberals opposed far more so than what they collectively represented. Liberals rejected communism and, with that, Labor's brand of socialism. It was an easy political kill for Menzies during the heady days of the Cold War.

In 1972, after 23 years in opposition, Gough Whitlam tried to do too much in too little time as prime minister, shortening the life of his Labor government in the process. Three years later and Labor was out of power, suffering the largest defeat in federal political history. But the re-elected Liberal Party was back without having thought sufficiently about what its core values were. Opposition to socialism (and interventionist government) only got the party so far. Members were calling for a positive agenda to reflect the times. With Malcolm Fraser and much of his inner circle largely void of political ideas, a new agenda was proffered by the dries – a collection of radical free-market thinkers who wanted to reform the economy and in particular the industrial relations system. For their time this grouping were certainly *economically* progressive, even if the Liberal Party writ large was yet to embrace such thinking, and certainly remained a socially conservative collective.

While the economic philosophy of the dries wasn't electorally popular, and support for it within the Liberal Party was spotty at best, it gave Howard the foundations for reforms he would go on to enact in government. Howard was a sympathetic ear to the dries during the Fraser years, even if as Treasurer he rarely championed their cause in cabinet. It ultimately gave the Howard prime ministership policy and ideological ballast, something the Fraser years didn't have because the remnants of the Menzies era – dominant in the upper echelons of the ministry – were catapulted back into office before the party had learnt the lessons of defeat.

Abbott's two years as Prime Minister suffered from the same lack of readiness for office Fraser's government had. Inadequate renewal of personnel, a failure to step back from the political combat of previous years and evaluate the policy setting the party should keep and discard for the future. The single mindedness of Abbott's pursuit of power was a different ethos to the traditional conservative reasoning behind seeking office. The question now is to what extent will a Turnbull led Liberal Party transform for the modern political era. At one level, the need to do so is diminished because of the lack of introspection Labor has undergone in recent times. Failure to reflect seems to be a bipartisan problem in the body politic.

Denying Progressives while also Keeping Labor out of Power

The Liberal Party, within our entrenched two party system, is organisationally unlikely to transform into 'Labor-lite', as conservatives disparagingly like to describe it, despite the window of opportunity for doing so given Labor's reluctance to modernise. The conservatives within the Liberal Party, including the former prime minister, have flexed their collective political muscles at the start of the 2016 election year. A series of steps have already been embarked upon to prevent Turnbull from transforming the historical conservatism of the party, even if under new leadership the Coalition is successful at this year's election.

Turnbull knows that the party membership at the organisational level are more conservative than he is. The parliamentary membership is largely careerist, but the conservative voices know that they can loudly announce their disagreements with government policy, especially from the backbench. This will temper any internal efforts to embrace progressive ideas, because the subsequent public debates will feed into a modern construct of 'disunity' and 'tensions', which can harm leaders via the impact these stories can have on opinion polls. Having removed Abbott on the pledge to make the party more competitive in the polls, Turnbull is now beholden to them. This will create a tension between the need to continue appealing to new voters, especially younger voters, and the reality that the base of support for the Liberal Party comes from an older demographic.[4]

The role of the National Party is also important when coming to understand Turnbull's institutional limitations on modernising his party, another reason to doubt Turnbull's capacity to shift the cultural lines within his party. We have seen in the same-sex marriage debate the more conservative leanings of the Nationals compared with the Liberal Party.[5] Also in what action to take on climate change. Liberal governments generally rely on their coalition partner for a working majority, and even where they can govern in their own right the coalition is rarely broken. While a Liberal leader isn't bound to limit his or her support for progressive policy setting within their own party because of the shared governing arrangements with the Nationals, government policy is impacted by Nationals. And close debates within the Liberal Party room are subject to informal influence by the Nationals.[6]

While a Turnbull leadership will be different to Abbott's, or indeed Howard's, the changes will need to be more incremental

---

4   For a detailed examination of the factors which led to Abbott's demise, as well as some of the positioning that Turnbull and his supporters engaged in prior to challenging Abbott, see Wayne Errington and Peter van Onselen, *Battleground: Why the Liberal Party Shirtfronted Tony Abbott*, Melbourne University Press, Carlton, 2015.
5   It should be noted that the meeting of the Coalition party room highlighted that a majority of BOTH party rooms were opposed to same-sex marriage. The margin was greater within the Nationals.
6   The merger of the parties in Queensland has heightened the applicability of this point.

than substantial. Voters who seek genuine progressive agendas from their political leaders will likely be disappointed by Turnbull's prime ministership. But this shouldn't blind us to the ways in which he may change politicking, and indeed the subtle differences between a Turnbull agenda versus that of a more conservative alternative leader.

Abbott's removal as Prime Minister wasn't a rebellion against his philosophical positioning. Indeed it is questionable whether Abbott really moved the party onto a more conservative footing than it had been under John Howard's leadership. Abbott was heavily criticised by his 'base' early on in his prime ministership, for the generous paid maternity leave proposal and his retreat from a commitment to amend the *Racial Discrimination Act*, for example. In the end Abbott's base fell in behind him despite their reservations about his leadership. This was partly because of a cultural response to threats to a first term prime minister, and partly to block Turnbull, who going back to his time running the Australian Republican Movement has been a figure of disdain for many conservatives.

The support Turnbull was able to muster was cobbled together in response to deficiencies in Abbott's leadership style, and the choice of Turnbull was simply because he was the most viable alternative candidate. His personal polling numbers, perceived political charisma and name recognition in the electorate put him ahead of alternatives such as Julie Bishop and Scott Morrison. The fact Turnbull had a more moderate pedigree than either of these candidates was a mere coincidence.

In fact, the votes within the parliamentary party, which shifted enough support for a successful challenge, came from

MPs and Senators historically doubtful about Turnbull's suitability to lead the Liberal Party. This will check any progressive political instincts Turnbull might have. Mitch Fifield was one of the three shadow parliamentary secretaries who got the ball rolling on the removal of Turnbull back in 2009 when he resigned his front-bench position.[7] Scott Ryan is a powerful factional figure from Victoria who describes himself as a dry, and let me know in no uncertain terms the error in my book *Battlelines* describing him as a 'moderate'. Both men accompanied Turnbull on his walk into the party room for the vote. Michaelia Cash, a minister from Western Australia, is a close ally of conservative factional leader Mathias Cormann, yet two weeks before the coup she went to see Julie Bishop to let her know Abbott had lost her support. Turnbull would do as a competent alternative was her message. And of course the spearhead of Turnbull's strategic push to oust Abbott was Arthur Sinodinos, Howard's long-time chief of staff, who could never be accused of being a dripping wet moderate. He also accompanied Turnbull on the walk into the party room.

The point of reeling off such names and circumstances surrounding Abbott's demise isn't to walk readers through the history of how Abbott came to be flung aside as PM, but simply to highlight that the September 2015 coup was no moderate push to oust a conservative leader. In fact sections of the conservative wing of the party long complained that when Abbott seized the leadership off of Turnbull he retained moderate faces in the inner circle – Christopher Pyne as manager in the House, Brandis in a leadership role in the

---

[7] The other two were Senators Mathias Cormann and Brett Mason. The three penned a resignation letter to Turnbull and released it to the media.

Senate. These players remain in Turnbull's inner circle now. Why would voters think that the elevation of Turnbull will suddenly see them begin championing progressive causes they never did under Abbott's leadership?

The Liberal Party has always been more pragmatic than ideological, seeking to retain power as a guiding principle. It naturally shuns progressive goals, which may include difficult (and untested) reforms. This of itself is a conservative ethos – keep Labor away from the treasury benches. Howard extended that thinking to a need to keep progressives away from power altogether, thus ensuring only incremental policy development as society modernises – again a very conservative agenda. To the extent that Howard included senior figures from the moderate wing of the party in his cabinet, he gave them portfolios where they were charged with enacting conservative policy settings as part of his government. The most obvious examples include Philip Ruddock in immigration, Robert Hill as environment minister and Amanda Vanstone in education.[8]

Keeping radicals away from power and incompetent Labor ministers away from the levers of Treasury are worthy goals for traditional conservatives. But what does doing so offer progressives or liberal economic reformers? Or indeed social liberals? Even Howard, who was unashamedly socially conservative, would not have tolerated governing for its own sake (as was clearly apparent from his final-term push for further industrial relations reform in the shape of WorkChoices). While the conservatives undoubtedly entrenched their power base within the Liberal Party during the dominant and strong leadership of Howard, conservatism has become a common

---

8 Wayne Errington and Peter van Onselen, *John Winston Howard: The Biography*, Melbourne University Press, Carlton, 2007.

ideological choice amongst Liberals today because it fits with the pragmatic goal of winning elections. This being an election year expect Turnbull, despite his progressive tendencies, to be captured by the goal of securing re-election. He will join the careerists who see attaining and retaining power as a goal in and of itself.[9]

Turnbull as Prime Minister

While Abbott is no progressive, he was more reactionary than conservative on many policy fronts during his prime ministership. Some of that positioning is what Turnbull will seek to alter. At most the party will lose its reactionary edge, and reform as a traditional centre-right party. To the extent that Turnbull can mollify conservative tendencies within the Liberal Party, it is likely to only be on the margins. Generational renewal may assist with this process. But Turnbull won't be able to transform the party into a progressive outfit as much as he may wish to. The early policy evidence highlights why not.

In just the first six months of the Turnbull government, this one time progressive public policy thinker has affirmed that he will not seek to re-embrace an Emission Trading Scheme; will stick to the plebiscite on same-sex marriage rather than give colleagues a free vote in the parliament; has refused to discuss a Republic until after the Queen passes away; and his rhetoric on radical Islam has gradually become less nuanced than his early commentary in this space. Where Turnbull once mocked Direct Action he now presides over its continued rollout, with

---

9 For more information on the rise of the careerist politician, see Peter van Onselen and Wayne Errington, 'Ruling, not governing', in *Griffith Review 51: Fixing the System,* eds Julianne Schultz and Anne Tiernan, 2016, 105–116.

suggestions that he may widen the funding envelope for the scheme. The opposition leader who took a softer approach to asylum boat arrivals in 2009 is continuing Operation Sovereign Borders in 2016, keeping one of the parliament's hard right conservatives, Peter Dutton, in the immigration portfolio. While Turnbull claims that there has never been a more exciting time to be alive, it's apparently not exciting enough (nor is the government prepared to be agile enough) to juggle a republic debate with the myriad other issues on the agenda.

At the same time a moderate push to dominate pre-selection showdowns in New South Wales, as already alluded to, has been crimped by prime ministerial intervention to avoid disagreements impacting on the government's performance. And little has changed in terms of the government's approach to social services – the portfolio has been handed to a rising star amongst conservatives, Western Australian Christian Porter.

We shouldn't overstate Turnbull's track record for progressive political outcomes. Turnbull, while progressive on some social issues when religion doesn't get in the way, defines himself more as an economic reformer – a policy script that no longer divides progressive and conservative Liberals. But it's not all despair for progressives on the Liberal side now that Turnbull has taken over the leadership. It's just that the changes have been far more muted than some might have hoped for, especially nonpartisan observers.

There are more women on the front-bench, as there should have been years ago. The agenda now includes an embrace of innovative industries, even if the minister charged with carrying out these duties is one of the parliament's most careerist representatives. While Turnbull, like Abbott before him, comes from the NSW division, the power sharing within the government has seen the Victorian division rise in stature. Victorian Liberals are a more progressive collective than their counterparts in NSW, WA or Queensland. This shift has more potential to alter the progressive approach of the Liberal Party than the rise of Turnbull to the leadership, although it must be acknowledged that Turnbull has facilitated this. On the economic front Turnbull has shown a willingness to discuss reforms to tax and federation structures. Such adjustments if they are pursued represent a form of progressive political thinking, albeit limited to the economic sphere.

Where disagreements emerge between differing Liberal Party ideological tendencies, they are more defined by what approach best suits the political situation of the day than any guiding principles of philosophy. It has been quickly forgotten that this was the case even when Malcolm Turnbull was arguing for putting a price on carbon. The approach was based on a belief that if the conservatives didn't do this they would suffer severe electoral repercussions at the hands of Kevin Rudd and his advocacy for action to address the 'greatest moral and economic challenge of our generation'. Turnbull wasn't initially standing on pure principle: slowness to act on climate change had been one of the factors that harmed Howard in his quest to win a fifth straight election. Turnbull lost the support of his party when the small number of strong opponents to the emissions trading scheme was joined by a larger number of Liberals who started to question the strategic electoral value in backing Rudd's plan. The pragmatic origins of Turnbull's support for a progressive climate change approach is crucial to understanding why he is now likely to be more pragmatic than progressively ideological.

Conclusion

Ultimately, Turnbull will not want to risk a split within the Liberal Party on ideological grounds. This will temper his policy positioning, certainly in an election year. It will be interesting to see if Turnbull emboldens his progressive approach on the other side of an election, secure in the knowledge he has obtained something of a mandate in his own right. That is the hope of moderates within the parliamentary team, and indeed within the party organisation. Of course critics might point out that without having spelled out an agenda with progressive policy scripts any mandate would be thin – at best built on the assumed intentions of Turnbull the individual.

The patronage of power has become the primary goal for many players from both major parties. The trappings of office – the cars, the travel, the extra staff and the salaries – matter as much, if not more so, than do the opportunities for reform that incumbency affords. Indeed the pursuit of reform becomes something functionaries who feel strongly about retaining power are cautious about because 'doing stuff' entails risks. Such thinking is the enemy of progressive politicking within both major parties, and presumably will be the subject matter of other chapters in this collection. Turnbull is not immune from it, and his capacity to change the culture of a conservative Liberal Party is limited. In an election year Turnbull may prize the legitimacy of victory above the policy goals he desires to implement.

Chapter 15

Labor or Green:
The Left and the Crisis of Politics

Simon Copland

This book asks *'how do we elect a progressive government?'* I am going to turn this question on its head, instead asking *'can we elect a progressive government?'* I argue that electing a truly progressive government is impossible within our capitalist political system. Given this, left-wing activism needs to shift away from standard political interventions (elections, lobbying etc) to instead focus on direct political intervention that aims to reabsorb the power of the state back into local communities.

I first got engaged in electoral politics in 2007. John Howard had been Prime Minister for almost as long as I could remember and I was extremely excited about the possibility of him being deposed at the next election. But at the same time I was already feeling betrayed by Kevin Rudd. During the campaign I saw Rudd take the party further to the right – particularly around workplace relations – and that disappointed me greatly.

The Greens therefore made perfect sense. I had great faith in their leadership and ideological positions and was excited to see how the party would grow. I soon joined and threw myself into the ACT Senate campaign.

Over the following years the Greens remained my main focus of political involvement. In 2010, I managed the ACT

Greens' election campaign and was convenor of the ACT branch from 2011–12. After moving to Brisbane, I worked on the Queensland Greens election campaign in 2013.

Throughout this time my main aim was to build the Greens as a viable alternative to our two 'old parties'. The ALP, as I saw it, had failed. Betrayals on climate change, asylum seekers, industrial relations and welfare payments were all deal breakers. Most importantly, I could never see the party turning back. The ALP had gone too far to the right and there was no chance of change – an alternative was what we needed. The Greens, I thought, were that party.

As I said, I was heavily involved with the Greens up until the 2013 election – after which I have not been involved at all. This partially due to needing a break, but over time it has developed into a changing perspective on how we create progressive change.

Particularly since the election of Richard Di Natale to the leadership, I have become disillusioned with the idea the Greens will ever become an alternative progressive government. Not because I don't believe the Greens have the capacity to grow, but instead because our system of capitalist governance[1] requires such compromise for that growth to occur that any semblance of progressiveness will disappear. Our system, as I see it, will never allow for a true progressive government to actually occur.

---

1 When I refer to capitalist government I am discussing what most would call 'liberal democracy'. Whilst capitalism is usually discussed solely as an economic system, modern liberal democracy is just as important for its survival. The two – economics and government – are inherently interlinked, making a 'capitalist government' synonymous with a 'capitalist economy'.

Can We Elect a Progressive Government?

What is a Progressive Government?

For many the answer to this is simple – one that invests heavily in public services (health, education etc), defends the rights of unions and workers, invests in clean energy and genuinely tackles climate change, has a compassionate response to refugees and asylum seekers, is willing to give a 'fair go for all' (such as allowing same-sex marriage), stands up for civil liberties, and provides adequate support for the poor (through a welfare state). These are the areas that consistently form the basis of progressive campaigns and in turn end up as a yard stick of whether a government is progressive or not.

It is also these issues that inform both the ALP and the Greens. Most MPs and members of both of these parties would likely agree with the list above, something which often makes the rhetoric of the two look almost indistinguishable. Most within these parties, particularly at the grassroots level, are in agreement on our basic values.

Yet, when actually placed into government, or even close to it, these values disappear. In its previous term of federal government, for example, the ALP reintroduced mandatory detention for asylum seekers, cut welfare payments for single mothers, campaigned on extremely weak targets for carbon emission reduction and refused to legislate same-sex marriage. In their latest experiment of government in Tasmania, Greens Minister Nick McKim was responsible for the closing of schools across the state. The moment parties get into government, many of the progressive ideals fall away. Why is this so?

The reason, I argue, is that our capitalist and political economic system is designed specifically to hold any form of progressive governance back. This is an argument that has a long standing within leftist thought, dating back primarily to the work of Karl Marx and his colleague Friedrich Engels. Our capitalist democratic system, they argued, was designed by the capitalist class. In doing so the systems were developed primarily to ensure the protection of their interests.

Our economic and political system is based on the survival of what we call a 'strong economy', and a strong economy relies on placing the interests of the capitalist class above all others. Jolasmo describes this best in their response to the election of Jeremy Corbyn to the leadership of the British Labour Party:

> Governments, of any political stripe, can act only by wielding the power of the state. To maintain a powerful state, governments need a strong economy, and that means managing capitalism and maintaining a capitalist social order. Different governments can try to do this in different ways, but they're all bound by the same basic logic, and none of them offer any real hope of a way out of the cycle of capitalist domination and human misery. That is why left wing and socialist governments routinely disappoint us.[2]

Governments of all stripes are required to ensure the maintenance of the capitalist system or face collapse and complete failure. The state is based in a capitalist economy, meaning that the economy must come first, despite the costs.

---

2 Jolasmo, 'This is not our victory. Red and black Leeds,' 9 November 2015, https://wearetherabl.wordpress.com/2015/09/11/this-is-not-our-victory/.

This is why the ALP spent years in government talking about debt and the surplus despite the political trouble that brought,[3] why the new Corbyn Labour leadership in the United Kingdom has already bought into the same conservative lexicon,[4] and why the Greek Syriza Government negotiated a harsh austerity package in order to stay in the European Union. Without conforming to these rules these parties, and their Governments, would not have been able to survive.

I don't state this with the intention to tarnish individuals who enter politics – particularly those on the progressive side of the aisle. I still believe the vast majority of people go in to politics to do good for their community.

The problem is that the political process itself corrupts these often very excellent people. When you enter politics you enter into a bubble or what some call the political class. As a member of this class your focus soon becomes narrowed around the day-to-day mechanics of politicking, which in turn is focused on the values of a capitalist economy. Faced with the demands of upcoming elections and the desire to grow your party you are forced to make important decisions – conform to the rules of capitalism and be taken seriously (hence helping your election chances) or don't and be rejected. While some manage to stay away the majority don't. In doing so politicians become disconnected from the very people they are meant to represent.

---

3   S. Copland, 'Surplus debacle a problem of leadership,' 2 January 2014, http://www.abc.net.au/news/2013-01-03/copland-surplus-debacle-a-problem-of-leadership/4451046.
4   J. McDonnell, 'Jeremy Corbyn would clear the deficit – but not by hitting the poor,' *The Guardian*, 11 August 2015, http://www.theguardian.com/commentisfree/2015/aug/11/jeremy-corbyn-close-deficit-poor-labour-economy.

It is worth considering a few examples of the way this works. How does a capitalist system shape political representation and discourse? For the sake of balance I will take an example from both the ALP and the Greens.

In the middle of 2015, Opposition Leader Bill Shorten came under significant pressure after details of a number of deals he did as the secretary of the Australian Worker's Union (AWU) came to light. It was revealed that Shorten had negotiated a workplace agreement with Thiess John Holland that cut worker conditions, saving the company millions of dollars.[5] At the same time, Thiess John Holland made a donation of $300,000 to the AWU. Further allegations included claims that during Shorten's leadership Winslow Constructors paid the union $40,000 to cover the memberships of 105 workers,[6] and that the chemical manufacturer Huntsman paid the union's Victorian branch hundreds of thousands of dollars to ensure workers 'didn't disrupt' their operations.[7]

Responding to these claims Shorten came out swinging, stating in essence 'this is how modern unionism is done'.[8]

---

5   B. Schneiders, R. Millar, N. Toscano, 'Bill Shorten's union took hundreds of thousands from building company,' *Sydney Morning Herald*, 17 June 2015, http://www.smh.com.au/victoria/bill-shortens-union-took-hundreds-of-thousands-from-building-company-20150617-ghq5si.html.

6   'Bill Shorten attacked from both sides over deals done while union secretary,' *The Guardian*, 14 June 2015, http://www.theguardian.com/australia-news/2015/jun/14/bill-shorten-attacked-from-both-sides-over-deals-done-while-union-secretary.

7   'Firm allegedly paid Bill Shorten's AWU to ensure workers "didn't disrupt" operations,' *The Guardian*, 17 June 2015, http://www.theguardian.com/australia-news/2015/jun/18/firm-allegedly-paid-bill-shortens-awu-to-ensure-workers-didnt-disrupt-operations.

8   J. Bennett, '"Entirely possible" companies paid AWU fees, Shorten says,' ABC Online, 21 June 2015, http://www.abc.net.au/news/2015-06-21/

Shorten defended his record, arguing that a more consultative approach where union leaders and employers come together to negotiate agreements is the only way forward.

Here we can see how our capitalist system has shaped Shorten's and the AWU's engagement. Key to Shorten's argument is the idea that capitalism relies on a more conciliatory approach from workers. This means the rejection of what some call the previous 'militancy' of the union movement, or what I would call the working class standing up for their rights. This approach to unionism has rightly been perceived as a threat to the interests of capitalism, and in turn has been squashed. Hence we get deals from union leaders that result in cuts to workers' conditions. Keeping the interests of capitalism alive was more important than defending the working class, making Shorten's argument come across as completely reasonable even as the interests of workers were eroded.

It's not just relationships with the capitalist class that shape the problematic relationships that form within the political class. Politics also has a way of reshaping the way in which the political class engages with its own values and those of the general population.

For example one of the most interesting, and at times frustrating, parts of my involvement with the Greens was tackling the idea that we needed to present ourselves as being a more 'serious' political party. To build our vote, many argued, the Greens need to drop our radical roots and present ourselves as professional and authoritative. This discourse is particularly strong around economic policy, with many arguing that because our messaging doesn't fit the standard

---

entirely-possible-companies-paid-awu-fees-shorten-says/6561362.

debate we'll never be taken seriously. To be taken seriously we need to become like the other political parties.

We can now see these debates play out in real time. When elected to the leadership of the party Richard Di Natale declared he was going to represent 'mainstream' progressive values,[9] a clear attempt to break from previous leadership. The Greens have since tried to emphasise their 'new look' economic team (Di Natale alongside Senator Peter Whish-Wilson and MP Adam Bandt),[10] an attempt to make the party look more 'serious' and 'realistic'. At other times Di Natale has emphasised his willingness to work within our political system, whether it was offering to quit politics if Malcolm Turnbull changed positions on key issues,[11] or offering himself as a potential Minister in a future ALP government.[12]

While presenting itself as the more radical left alternative in Australian politics, in order to fully participate in our system the Greens are being forced to make serious compromises. The capitalist state requires parties that fit particular moulds – ones that we can take 'seriously'. The Greens are increasingly

---

9   B. Siebert, 'Revealed: Greens' Senate candidate report cards,' *InDaily*, 20 August 2015, http://indaily.com.au/news/2015/08/20/revealed-greens-senate-candidate-report-cards/.

10 G. Hutchens, 'Meet the new Greens economics team preparing to shake up Australian politics,' *Sydney Morning Herald*, 26 June 2015, http://www.smh.com.au/federal-politics/political-news/the-greens-have-a-new-economics-team-they-are-not-what-youd-expect-20150624-ghw747.html.

11 M. Farr, 'Di Natale outlines price for Senate peace to the PM,' News.com.au, 30 September 2015, http://www.news.com.au/finance/work/di-natale-outlines-price-for-senate-peace-to-the-new-pm/story-fn5tas5k-1227550943730.

12 Massola, 'Richard Di Natale eyes cabinet post' (see chap. 1, n. 8).

disconnecting themselves from their political roots, and the people they are elected to represent.

These examples, and the broader issues above, highlight the problem with the question of 'how do we create progressive governance?'. This question is impossible to answer because our current system is not designed for progressive governance. A system built and based on the interests of capitalists will never truly be able to be progressive.

What Role for Politics?

Given that we are unable to elect a truly progressive government, we must then turn to the question, 'what role for politics?'

I see two key ways in which the left should interact with the state, which I am aim to illustrate through some current key issues. These strategies are: (a) drag the state left when opportune; and (b) repudiate and reabsorb the power of the state. Both of these approaches require a repudiation of standard political engagement (elections, lobbying etc) and instead a focus on direct intervention with the state only when strategic.

Despite my critiques of the state, I'm not saying we cannot work to make government more left wing. Whilst I critique the power of the state, I acknowledge its existence and its capacity to do good. I do for example believe that governments should invest more heavily in health, education and other social services. I also see the capacity for governments to help fix major problems such as climate change, whether it is investing in renewable technology or regulating dirty polluters to help see their demise. The state can play an important role in advancing progressive ideals.

Our interaction with the state however has often focused too heavily on a search for it to be a leader on all issues, rather than using our own leadership to drag it in the right direction.

The perfect example of this is climate change. Climate change is an issue of huge concern for the Australian population, with a majority wanting serious action.[13] Climate change has often been a vote-turner, responsible, at least in part, for the collapse of five Australian political leaders – John Howard, Brendan Nelson, Malcolm Turnbull (as opposition leader), Kevin Rudd (the first time) and Julia Gillard. The issue has also helped to stimulate a significant political movement, which has interacted with successive governments in a number of different ways.

The climate movement has spent large amounts of time and energy campaigning for leadership from government. Initially climate groups demanded governments implement emissions trading schemes, but are now turning towards mass direct intervention in the economy. This shift has been led by the ideas outlined by Naomi Klein, who in her book *This Changes Everything* argues world governments should engage in a mass economic reengagement similar to the size of the New Deal or Second World War economic programs.

This call for government leadership has shaped all elements of the climate movement. Even with the election of Tony Abbott to the Prime Ministership many activists turned to government for 'leadership'. Former head of the

---

13 2015 'Lowy Institute Poll finds rapidly shifting attitudes on climate issues and strong views about solar,' Lowy Institute for International Policy, 2015, http://www.lowyinstitute.org/news-and-media/press-releases/2015-lowy-institute-poll-finds-rapidly-shifting-attitudes-climate-issues-and-strong-views-about.

Australian Conservation Foundation Don Henry headed up Parliamentary negotiations to create a 'grand bargain' on the Abbott Government's direct action policy, seeing the very existence of a government policy on the issue as important in and of itself.[14] Government, according to this theory of change, had to be a 'leader' no matter what that leadership actually looks like.

These strategies however have failed time and time again, with each call for political leadership being met with weak or even dangerous alternatives. Across the world emissions trading policies have failed to stop emissions and handed billions to polluting companies. The push for a 'Green New Deal' in response to the Global Financial Crisis was met with a mixture of surplus policies that promoted mass consumption on one hand and austerity policies that crush the poor on the other. Pushes for mass investment in renewable energy have failed in most states, with governments often using 'renewable' policy as a way to promote dirty alternatives. Each push for political leadership has hit a wall when faced with the realities of capitalism.

But it is in climate change where we can see the birth of new and different forms of political engagement, which have much greater capacity to create change. Learning in particular from the failures of campaigns for emission trading schemes, in recent years the environment movement has turned to new tactics.[15] These tactics have been twofold: fossil fuel

---

14 L. Taylor, '"Grand bargain" may secure enough support for Direct Action to pass Senate,' *The Guardian*, 22 August 2014, http://www.theguardian.com/world/2014/aug/22/grand-bargain-climate-change-action-ret.

15 S. Copland, 'Turning values into (direct) action,' *Inside Story*, 24 September 2013, http://insidestory.org.au/turning-values-into-direct-action.

divestment and the targeting of new and existing fossil fuel projects, largely through non-violent direct action.

These campaigns are important for a couple of reasons. First, they have actively bypassed politicians as decision-makers, instead going after the source of the problem – fossil fuel companies. Having been involved in the movement for a number of years this came from a direct recognition that politicians were not going to take the action needed on the issue, and that we therefore needed to take it ourselves. This has resulted in significant progress – whether it is the hundreds of people who took direct action at the Maules Creek Coal Mine, or the thousands who have been involved in divestment campaigns across the country, and world.

That does not mean however that government is completely removed from the process. Instead the movement has used standard political avenues more strategically. In 2015, for example, Green groups successfully won a legal challenge to the approval of the Carmichael Coal Mine in central Queensland.[16] Seeing faults in the state's decision-making process environmentalists built on the strong on-the-ground movement to make a direct intervention. Whilst the government has recently re-approved the mine, the action brought with it significant attention and delay, which are likely to have a long-term impact.

Government in this strategy is secondary, with political interventions being used only as a way to drag the state to the leadership we have already shown. Whilst the strategy of using the courts for example accepts the existence of the state and its

---

16 J. Robertson and O. Milman, 'Approval for Adani's Carmichael coalmine overturned by federal court,' *The Guardian*, 5 August 2015, http://www.theguardian.com/australia-news/2015/aug/05/approval-for-adanis-carmichael-coalmine-overturned-by-federal-court.

institutions, it is not one based on asking the government for all the answers. Instead of looking to government leadership, or lamenting the lack of it, this strategy is based on using direction intervention – whether it is non-violent direct action at the coal source or exposing the failures of successive governments to put the interests of the community first.

Unlike many of the campaigns of the past, these strategies have seen significant success. The divestment movement has become an international phenomenon, with billions of dollars being removed from the fossil fuel industry. Anti-fossil fuel campaigns are leading to genuine success with the closure and cancellation of fossil fuel projects across the world. And politicians are being dragged along as well – whether it is Barnaby Joyce speaking out against the proposed Shehua Coal Mine in the Liverpool Plains, US Presidential Candidate Hillary Clinton arguing against the proposed Keystone XL Pipeline, or the Chinese Government announcing a three-year ban on new coal mine approvals.

This leads me to the second area of political action. When not dragging Governments to the left, progressives should be doing all we can to take back power from the state and instead place it in the hands of local communities. Here, I turn to recent debates around same-sex marriage.

In August 2015, the Tony Abbott Government was thrown into turmoil after the Coalition party room decided to block a conscience vote on same-sex marriage. In response Abbott publicly suggested a plebiscite on the issue, framing it around being about a 'public vote' versus a 'politicians vote'. Polling has shown that a people's vote is extremely popular,[17] and under

---

17 'Decision on same sex marriage,' *Essential Report*, 22 September 2015, http://www.essentialvision.com.au/decision-on-same-sex-marriage-2.

pressure from his conservative base Prime Minister Malcolm Turnbull has continued to pursue the policy.[18]

Many marriage equality advocates however have reacted strongly against the idea,[19] arguing it is not up to the public to vote on 'our rights'. This got to the point where former Prime Minister Julia Gillard publicly changed her position on same-sex marriage, particularly targeting the plebiscite. Gillard stated that the 'only foundation stone for the idea of a plebiscite or referendum is an appeal to the all-too-popular sentiment that politicians are inadequate, that their decision-making is somehow deficient'.[20] Pushing aside the irony of this coming from the Prime Minister who once suggested a 'Citizens Assembly' on climate change, the message was clear – it is up to Parliament to decide and the people should have no role.

This represented a failure to grasp an important opportunity. Whilst I fully appreciate and understand the concerns of many within the marriage equality movement, a plebiscite offered an important opportunity to highlight exactly what Gillard

---

18 D. Hurst, 'Malcolm Turnbull holds the line on climate policy and marriage equality plebiscite,' *The Guardian*, 15 September 2015, http://www.theguardian.com/australia-news/2015/sep/15/malcolm-turnbull-holds-the-line-on-climate-policy-and-marriage-equality-plebiscite.

19 'Gay and lesbian rights lobbies' community survey rejects marriage equality public vote,' *Sydney Star Observer*, 8 September 2015, http://www.starobserver.com.au/news/local-news/gay-and-lesbian-rights-lobbies-community-survey-rejects-marriage-equality-public-vote/140539.

20 S. McDonald, 'Gillard says she supports same-sex marriage, condemns referendum,' *ABC Online*, 26 August 2015, http://www.abc.net.au/news/2015-08-26/gillard-says-she-supports-same-sex-marriage-condemns-referendum/6727638.

was concerned about – that our politicians are far behind the general population when it comes to LGBTIQ rights.

Much of the marriage debate has been focused heavily on standard political engagement. Marriage activists have worked mainly in two areas – political lobbying and attempts to influence election campaigns. In turn the campaign has lost much of its community spirit – fights happening in the halls of Parliament rather than the streets of our cities and towns.[21] All the power to fight homophobia has been largely given to Parliament, and taken away from local communities.

A plebiscite has the capacity to change this. It would put the fight back on our streets, empowering local communities and community leaders to be advocates for change. On an issue like anti-queer prejudice, this couldn't be more important. We fight prejudice street by street, not through wielding the power of a state, which largely has little power to do anything anyway (even when changing legislation).

It is here where I see the second form of political action. The state has become too powerful. As John Harris states:

> The state comes to the rescue of banks while snatching away benefits. It strides into sovereign countries, and commits serial human rights abuses. It subjects doctors, nurses and teachers to ludicrous targets. It watches us constantly via CCTV, and hacks our email and phone data. It farms out some of its dirtiest business to private firms.[22]

---

21 S. Copland, 'The "new" marriage equality strategy is bound to be a failure,' 15 October 2015, http://www.starobserver.com.au/opinion/the-new-marriage-equality-strategy-is-bound-to-be-a-failure/141679.

22 J. Harris, 'The left is too silent on the clunking fist of state power,' *The Guardian*, 5 January 2014, http://www.theguardian.com/commentisfree/2014/jan/05/left-silent-state-power-government-market.

For Harris the left has become too silent on this 'clunking power of the state', arguing that an 'arrogant and centralised state is as big a problem as the out-of-control market'.

Political action should therefore be focused on breaking down this entrenched power, treating the state with just as much suspicion as neoliberal markets. The left already engages in this sort of activity, whether it is nurses and doctors refusing to release children from hospitals so they are not put back in detention centres,[23] to Greens' Senator Scott Ludlam publicly publishing information on how citizens can avoid data retention.[24]

This sort of non-violent direct action is an important way for the left to repudiate the state but we need to do more. If we want true representative and progressive governance structures we should not just be looking to repudiate the power of the state when it is being used for evil, but aim to do so in all cases. While marriage equality can technically be done through a bill in Parliament a plebiscite is significantly more powerful. It highlights the deficiencies of the state and our conservative parties, whilst empowering local communities at the same time. In turn it promotes actual grassroots democracy, something the left often promotes, but rarely actually tries to implement.

We can therefore see the alternatives available to us other than our standard political engagement. With an acknowledgement that the capitalist state will be sticking around at least

---

23 P. Hatch, J. Ireland and C. Booker, 'Royal Children's Hospital doctors refuse to return children to detention,' *The Age*, 11 October 2015, http://www.theage.com.au/victoria/royal-childrens-hospital-doctors-refuse-to-return-children-to-detention-20151010-gk63xm.html.

24 S. Ludlam, #StopDataRetention, 2015, http://scott-ludlam.greensmps.org.au/campaigns/stopdataretention.

for the short term the left needs to rethink how we engage with it. Instead of turning towards the state for leadership at all times (which despite some alternative trends is something that is becoming the norm at least within mainstream organisations), I argue we should instead emphasise the leadership of local communities instead. This means dragging governments left when we have the capacity to do so, but more importantly it means working to re-absorb political power back into our communities. This is a more direct form of intervention, one that places faith in our local communities and does everything it can to empower communities to take action of their own rather than relying on government to do it for them.

Labor or Greens?

If standard political interventions – in particular the pursuit of electing a progressive government – are a failure, then how should progressives engage with elections? What party should we support, if any at all?

There is a lot of tribalism in progressive politics, some of which I have shared. On reflecting on this essay though I am increasingly of the position that our political engagement should be far more flexible, supporting the party or parties who can best play a role in the political strategies I've outlined above.

Over the past decade or so I believe the Greens have been the party which has best played this role. This is why I remain a member of the party – although an increasingly wary one. The Greens have advanced radical strategies in two ways.

First, unlike the ALP, the Greens are less focused on the 'realities of government' and more on using political interventions to drag politics left. Whilst many of the Greens, including the current leadership, have fallen in to the trap of thinking of government as the agent of change, a significant faction of the party still sees the world differently. The Greens are both actively willing to challenge the growing power of the state (see for example data retention) and to spend more time presenting social movements as the agents of change rather than ourselves.

Building on from this the Greens are more willing to spend their energies on breaking up the standard political order. Despite his negotiations with Labor Prime Minister Julia Gillard, Bob Brown was the typical anti-politics politician: a man who refused to stick to the games of the political class and gained support from this. The best example of this was Brown and Senator Kerry Nettle's disruption of George W. Bush as he spoke in federal Parliament – an act that caused significant controversy. Whilst Brown's successor Christine Milne was often weighed down by the deal with former Prime Minister Julia Gillard, I believe she significantly learnt the lesson from that experience, and worked internally against the idea of future deals. Milne focused her 2013 campaign on the idea that 'we live in a society not an economy', trying to challenge the idea that a 'strong economy' is the sole indicator of a good government. Of the major political parties the Greens do the most to disrupt standard politics, challenging both the way politics is done, and the power it uses to do so.

But it is here where there is cause for concern, and the need for flexibility which I have described. Recent months, particularly since the election of Richard Di Natale to the party leadership, have seen significant shifts away from these agendas. As noted above Di Natale has not just shifted the party to the right, professional and serious end of the political spectrum, but he has also placed significant faith in the leadership of politics to create change. Di Natale comes from a highly technocratic political background,[25] one which values 'evidence-based policy' as the solution to our social, economic and environmental ills. This not only lacks any form of ideology, but disempowers local communities through placing power in the hands of experts, scientists and unfortunately politicians.[26] In doing so I believe Di Natale has the potential to shift our party away from its anti-political roots and into becoming a highly technocratic and political one.

To me these shifts are extremely worrying. At the same time however they seem inevitable given the way progressives engage in our political system. This is the outcome of the drive to find a 'progressive government' in a system that does not allow it. Whether it was the ALP of the past, or the Greens of the future, an obsession with parliamentary politics warps our capacity to create progressive change. It is only natural that as the Greens become entrenched in Parliament and gain more power that they would head down this direction.

I remain a wary supporter of the Greens, hopeful that recent shifts will be resisted and end up being temporary. But I do not believe that will be the case unless we reshape progressive engagement to parliamentary politics. The question of Labor vs Greens therefore seems moot. It is not about which party is better, but about how we should engage in political processes. That is what the left needs to change.

---

25 T. Tietze, 'The Greens after Milne: Running out of options?,' *Left Flank*, 8 May 2015, http://left-flank.org/2015/05/08/the-greens-after-milne-running-out-of-options/.

26 S. Copland, 'Against experts,' *Overland Journal*, 3 October 2014, https://overland.org.au/2014/10/against-experts/.

This book asks the question, '*how do we elect a progressive government*'. In this essay I've argued that in a capitalist society this is impossible. We therefore need to turn our attention away from the state, and in particular stop relying on it to be the solution to our society's ills. We can do this in two ways – through showing community-based leadership that drags the state in a progressive direction, and through fighting against the increasing power of the state through reabsorbing this power into local communities.

We live in a time when this strategy could be extremely successful. The general population is turning sharply against politicians and we have the opportunity to harness that energy to help create deep social movements that reabsorb political power into community power.

When it comes to electoral politics I believe the Greens remain the best avenue to do this work. However I state that very warily, with a concern that this reality may soon be coming to a close. It is up to the party to stay true, to disrupt, and to challenge the power of the state.

Contributors

Dennis Altman, a Professorial Fellow in Human Security at LaTrobe University, has published thirteen books, most recently *The End of the Homosexual?* and (with Jon Symons) *Queer Wars*. In 2006 *The Bulletin* listed Dennis Altman as one of the 100 most influential Australians ever, and he was appointed a Member of the Order of Australia in 2008.

Van Badham is a Melbourne-based writer, critic, trade unionist, feminist, activist and occasional broadcaster, an internationally award-winning theatre maker and one of Australia's most controversial social commentators. She is currently employed as a weekly columnist for *Guardian Australia* and is Vice-President of MEAA Victoria. She is a proud alumnus of the University of Wollongong and has a Masters from Melbourne. She tweets via @vanbadham.

Adam Bandt is the federal Member of Parliament for Melbourne. In 2010 he became the first Greens elected to the lower house at a general election and was re-elected with an increased vote in 2013. Adam previously worked as an industrial and public interest lawyer for over a decade, representing many workers and unions. He holds a PhD in legal and social theory. He is the Greens' Treasury, Industry, Employment and Arts spokesperson and was formerly the party's Deputy Leader.

Nicholas Barry is a lecturer in the Department of Politics and Philosophy at La Trobe University. His current research interests are in the areas of egalitarian theory, constitutions and political parties.

Simon Copland is a freelance writer focusing on sex, the environment and politics. He worked for the Greens in the 2010 and 2013 federal election campaigns and as campaigner at the climate organisation 350.org. In his spare time he is a rugby union and David Bowie fanatic.

Andrew Giles is the federal Member of Parliament for Scullin, having stood for the seat as ALP candidate in 2013. Before that he was an employment lawyer at Slater and Gordon in Melbourne.

Stewart Jackson is a lecturer in the Department of Government and International Relations at the University of Sydney. Stewart researches Green and environmental parties and politics in the Asia Pacific, and is the author of *The Australian Greens*.

Carmen Lawrence is Director of the Centre for the Study of Social Change at University of Western Australia and Chair of the Australian Heritage Council. During 21 years in politics she held various ministerial positions including Premier and Treasurer in Western Australia and Minister for Health and Human Services in the Keating Government.

Andrew Leigh is the Shadow Assistant Treasurer and Federal Member for Fraser in the ACT. Prior to being elected in 2010, Andrew was a professor of economics at the Australian National University. Andrew holds a PhD in public policy from Harvard, having graduated from the University of Sydney with honours in Law and Arts. A Fellow of the Australian Academy of Social Sciences, his books include *Disconnected*

(2010), *Battlers and Billionaires* (2013), *The Economics of Just About Everything* (2014) and *The Luck of Politics* (2015).

Scott Ludlam is an Australian Greens Senator for Western Australia. Elected in November 2007, he is one of eleven Australian Greens in Parliament and is the spokesperson for Foreign Affairs, Communications, Nuclear Issues, Housing and Sustainable Cities. Scott, a former film maker, artist and graphic designer, likes the internet.

David Mejia-Canales is a lawyer based in Melbourne, Australia. He has a keen interest in human rights issues, particularly as they intersect with questions of sexuality, gender, migration and refugees.

Narelle Miragliotta is a senior lecturer in the Department of Politics and International Relations at Monash University. She researches in the areas of political parties, electoral systems and parliaments.

Ellen Sandell is the first Greens MP elected to the lower house of Victorian Parliament. She holds a Bachelors of Arts/Science Degree from the University of Melbourne, majoring in genetics, linguistics and Spanish. Ellen began her career as a researcher with the CSIRO. She then worked on climate change policy for former Labor premier John Brumby's Department of Premier and Cabinet, and later became the chief executive of a national climate change non-profit organisation, the Australian Youth Climate Coalition. Ellen is the Victorian Greens spokesperson for housing, climate change and energy.

Sean Scalmer teaches History at the University of Melbourne. His books include *Dissent Events*, *The Little History of*

Australian Unionism and *Gandhi in the West*. He is a co-editor of the journal *Moving the Social*.

James Tierney is an industrial relations and employment lawyer in Melbourne. He recently completed a Masters of History at the University of Melbourne, focusing on trade union mobilisation and social movement theory.

Peter van Onselen is foundation chair of journalism and professor of politics at the University of Western Australia. He is a contributing editor at *The Australian* and hosts *PVO News Day* and *Australian Agenda* on Sky News. Professor van Onselen is the author or editor of six books on Australian politics, most recently (with Wayne Errington) *Battleground: Why the Liberal Party Shirtfronted Tony Abbott*.

Felicity Wade is an environmental activist and National Co-convenor of the Labor Environment Action Network (LEAN). She spent over a decade leading the Wilderness Society in New South Wales. She is proud of her role in defending the Great Barrier Reef's Hinchinbrook Island, protecting wilderness, establishing forested National Parks in the state's south-east, and ending broad-scale land clearing. She was environment and climate adviser to Luke Foley.

Shaun Wilson is a Senior Lecturer in the Department of Sociology at Macquarie University. He researches and teaches in the areas of political sociology, the sociology of work, and social survey research and social attitudes. Shaun is presently serving as Secretary of the Australian Consortium of Social and Political Research Incorporated (ACSPRI), which runs social research training for Australian university researchers and students.